PORTRAIT OF MEXICO

PORTRAIT OF
MEXICO

Paintings by Diego Rivera and Text by Bertram D. Wolfe

NEW YORK COVICI · FRIEDE PUBLISHERS

ACKNOWLEDGMENTS

The reproductions in this book are from photographs made by Lupercio, Tina Modotti and Manuel Álvarez Bravo. The earlier murals in the Secretariat of Education were photographed by Lupercio. Upon his death Tina Modotti became Rivera's photographer until her deportation from Mexico. Most of the pictures, however, including the majority of the frescoes and all of the individual canvases reproduced, represent the camera work of Álvarez Bravo and I am deeply indebted to him for his patient and expert cooperation in the assembling of these pictures. Grateful acknowledgment is due S. A. Jacobs for the planning of the book and unusual care in its technical preparation.

I also wish to express my indebtedness to Frances Toor, editor of *Mexican Folkways*, and to Diego Rivera and Frieda Kahlo de Rivera for reading the manuscript prior to publication, as well as to Martin Temple and Ella G. Wolfe for their generous and many-sided assistance and encouragement. This must not be taken to imply the responsibility of any of the above for the views expressed here or for any deficiencies to be found in the text.

BERTRAM D. WOLFE

January 19, 1937

CONTENTS

Chap. 1   THE MEXICAN LAND   Page 13

Chap. 2   THE MEXICAN PEOPLE   Page 20

Chap. 3   LIFE AND LABOR   Page 31

Chap. 4   DEATH AND LAUGHTER   Page 46

Chap. 5   BEFORE THE SPANIARDS CAME   Page 61

Chap. 6   THE CONQUEST   Page 76

Chap. 7   NEW SPAIN   Page 90

Chap. 8   THE STRUGGLE FOR INDEPENDENCE   Page 100

Chap. 9   "MEXICAN MAZE"   Page 114

Chap. 10   REIGN OF DON PORFIRIO   Page 138

Chap. 11   REVOLUTION OF 1910   Page 148

Chap. 12   MEXICO TODAY   Page 170

Chap. 13   LAND OF THE SIX YEAR PLAN   Page 196

REPRODUCTIONS

EASEL PAINTINGS

1. THE LAND AND THE PEOPLE   *Plates 1-102*

FRESCOES

2. THE COURT OF LABOR

   Frescoes in the First Patio, Ground Floor
   Ministry of Education, Mexico City   *Plates 103-111*

3. THE ASCENDING LANDSCAPE

   Elevator Entrance and Stairway Frescoes
   Ministry of Education, Mexico City   *Plates 112-120*

4. COURT OF FIESTAS

   Second Patio, Ground Floor
   Ministry of Education, Mexico City   *Plates 121-135*

5. REVOLUTIONARY BALLAD SERIES

   Third Floor, Court of the Fiestas
   Ministry of Education, Mexico City   *Plates 136-161*

REPRODUCTIONS

6. NATIONAL AGRICULTURAL SCHOOL AT CHAPINGO
Stairway Frescoes   *Plates 162-171*

7. NATIONAL AGRICULTURAL SCHOOL AT CHAPINGO
Chapel Frescoes   *Plates 172-187*

8. MINISTRY OF HEALTH, MEXICO CITY
Meeting Hall Frescoes and
Stained Glass Windows   *Plates 188-194*

9. CUERNAVACA MURALS: PALACE OF CORTÉS
                                                     Plates 195-219

10. MEXICO: PAST, PRESENT AND FUTURE
Murals on the National Palace Stairway,
Mexico City   *Plates 220-241*

11. MEXICAN CARNIVAL: YESTERDAY AND TODAY
Frescoes in the Banquet Hall of the Hotel Reforma,
Mexico City   *Plates 242-249*

PORTRAIT OF MEXICO

I. THE MEXICAN LAND

One's first impression of Mexico is one of elevation. Great volcanic mountain ranges line each coast. The bulk of the country is high table-land gently uptilted from north to south at an elevation rising from four to eight thousand feet above the sea, broken in turn by towering mountain chains many thousands of feet higher, and seamed by precipitous *barrancas* or canyons many hundreds of feet in depth.

The land culminates in three mighty volcanoes which continue to smolder and smoke in the moonlight, and by day thrust into the brilliant blaze of a tropical sun the shining luster of their eternal caps of snow. Popocatepetl and Ixtacihuatl lift from the highland regions to elevations of over seventeen thousand feet, while the sleeping conical peak of Orizaba rises from the tropical jungle to a height of over eighteen thousand feet above the level of the sea.

TIME AND SPACE

As the sensitive observer ascends the rocky tree-filled canyons to the great elevated table-land of the *mesa central*, he becomes increasingly aware of the fourth dimension in this space-time journey: he is not only travelling upward in space, but also backward in time. Feudal fortresses, battlemented and slotted and impregnable of wall, flash past his train or auto. Medieval churches lord it over scrubby little clusters of mud or reed huts. As he exchanges railroad and concrete highway for burro trail and footpath, he comes upon unexpected little villages hidden on the steep flanks of canyons where medievalism has not yet arrived, villages on whose trails no wheel has ever turned, where iron and steel and power have not even extended their first premonitory filaments. And beyond these, in the remoter mountain regions of the center and north, he may find settlements where men still live in caves and fulfill all the essentials of living with the instruments and techniques of the Stone Age on the last or outer edge of barbarism.

THE PAINTER'S LAND

To the painter Mexico presents every conceivable variety of landscape. At sea level the rank luxuriance of the tropical jungle thrusts powerful green hands into the feeble clearings and dwellings and monuments of men, and time and again tears them apart and buries them beneath its overwhelming fecundity. Man's very hut is a scarcely transformed bit of jungle growth made of palm or cane brake and thatched with reeds. Taken from the surrounding forests, it blends with them, and is soon lost in the all-pervading vegetation from whence it came.

Here Nature offers her products in abundance: the mango, the *mamey*, the banana, the *zapote* and other wondrous fruits of taste exotic and indescribable for Northern peoples; cacao, coffee, vanilla and tobacco and drugs and herbs innumerable; dye-products; ebony, mahogany and other precious woods. The forests are filled with sound and color: the chatter of monkeys, the screech and gossip of parokeets, the blaze of tropical flowers and the flitting flame of birds of brilliant plumage, the hum and whir of myriad insects great and small and the hushed and rumor-filled silence of forest noons.

The jungle gives the means of living freely, so freely that it takes much work of missionaries and much use of barbed wire and battleships and bayonets to teach the inhabitants to wear more clothing than they need, pick more fruit and consume less of it than meets their requirements, so that the United Fruit Company can ship the still green "banana gold" and pineapples and such, profitably to the four ends of the earth.

The jungle gives the means of simple living freely and almost without human effort, but it is deeply intolerant of that effort, swiftly overwhelms the work of man and chokes his planting. It abounds in poisonous insects and reptiles, parasitic diseases and malarial fevers. The aboriginal, living in close harmony with and subordination to his overwhelming surroundings, develops a relative adjustment and immunity. But the outlander, and even the native, once he has been "uprooted" by the enforcement upon him of alien standards of "civilization," is likely to suffer the ravages of epidemic disease and an incredibly elevated death rate.

The swamps and forests of much of Chiapas, Tabasco and Quintana Roo have defeated Spanish conquerors, Mexican administrators, census-takers, tax-collectors and road-builders alike, and its inhabitants live largely in their jungle primitiveness undisturbed by and unaware of changes of government and regime in the far away capital of a scarcely even legendary republic.

14

On the sun-and-rain-soaked Isthmus of Tehuantepec, men go to work in the fields many hours before dawn under the black-blue of a star-filled tropic sky, and no man can stand the merciless rays of the sun in the open fields from ten o'clock in the morning till evening casts its cooling shadow over the earth. Here one finds stately and beautiful women, the most beautiful in the Republic, bearing their statuesque bodies and their colorful and lovely garments with the grace of queens—lusty, forceful, free women, who seem to maintain a relation of almost matriarchal dominance over their less impressive menfolk.

To the east of this fascinating isthmus faintly reminiscent of ancient Egypt, lies the legendary Peninsula of Yucatán. There is no road, no railroad, no burro trail, uniting Yucatán with the rest of the country. To get there from the capital of the Republic the administrator or commercial agent must have recourse to American or other foreign boats that ply their way between Vera Cruz and Havana, New York or some European port, or he must wing his way over the trackless jungle and swamp land by plane. On the Pacific coast, the rocky, semi-barren peninsula of Lower California is in a somewhat similar plight, since it can be reached by rail or auto from the heart of Mexico only by taking a journey into the United States.

Yucatán is a low-lying coral reef formation, rising very slightly above the level of the sea. So porous is this ancient reef that it thirstily soaks up the gulf-coast rainfall, and its inhabitants have to dig hundreds of feet down into limestone grottos to locate *cenotes*, or underground pools, and subterranean rivers from which to draw their water supply. On this inhospitable peninsula in which the Mayans took refuge after their defeat and the collapse of their civilization some thousand years ago, the top soil, where it exists, averages less than a few inches in depth; limestone rock juts out everywhere; and the casual traveller, impressed by the tropical beauty of Merida, little dreams that each tree casting its grateful shade over that pleasant capital represents a miniature epic of human effort to force nature to its will. While much of the peninsula is covered with scrubby sterile forest vegetation or overwhelming jungle swamp, in the cultivated portions no tree grows till man has dug a ditch and filled it with transported humus-soil. Every vegetable and garden patch represents a similar labor. Fruits and fresh vegetables and even drinking water are scarce and precious, and Nature yields her products grudgingly and under compulsion. Only the henequen cactus (Yucatán hemp or sisal) grows readily here; but its exploitation to produce the binder twine used by the American harvester manufacturers, and the sleeping hammocks and other fiber products used locally, represents an incalculable cost in the enslavement of the henequen peons. Nor is the casual traveller likely to remember, as he revels in the "dream-city" of Merida, that its wonders are the parasitic fruit of this nightmare of exploitation.

On the walls of the Secretariat of Education Rivera has portrayed the *cenotes* and reed huts of the Yucatán peninsula; and he has gone again and again to Tehuantepec to sketch and paint the tropical beauty of its landscapes, the "Egyptian" blue of its water and sky, the swing and rhythm of its regional dancers, the stately grace of its women and the almost feminine-featured delicacy and slightness of its men.[1]

In the building of the Ministry of Public Education, the painter has taken advantage of the stairway walls to portray the vast ascending background of the Mexican landscape.[2] At the base of the stairway we see rivers and subterranean streams pouring their waters into the sea; symbolic figures represent the islands of the Gulf of Mexico and the clouds that pour their fertilizing rains upon the fecund earth. From the sea rise precipitous mountain walls, jungle-green at their base, pine and fir-clad higher up, then sparsely covered with cactus and sage and chaparral, then bare and brown and *barranca*-seamed from the ravages of rainy season torrents, clear of outline and airy blue in the distance, purple and lavender in the light of the setting sun, slate-gray under the burden of gathering rain clouds, and black against the deep cobalt blue of the late twilight.

Near sea level Rivera has portrayed oil fields and clearings and buzzard-crested trees; then the rank luxuriance of the tropical jungle where naked women bathe or, clad in a single garment, rest in idyllic peace in tree-swung hammocks (the favorite bed of the people of Yucatán and other torrid regions). The green jungle walls grow denser and thick vines twist around the moss-hung trees brilliant with flaming flowers and the plumage of tropic birds. Amidst the foliage Rivera has painted two nude female figures, one representing woodland silence and

[1] Plates 8, 13, 14, 18, 19-21, 25, 54, 55, 58, 59, 60-69, 113, 135.
[2] Plates 112-120.

one woodland sound, and has portrayed the cult of Xochipilli, the ancient god of flowers. As we ascend the stairway we ascend in vision the mountain canyons and reach the rich sub-tropic lands of abundant fruit and vegetation, and of sugar mills and sugar plantations. Then wheat and corn fields appear, and with them the symbolic figure of *Centeotl* the corn goddess, while plows and tractors break the semi-arid background and mine shafts thrust deep into the bowels of the earth. With agriculture and industry come the more developed aspects of the class struggle and the allegory takes on social rather than natural significance. The landscape grows bare and brown; the hills, more monotoned and barren, culminate in ice-and-snow-clad peaks, source of continuous streams that will provide water-power to a future indus-trialized Mexico. Now the foreground is peopled with figures symboliz-ing the coming union of worker, soldier and peasant ruling their own destinies in a workers' land. Such is the painter's epitomized portrait of the Mexican land.

THE MESA CENTRAL

Rivera's landscape varies as his region and conception vary, for in landscape as in social life Mexico is a land of infinite variety! Yet Diego Rivera is essentially a man of the cool uplands, of the great *mesa central* that is the region of greatest agricultural and mineral and industrial development, of governmental and intellectual and cultural predominance, of greatest population, largest cities and most advanced civilization, of sharpest class struggle and highest social potentialities. And therefore the bulk of his painting, especially his mural work, has as foreground figures and scenes from the sun-scorched and water-carved plains of the *mesa central*, and as background the never altogether absent horizon of brown or gray or blue or purple hills.

In the lowland man is overwhelmed by the green fecundity of the jungle, but on the upland plateaus he seems dwarfed by the limitless expanse of great semi-arid elevated plains and the lofty reaches of the distant mountain peaks.

LAND OF CACTUS AND MAGUEY

Especially on the northern *mesa* there are day-long distances on mule or burro where one sees only sun-drenched desert land, well-nigh bare of vegetation save where cactuses lift grasping hands against the sky and cast purple shadows of misshapen waving arms upon the salty stony unyielding land.[3] Or one sees endless rows of the fleshy-thick, spine-edged, gray-green whorls of the *maguey*,[4] often mistaken by the foreigner for "just another cactus," but actually, together with beans and Indian corn or maize, one of the three life-givers of primitive Mexican agrarian economy. Indeed there are regions of Mexico, remote from highroads and centers of modern culture, where the *Agave Americanus* or *maguey* is almost the sole support of indigenous communities. It still provides fiber for rope and coarse woven cloth, and spines for piercing and sewing. It once was a source of primitive paper, while an insect found upon its leaves supplied the coloring matter for dyeing the cloth and ink for writing on the paper. Ground up, the pulpy leaves provide food for animal and man, and a prized delicacy is prepared by frying the long white grubs that live within. Used entire, the leaves serve as thatch for roofs and walls of primitive homes.

The plant thrives in semi-arid desert land where water is scarce. It slowly gathers the meager rainfall through the years, storing it for the supreme effort, not of an annual flowering, but of the production of a rare desert flower perhaps once a decade, whence it has gained the symbolic if not exactly accurate name of century plant. When the long preparatory period is over, there is a rush of sap to the base of the young flower stalk. Then man intervenes. He cuts out the stalk and, from the natural bowl thus formed in the very heart of the plant, draws out the life-giving juice into the long bulbous sucking tube which he holds to his lips. This *aguamiel* or "honey water" continues to seep into the excised bowl of the plant at the rate of a liter or more a day for several months; then the plant is exhausted, but can be reproduced anew from the shoots that germinate at the bottom of the *maguey*. The *aguamiel*, carried off on the backs of the *tlachiquero* in a goatskin sack, serves as a sweetening for other foods and beverages; fermented, it is the gentle *pulque*, Mexico's wine and beer in one, now coming to be recognized as the chief source of vitamins in the ill-balanced bean and maize diet of an undernourished people; and distilled it provides the strong and fiery yet deceptively soft-tasting *tequila* and *mezcal*. Thus this miracu-

[3] Plates 2, 3 and 4.
[4] Plate 125, section above portal.

lous plant, which grows in barren and arid land that will scarce support any other vegetation, has been curse and blessing in one: a curse because when its fermented and distilled juices are imbibed to excess or taken in improperly fermented, adulterated and bacteria-contaminated form, it is a source of chronic drunkenness and stupefying brutalization and a maintainer of the bondage of the Mexican masses; an illusory "blessing," because like the church, it has served as anodyne and narcotic to help the peon forget his hard lot while that lot was still unalterable and to continue his subjection now that the means of freedom are within his grasp; and it has been a source of positive good because in hard, unyielding, semi-desert land this plant of many uses has been more truly a "staff of life" than bread itself. Hence it is not to be wondered at that it became an object of legend and worship, and of a tradition of evil as well,[5] in the lore of the pre-conquest Mexicans, or that among the primitive Otomi Indians of the barren isolated north-central upland it is known not as *agave* or *maguey*, but is referred to simply as *the plant,* since even today it is the central growing thing of the centuries-old economy of this tribe.

[5] The defeat of Quetzalcoatl and the downfall of the great civilizing and constructing Toltec culture is connected in legend with the discovery of the method of fermenting and distilling the juice of the *maguey*.

II. THE MEXICAN PEOPLE

When we say "the Mexican People" we must specify *which people.* Are we talking of the handful of whites? or the millions of *mestizos?* or the other millions of indigenous peoples? Of those who read and write and talk of "capital and labor" and the "republic" and "socialist education"? or those who do not even speak Spanish, but continue to use an unwritten indigenous tongue? Of those who live in the jungle-swamps of Quintana Roo and drive out government officials (if the latter ever dare to approach their "territory") as they would drive out any other foreign invader? of those who lead a nomadic existence under a predominantly hunting economy in the northern sierras? or of those, not far distant from them as the crow flies, who extract gold and silver and copper and lead from these same sierras with modern power-driven instruments, and belong to *sindicatos* or unions and are developing the viewpoints and customs of the modern industrial proletariat? Of those who travel and ship in auto and plane and train and boat? or those who have never used a cart nor seen a cartwheel turn but carry all their burdens with a head-strap on their backs?

LAND OF MANY TIERRAS

Floods of official oratory and reams of editorial odes to the contrary notwithstanding, Mexico has not yet formed itself into a nation. Its independence as a political entity does not carry with it a corresponding economic independence. Its unity as a geographical expression does not reflect a unified national economy. It is divided "horizontally" into innumerable and variegated regions, and "vertically" into at least three distinct social-economic cultures superimposed upon each other like the layers, constructed in successive epochs, that reveal themselves during the excavation of a Mexican pyramid.

The great mountain ranges and canyons, the absence of navigable rivers and good natural harbors, the absolute lack of beasts of burden before the conquest and relative lack since, the inadequacy of internal means of communication—save where by accident a village finds itself on some rail or highroad built not to connect the parts of Mexico with each other, but to link up some oil or mineral deposit or some export-crop center with the outside world of foreign exploitation—all these combine to preserve the ancient regionalism and localism of the country. Mexico is not so much one land as many lands: a number of isolated, relatively stable and unchanging local economies, loosely united under a single unstable superstructure, a constantly changing and shifting central government.

Each region has its own characteristic dress, its own arts and crafts, its own blanket and pottery patterns, its special local products, its distinctive cuisine, its exclusive fiestas, its regional music and dance and legend, its unmistakable folk of easily distinguishable features and stature and temperament and language, or, where Spanish is spoken, its own peculiar intonation. Mexico's people and customs and ways of living are as infinitely varied as its landscape, and when the Mexican says "mi tierra" he does not as a rule mean the Mexican Republic, but rather Yucatan or Sonora or the *Bajío*,[1] or more often, some little village which for him preserves a separate identity even within the region of which it is a part.

On a national scale, Mexico is a land of great diversity and infinite variety: locally there is marked homogeneity and uniformity. Its political apparatus is excessively centralized, but at the first moment of weakness of the central government it tends to fly apart into excessive decentralization. Its big cities are characterized by close union with the outside world; its villages by virtual self-sufficient isolation. City life is marked by restless and unceasing change; the village by relative stagnation and continuity. If a village has been in the path of a railroad or highroad, or in the orbit of a mine or factory district, or a "mecca" of tourists and folklorists, or too close to the gravitational field of some big city, then change and diversity have set in with ever accelerating tempo. But in the remoter villages, the present generation often lives according to patterns essentially undistinguishable from those followed by its village ancestors in colonial and even in pre-colonial times.

It is to these patterns, markedly different from the life patterns of Europeans and "Americans," and even from those of upper-class and urban Mexicans, that the much used but little understood term "folk"

[1] A name applied to the great central agricultural and mining region which cuts across state boundaries and includes the richest sections of Guanajuato and Michoacán.

properly applies. In these isolated villages there is truly a folk life, folk ways, folk culture, folk song, folk lore. Here there is also a high degree of communal similarity and solidarity. The villagers know each other. They are all related by infinite criss-crossed threads of intermarriage, by a common stock of beliefs and traditions, by local economic interdependence. They have a common enemy in the local *hacendado* or village tyrant, and in the remoter government and outside world as represented by the political *cacique*, the tax-collector, the agent of fruit company or trading corporation that purchases such local products as are destined for the external market.

Slowly but inevitably, these "outside" influences are changing and disrupting the ancient village ways. The army, the "revolution," the distant mine or factory or city, are taking the menfolk from the village and returning them quite other people—if they return at all. Local, self-chosen village leaders or "presidents" are being replaced by political chieftains imposed from outside. Administrative measures, when they do not remain on paper, introduce uniform, nationwide changes into this diversity of national life. Tourists, and agents of trading companies, introduce money and machine products and processes and modifying demands and desires into this world of folk-products and hand-processes and agricultural self-sufficiency and relatively moneyless economy. The radio, the newspaper, the political campaigner, the administrator, the travelling governor, or president or investigating commission, introduce new phrases, new ideas, new decrees, new ways of living, at the same time modifying and undermining the old. Village homogeneity and stability and solidarity grow weaker and weaker: diversity, deeper class conflict, progressively faster changes set in. The variegated villages become more like each other: but inside each of them the local villagers become more and more unlike each other. National uniformity grows: local homogeneity weakens. Mexico is a land in transition: it is in the process of changing from pre-capitalist to capitalist, from handicraft to machinofacture, from local to national-international economy—from a conglomerate of folks and regions into a nation.

BLEND OF PEOPLES

Properly speaking there is no "race problem" in Mexico. The Spaniard intermarried freely with the Indian and the resultant offspring provides every conceivable proportion of "blood-mixture" and every conceivable variety of feature: blue-eyed, fair-skinned and blond-haired; green or gray-eyed, olive-skinned and black-haired; glowing black-eyed, bronze-skinned and black-haired—all living side by side and blending and producing by free intermarriage an ever greater homogeneity of appearance.

Efforts have been made to measure "racial purity": how many "pure" Indians, how many "hybrids" or *mestizos*, how many "pure" whites. In vain! There is no "purometer" that will tell us anything significant, and racial "purity" among the very whites who conquered Mexico (mixture of Celt and Roman and Moor and Jew and what not!) was never more than a myth. One thing, however, is certain and unmistakable: the total number of whites who have come to Mexico from the days of the Conquest to the year of this writing is infinitesimally small compared with the great native Indian mass, and as their "bloods" have mingled in accordance with the inevitable biological laws of cohabiting peoples, the "pure" Indian and the "pure" white European alike have been steadily losing ground to the *mestizo* while the tiny stream of white "blood" has been gradually overwhelmed by the great river of Indian "blood." The resultant admixture partakes ever more of the physical features of the original inhabitants of the land.

At the same time, the land itself in sure and subtle and unexplored ways continues to exert its influence upon its native sons to make them ever less European and ever more Mexican in constitution.

In keeping with these facts as grasped with a painter's powers of observation, Rivera's human figures are predominantly a coppery, almost chocolaty brown. There are whites to be sure: the Spanish *conquistadores*, the American participants in military, financial or tourist invasions, and the "near whites" who strive in vain to preserve a "distinguishing" and "snobbish" resemblance to the conquerors with the aid of bleach and paint and clown-like powdering. But they are lost in the total effect of his painting as they are lost in the total effect of the people of this land; they are but dramatic or humorous counterpoint to the all-pervading color and feature of the Mexican people that fill his canvases and murals with abounding life, even as they fill the Mexican land.

23

There are whiter faces and browner ones in the remotest Mexican village. There are browner faces and whiter ones in the *cines* and cabarets and workshops and government secretariats of Mexico City. Not blood nor race nor complexion but the mode of living determines psychology and temperament and outlook on life. Between the outlook of the villager and that of the city dweller, between the outlook of the big landowner and that of the industrial worker, are gulfs impassible, though both may be creamy white or both may be dusky brown. There are many Mexicos, not because there are many degrees of blood admixture, but because there are many distinct socio-economic cultures existing side by side in uneasy cohabitation.

In the remoter regions of the country there is the indigenous civilization, degenerate and fallen on evil days but still giving answers, if pitifully inadequate ones, to all the elementary problems of living. Peoples like the remoter Mayas, Huichols, Yaquis, Tarahumaras and Otomis, inhabiting the jungle swamps and the solitary sierra regions, preserve the stubborn remnants of pre-conquest tribal civilization. Among these peoples are cave dwellers and nomads, groups that live by hunting and fishing poorly supplemented by the most rudimentary agriculture. They use mainly the primitive instruments and weapons of the late Stone Age. They speak no Spanish, forming a considerable portion of that one to two million Mexicans who speak exclusively an indigenous tongue. They are not truly comparable to the pre-conquest Indians for they inhabit only the least desirable regions of the Republic, suffer from centuries of oppression, isolation and stagnation, and show many signs of physical and cultural degeneration.

Towards these peoples Mexican policy has been contradictory and inadequate: at times it has inclined toward that of the North American Indian reservation with its theory of perpetual benign guardianship and its all-too-frequent practice of ruthless exploitation, wholesale enslavement and extermination; and at other times it has inclined to the theory and practice of forcible incorporation into the national life by means of deportation into other regions, appointment of alien (though Mexican) administrators, obligatory use of Spanish as the official language, and forced labor on a mass scale. There have been periods of virtual disregard of their existence and sufferings till some eruption of outraged patience has compelled military "attention"; alternating with periods of demagogic and fantastic flattery and the use of the more warlike tribes as blind pretorian instruments of one or another political leader. Thus far in revealing contrast to all the "socialistic" phraseology of the government, there has been no attempt to follow the procedures already made classic by the folk or national policy of the Soviet Union, a policy which would involve aiding them to construct a written language, to preserve and develop further and contribute to the general stream of human culture what is worth while in their traditions and literature and dances and songs and decorative arts, and to lead to their voluntary incorporation into a free union of peoples on the basis of a common national, and ultimately international, economy, in which their immediate part in the national and world division of labor would flow from the climatic-telluric nature of their regions, the local fauna and flora, their special temperaments and aptitudes, and the application of the methods of modern science to the development of the possibilities latent in each of these factors.

Next there is the wide area of semi-feudal culture based on the *latifundio* or great landed estate, on forced labor, debt peonage, terrorization by private armed bands of retainers, indoctrination by a feudal-minded and feudally organized ecclesiastical apparatus, the existence of thinly disguised feudal prerogatives ranging all the way from arbitrary administration of self-willed decrees by the landowner or his agents vested with political power to the still living remnants of the right of the first night—privileges that are further aggravated by absentee ownership and their delegation to local overseers. Despite the constant uprisings of an outraged peasantry and the grandiloquent phrases of agrarian programs that remain largely, though not entirely, on paper, it is this "culture" that comprises in its areas the bulk of the Mexican land and people.

A lesser rural area, favored by the circumstances of the agrarian struggle, or by location in geographically predisposing or administratively favored areas, is characterized by a fairly widespread distribution of small parcels of poorly watered and infertile land and village commons. Here they raise mainly beans and corn and wheat and a few chickens or cattle for domestic consumption on the basis of a largely self-sufficient domestic economy, occasionally supplementing these meager means of living by work on some nearby great estate or by the precarious production of a bit of some staple cash crop for the external market, or by work in the traditional handicrafts such as pottery, weaving, the production of lacquer ware, and the like.

Lastly there are the industrialized areas with a modern capitalist economy strongly colored and distorted by elements of pre-capitalist culture. Here we find side by side the most anachronistic hand processes and the very latest power-driven machinery and techniques; a powerful foreign and a still weak but aggressive and growing native capitalist class; a literate and semi-literate proletariat still carrying with it the visible signs of its not yet outgrown peasant origin and outlook; the beginnings of labor organization and consciousness complicated and distorted by a skillful and systematic governmental corruption of its leadership and most capable elements, and by the employment of the arts of political demagogy, on a scale never surpassed and scarcely equalled anywhere else in the world.

Thus there exist, side by side, all the ranges of human development from the stone age to the age of power. Nor are the dividing lines as sharp and clear nor the picture as simple as the above account might seem to make them. Into the remotest and most backward regions extend the precursory filaments of dominant, destiny-backed and slowly spreading modern capitalist industry. And even the most advanced centers of industry are permeated through and through with the powerful and living, if slowly weakening, elements of the earlier cultures that have preceded it.

Before the eyes of the observer is spread a vast temporal panorama: the decaying remnants of indigenous civilization; the persistent, omnipresent but slowly yielding Mexican village and agrarian-feudal regime; the weak, young, lusty-growing and disproportionately powerful and articulate industrial city, slowly spreading the influences of money, machinery, markets and manufactured materials, and urban phraseology and outlook and administration over the land: Mexico's past, Mexico's present and Mexico's future are spread out side by side. Far too much emphasis in the total picture has usually been given to the first and the third: to the remnants of autochthonous culture because of their picturesqueness, their anthropologic and folkloric interest and the fashion-

26

able cult of Indianism; to the city because of its expansive powers, because of its accessibility and articulateness, because of its stirring if misleading propaganda as to Mexico's "socialistic regime," "Bolshevik Constitution," "revolutionary government" and "socialist education."

THE VILLAGE STILL PREVAILS

Mexico's present is soaked through and through with the heritage of its Indian past; it is visibly pregnant with the longed-for burden of its industrial-proletarian future; but predominantly Mexico is still a semi-feudal, semi-colonial, agrarian land, and the great mass of its people and the ways of their living and their thinking, still center in the Mexican village.

In the village, despite the confusions of increasing transition, life is still simple, for it is regulated essentially by the simple and unchanging rhythms of soil and sun and seasons, and the patterns imposed by inherited custom and tradition. The scientific and experimental norms and fashions which the city takes for granted, however little it may really understand them, have no authoritative power here. The place of the authority of science is taken by the authority of lore: the professorial "brain trust" and commission of experts is represented by the village elders. The old women tell the young mothers what to do during pregnancy, supervise the birth of the child and its nourishment, care and upbringing. The old men initiate the young into the mysteries of times and seasons and planting and harvesting and the ways of the beasts of the field. Oral tradition, old wives' tales, the ripened wisdom of long-yeared experience of preceding generations, the tenacious continuance of beliefs and procedures that have long lost their foundations and reason for being, the advice of village priest and witch and wizard and local man of skills, the accumulated weight of inherited tradition adapted by generations of slow development to a stable or but slowly changing environment—these take the place of the experimental, rapidly changing, often fad-ridden, body of scientific and pseudo-scientific knowledge that regulates life in the cities.

When Diego Rivera had an infected eye and feared that he might lose his sight, he went to the American Hospital and sought the services of a radiologist, a bacteriologist, an optical surgeon and a trained nurse. He believes in germs, and in sterilized instruments and vaccination. But

27

when his god-children, two of whom he has painted so often, became ill only a few miles away in a nearby suburban but rural-folk village of Ixtapalapa, Rivera's *compadre* [2] invariably took them to a *bruja* or witch who used herbs and charms to avert the "evil eye" and to cast out live toads from their foreheads. Their distressed godfather, the science-believing painter, offered and urged in vain to secure and pay for the services of medical doctors. None of these children were ill; they were "bewitched": and for once the almost reverenced authority of the great and good painter, who had showered so many blessings upon this peasant family, was stubbornly ignored in favor of the superior authority of the local old men and women and of the witch who had cast out so many living toads from the foreheads of bewitched persons, as any number of ancient and worthy and credible eye-witnesses could personally testify. Not even the death of five of his seven children under this treatment has convinced Rivera's *compadre* that the treatment itself is at fault.

Yet not all of the village lore is so tragically inadequate. The accumulated experience of so many generations of relatively unchanging life in a relatively stable environment has produced an empirical folk-wisdom well adapted in the main to the needs of life—till sudden change disrupts the ancient ways of living! In the remoter and still unchanged regions of the country, life often reveals a simple grace and dignity, a sense of "belonging" to its surroundings, an elementary harmony between nature and man that to the observer is even esthetic in quality, a harmony and dignity of a kind that are lacking in the life of the cities of our day. Not that urban industrial life does not contain within it the potentialities for another harmony and another human dignity: it does, and ultimately on a far higher and wider scale than is possible to this poverty-cramped and horizon-limited adaptation of folk to land. But from the "megalopolis" of today, with its heartlessness and vulgarity, its slums and squalor, its speed and noise, its acquisitive madness and exploitative cruelty, its collective productive processes and autocratic individual ownership and control, its inhuman production for production's sake or rather for profit's sake, and its meaningless subordination of man to one

[2] Father and godfather are known as *compadres*, a ritual relationship much deeper and more significant than the formally similar one of other lands, and one involving eternal friendship and comradeship.

28

or another of the fragments into which his life has gotten subdivided, those who cannot look forward to and work for the possibilities of tomorrow are apt to feel a wistful nostalgia for the memories of yesterday and to flee, with a sense of relief, to the fading harmony and disappearing human dignity of these Mexican villages, overlooking their crumbling foundations and pitiful limitations and idealizing them into veritable paradises of human living.

Rivera has seen with unflinching and penetrating eye all the transition-ridden and contradictory realities of this Mexico. In his paintings you will find the color and savor and joyousness of the disappearing but still lingering yesterdays: the grace of the traditional garments (what European-American bourgeois fitted "suit" can match the fling and fold of a Mexican *sarape?*), the beauty of body of the free-walking women, basket or jar balanced lightly and surely on their erect heads; the lithe swing and rhythmic surety of the men wherever labor is not too hard nor exploitation too intense; the dream-filled eyes and precocious self-possession and gentle gravity of the children; the love of flowers and colors and patterns and rhythms that dominates all the humblest acts and products and possessions and movements of this folk; the brightness and unforced, unpurchased and unpurchasable gayety of their dances and songs and *fiestas*.

But he has painted also the back-breaking, brutalizing loads of Mexico's human beasts of burden; the ragged pitifulness of its hordes of beggars; the landless penury of its disinherited peasants; the arrogant tyranny of its landowners and generals and *mayordomos;* the deceitful demagogy and swinish greed of its newly rich "men of the revolution"; the wanton cruelty of its execution of agrarian leaders and shooting up and burning of whole rebellious villages; the heavy burden of stark poverty and misery and oppression that weighs upon its exploited masses.

Here is Mexico, at work and at play, rejoicing and sorrowing, building and dreaming . . . and fighting. His *machete*-wielders are not always bent in patient rhythm to swing their long knives against the wheat or cane, or in symbolic subjection before the figure of landowner or overseer. At times they straighten up with *machetes* raised aloft to be put to other ends, for the *machete*, as every peasant knows, is an instrument of a variety of uses:

El machete sirve para cortar la caña,
para abrir las veredas en los bosques umbríos,
decapitar culebras, tronchar toda cizaña,
y humillar la soberbia de los ricos impíos.

"The machete serves to cut the cane,
To open paths in shady woods,
To decapitate serpents, to cut down weeds,
And to humble the pride of the impious rich." [3]

Rivera knows also that the *machete* is powerless against the machine gun and the peasant incapable of redeeming himself except in alliance with and under the guidance of the urban industrial worker. Hence the recurring portrayal of the worker of mine and mill, in labor and in struggle, in meeting and demonstration and strike and in patient and earnest converse with his peasant brother. And hence the ever-recurring symbols of crossed sickle and hammer and the tripartite unity of worker and peasant and soldier in a common struggle for freedom.

[3] Verses borne at the masthead of the communist paper *El Machete* in the days when Diego Rivera was one of its editors.

III. LIFE AND LABOR

Today, as before the arrival of the Spaniard, the upland Mexican lives in a hut of *adobe* or sun-baked mud thatched with *zacate* or with shingles of the broad *maguey* leaf; and in the hot country his tiny one-roomed hut has latticed walls of palm and a roof heavily thatched with grass. The doorways, purple with shadow, lead into windowless and chimneyless interiors, dim and gray-black after the blinding brightness of the tropic sun. As our eyes grow accustomed to the shadowed gloom, we contemplate a scene such as would have made the pre-conquest Indian feel quite at home.

In the depths of the dim interior, even as in ancient days, there is an inevitable touch of illuminated color—a bunch of once brilliant artificial flowers, an image of the virgin or some saint, a cheap gaily colored chromo—something to redeem the dull gray-brownness of the smoky wall. Centuries of oppression and of overwhelming poverty have not been able to blot out that inevitable touch of brightness. It is in everything the Mexican creates, on every object of daily use; it gives richness to his inexpensive dishes and bowls of baked clay, lends gayety and grace to his meager store of clothing, and brightens and renders esthetically satisfying even the humble foods he eats. It gives an overwhelming sense of color to every aspect of Mexican life.

THE SYMBOLIC PETATE

The furnishings are so few that the hut seems almost bare to the alien eye. On the earthen floor, almost illuminated in the general gloom, lie *petates* or mats of woven reed. On these straw mats the great mass of the Mexican people sit, eat, sleep, are born, kick their legs in infancy, lie dreaming and playing in early youth, love and embrace and give birth in the time of their maturity, groan or suffer silently their hours in pain and illness, mumble or dream silently over the years that have passed as they husband out the last sparks of declining life. And when they breathe their ultimate breath upon its straw, they are wrapped within the folds of their last *petate* to be lowered into the ground.

The humble straw mat is an omnipresent symbol of the life of the lowly: their speech is full of homely metaphors which reveal the importance of the *petate* in all their acts of daily living. The belated guest who doesn't know when to leave "stays even to help pick up the *petate*." An intense but swiftly exhausted enthusiasm is a *"petate* flame." He who goes to live in another region has "tied up his *petate*." An inquiry after a deceased person may evoke the response: *"se petateó"*—he has betaken himself to his *petate* for an eternal sleep. Pride in one's own ways and views finds expression in the homely saying: *"De esas pulgas no brincan en mi petate"*—none of those fleas jump on my mat. And the snobbery of the self-confessed *gente decente* who sleep in beds reveals itself in the proverb: *"El que nace en petate siempre apesta a tule"*—he who is born on a *petate* always stinks of straw.

On the floor in a corner near an opening in the wall, or perhaps on the ground in a lean-to shelter in the patio is the primitive fireplace of pre-conquest origin and form. It consists of three stones perhaps covered with a grate, or a three-sided adobe or brick or stone or lava *brasero*, whose coals of charred wood are fanned into a red glow by means of an ash and smoke-scattering *petate* fan. Seated on straw, or on the ground, or squatting endlessly on their haunches, are women engaged in the time-consuming preparation, after the ancient manner, of a swiftly eaten and modest meal. In slightly hollowed-out lava grindstones and baked clay bowls they are grinding and mixing the corn meal dough for the *tortillas* [1] or they are chopping and cutting up fresh vegetables or reducing dried peppers to powder for the spicy sauces. If it is a rare feast day, or if there are guests, meager strands and fragments of meat or chicken are perhaps to be added to the tomato and chile pepper and pungent herbs to form the center of *tortilla* sandwiches or corn-leaf wrapped, corn meal mush *tamales*. *Tortillas* too will serve as plates betimes, and used as scoops for beans or gravies or *guacamole* (chopped and spiced alligator pear) they remain as the living representatives and exact latterday replicas of the stone-age spoon.

Corn and beans, *tortillas* and *tamales*, chile peppers and tomatoes—the diet is as ancient and primeval as the technique of its preparation. When Cortés was not yet an evil dream nor Quetzalcoatl even a shining legend, these same foods, prepared in the same time-consuming, color-and-flavor-producing manner, had so long been the staples of the diet

[1] Plate 87.

of the Indian people that the memory of man no longer recorded their origin.

THE MEXICAN MARKET

The same pungent odors of native herbs and infinite varieties of chile peppers that give a Mexican market of today [2] its characteristic smell, greeted the nostrils of Indian housewives on the way to the ancient *tianguis* a thousand years ago or stirred with its promising tang the inquisitive nostrils and eager palate of Bernal Diaz del Castillo five centuries back as he set down in delighted wonder his first impressions of an Aztec market. We can still see today, as he did then, *chirimoyas* and *zapotes*, *tunas* and *chilcayotes* (still bearing their ancient Indian names), sweet potatoes and squashes, strawberries and melons, *aguacates* and onions, beans and corn, *maguey* worms and pond scum "cheese," *ajonjolí* seeds to make *mole* sauce and melon seeds of numberless uses, native spices and pharmaceutical herbs, an infinite variety of peppers fresh and dried, whole and ground, of all sizes and colors and degrees of bite, cocoa beans and coffee beans, lemon tea and tobacco leaves, brilliantly colored and variegated refreshing drinks made of the juices of all kinds of tropical fruits, and numberless other herbs and fruits and flavorings and garnishings and colorings still unknown to the less colorful kitchens and less favored palates of the non-tropical world.

The market is an ever fresh surprise and delight to each new explorer, and we can still share the wonder of Bernal Diaz at gaily colored fabrics and embroideries, at gracefully molded bowls and water pitchers of painted and baked clay, at brightly lacquered gourds and boxes, and brilliantly painted baskets and carrying cloths, at incredibly diminutive and perfect toys of baked clay, at scowling, straw-maned, broom-bristly-moustached, *petate* lions, and *petate* burros and straw-sombreroed, straw-pistoled, straw-hatted, straw-bodied bandits seated on straw horses—toys that would delight the heart of any child and unbend the dignity of even the most self-important and disapproving tourist or *conquistador* in all the world.

We can find *huaraches* or sandals such as met the eye of Bernal Diaz and such as are pictured on the figures painted in the ancient codices; reed hats of primeval form; new fabrics and materials woven in old

[2] Plates 132 and 133.

ways and designs, to be worn with an ancient, timeless grace and dignity that can never be attained by our fitted clothes.

Now as then the meanest village market is redolent with enchanted odors: the spices and herbs, the fragrances of fully ripened fruits that have not been plucked prematurely, the perfumes, in all the seasons of the year, of great heaps of brilliant flowers. True, other foods and fruits and fabrics and utensils and materials and designs, even other flowers of alien origin, have come in great numbers to take their place beside the original native products, but the odor, the color, the flavor, the pattern, the human pose and gesture, the very chatter of the ancient *tianguis* still prevails.

Even Mexico City with its "Versaillese" mansions, its "Venetian" postoffice, its "Parisian" boulevards, its modernistic buildings, its "American" tea rooms and night clubs, its factories and department stores and movie houses and electric light advertisements, has not outlived its ancient heritage. Just off the main avenues, and often on them, are the *adobe* huts—matching much more closely in essential lines with the buildings of modernistic architecture than with the pseudo-colonial and pseudo-classic and "European." Elegant Porfirian palaces equipped "with all modern improvements" still have their kitchens provided with charcoal-burning *braseros;* their sunken bath tubs and tiled floors are still cleaned with *zacate* or *ixtle* fiber, and the Indian-looking, sandal-*huipil-* and-*rebozo* clad occupants of the servants "quarters" still prepare for their own and often enough for their masters' meals, the ancient foods cooked in the ancient ways. The roar and clang and clatter of the city's industry and traffic blends with the soft pad of bare or sandalled feet, and with the rhythmic clap-clap-clap of women's hands patting the corn dough of the *tortilla* into a round flat cake to be parched over a charcoal stove. Among the *gente de bien*, the well-to-do and snobbishly "decent" folk, there are those who pride themselves on their "civilized" manners and "European cuisine," but when they supply the housekeeper with a few cents to buy *tortillas* "for the servants' table," they are more than likely to filch some for their own consumption. The machine-baked, machine-sliced, wax-paper-wrapped white bread or Spanish *bolillo* lies neglected on the table while the *tortillas* still serve their ancient functions as hand-made wrappings for all sorts of fillings and as stone age spoons to scoop up rice and beans flavored with chile-

34

peppers or *mole* sauce. And often the burning mouthful is washed down with a draught of *pulque* to the neglect of French and Spanish wines and German beers.

THE TELESCOPING OF TIME

Thus in labor and in living all the ages of mankind from that of stone to that of power jostle and elbow each other, now in friendly, now in hostile cohabitation. It is hard to keep one's sense of time and historical development clear when one can step thus from age to age in a few kilometers, sometimes in a few paces. Here is the latest Ford or General Motors truck—and dodging it is a barefoot *cargador* bearing a burden of a hundred or more pounds of freight on his head and back. The truck is more impressive but the area it covers is but a tiny fraction of the country. Over the land as a whole, even the burro must yield precedence to man as the chief pack animal, today as he was in ancient times. Only touristic callousness can find "charm" and "quaintness" in the weight of that anachronistic burden. Let the reader contemplate Rivera's "Garbage Carrier" or *cargadores* or builders of churches and pyramids, and he will feel a sense of the strain and labor in those great head-compressing and back-breaking loads.[3]

Here and there an especially favored village changes over night from the sharpened stick or man-drawn wooden plow to the power-driven tractor, skipping the intermediate stages of the employment of draught animals. Or a woman ceases to grind her own corn on a lava grindstone or *metate* to purchase corn flour already ground at an electrically operated *molina de nixtamal*. In both cases there has been a sudden leap from the Stone Age to the age of power! No wonder that the Mexican time sense and historical situation is at times confused and confusing!

Nor is it any use asking rural Mexicans how far it is to the place one is seeking. Their concepts of space differ from ours too. Any place they have ever been to is "just over the hill" or "yonder a ways" or "only a little walk." The chief means of locomotion is foot power and men, women and even children will walk, or rather jog at a slow trot, all day and all night over hill and dale with a great pack of their handmade products on their backs, to get to some fair or market place at dawn and to begin the day's work of selling their wares. If it is a woman

[3] Plates 7, 12, 72, 73, 82, 83, 92, 93, 97, 201.

she may carry atop her load or in an Indian carrying-sash her youngest child as well. Two or three days of labor at home, a day and a night or more of walking and trotting to market over hilly ground (Indians have been known to come afoot to important fairs in Mexico from distant Guatemala!), a day of alert activity in the market place vending their wares, a night of rest somewhere on the road, and a day and a night or more of walking and trotting home again; and perhaps fifty centavos or at most a peso or two (certainly less than an American dollar) in cash is all that the skilled and patient craftsman will have to show for his labor.

Hence their good taste and preference for the cheap and lovely handicraft products over the imported, ugly, machine-made goods is preserved perforce by their own poverty and lack of ready cash. Time is surely not money here! Wages that range from a few centavos to a peso or so a day cannot afford even the cheapest and tawdriest of imported manufactured products. A Mexican craftsman can spend days and weeks in weaving beautiful *sarapes* or sashes or baskets or bags, in lacquering boxes and gourds, in hand-tooling leather purses or saddles, but he cannot spend a few cents on things not produced under the same pre-capitalist economy. Time is the most plentiful thing he possesses; cash the scarcest. Hence his concept of time, like his concept of space, is not that of the advanced-industry peoples. This explains, too, why the tourist can buy up his ridiculously cheap bargains in beauty, for he is purchasing with a money that has a different relation to time than prevails in Mexico.

MEXICANS HAVE NO "TIME SENSE"

The Mexicans have no "time sense." Or is it that they have more sense about time than the rushing, speed-driven, machine-broken people of more industrialized lands? Not that Mexicans do not like speed. It is one of life's joys—when you can turn it on or off at will. There are no gayer, faster, more reckless, mountain-curve-spinning, tree-and-boulder-missing auto drivers in the world! But like all peasant, pre-industrial peoples, the Mexicans are never in a hurry, and they refuse to be rushed.

Mexico has been called "mañana-land" because of its genial habit of never doing today what can be put off till tomorrow. But *"vuelva usted*

36

mañana" is really an inherited Spanish formula rather than a native one. The true native phrase is "*ahoritita*"—"right away": the Spanish word "*ahora*," "now," with the playful Indian love of adding on a string of softening diminutives—"in a little, little, little now." To the bewildered and indignant foreigner it seems to mean, "I'll do it, if you ever catch me again, maybe."

The foreign investor or business man hovers forever on the perilous verge of apoplexy because these stubborn, easy-going people simply will not be hurried or speeded up. The old-timer that survives into comprehension has learned that if he can arouse interest in a sudden emergency he will get unparalleled speed and energy and skill—that's fun! But by threats and bullyings he will get only an increase in slowness and resistance. "I must keep their wages down," business men will assure you, "for if I give them enough wages in one day to meet their living expenses for two, the —— —— ——s take a day off!" And there's some factual truth to the irate business man's assertion, for the Mexican never can quite comprehend the idea of spending all one's life working to the point of exhaustion in order to earn money in order to keep alive in order to go on working. . . . He wants to *live* sometimes as well.

Hence, as in all pre-capitalist lands, the frequent holidays, the gay and absorbing fiestas, the human dignity of slow speech, of thoughtful reflection, of quiet dreaming and lazing in the sun, the social sustenance of the not-yet-lost art of conversation, the graceful carriage, the easy swing of measured movement in harmony with the natural rhythms of the body that has not yet been broken to the clanky gait of the machine.

BATTLE WITH THE MACHINE

There are machines in Mexico: they have come to stay and their use and the flood of their products is spreading slowly over the land. But so far the Mexican spirit has refused to subordinate itself to the machine; rather does it insist on adapting the machine to itself. So the machines run a little more slowly; adopt peculiar rhythms their inventor never dreamed of, "miss fire" every so often, or some of their taxing multiple series of working tools whirl idly and untroubled through the air. "Lack of efficiency" say the foreign engineers. Quite so, less efficiency and, so far, more humanity.

But will this situation endure? Not likely, in the long run—unless

37

the Mexican people, thanks to some fortunate turn in domestic and world events, should succeed in developing soon the foundations of a post-capitalist social order on the basis of which machinery can be introduced in subordination to man. But if not, the Mexican spirit will give the machine—and its present owners and introducers—a fight worth witnessing.

"THE MEXICAN IS A QUEER BIRD"

The psychology of the Mexican people is still pre-capitalist. They have never learned to value quantity above quality, money above corn and wine or corn and *pulque*, things above their uses, the symbols of wealth above wealth itself. The foreigner is often puzzled, even enraged, by the refusal of a "ragged Indian" to sell some object of beauty he is using, regardless of the price offered and the importunity (to use a polite word) of the would-be purchaser. *"Es para el uso, señor."* (It's for use—not for sale), is the response delivered by this poverty-stricken peon with a dignity a prince might envy. Or more baffling still is the refusal of a craftsman to sell his most beautiful wares because he rightly feels that they adorn his humble workshop. Or again, to sell on the road, at any price, wares which he has prepared for the exciting adventure of carrying to market. In vain to argue that it will lighten his load, that you are offering better than the market price, that he intends to sell them anyway. Production is more to him than just a device for getting money as much and as quickly as possible; production, as in all normal human beings whose instincts have not been distorted by unpleasant and degrading toil or leisure-class ideology or money-commodity relationships, is still a way of life as well as a way of "making a living."

He cannot understand a life in which everything is for sale and money is the measure of all things. He knows that not everything is so measurable in terms of price: joy in work, for instance, or skill and beauty of workmanship. He will linger lovingly over an object of labor: he is to sell it, to be sure, but it's not "for sale" only: in his mind it is also for use, to serve and enrich the processes of living. So he stops to put the extra skillful workmanlike touch upon it, the extra loving care in design, the extra playful bristle into the broom whiskers of the little straw lion, the extra breath of bright reality into the little paper flowers, the added bit of cross-eyed bewilderment to the expression of the little clay

38

pig, the unpaid touch of color and pattern to the plate of *guacamole* which will not fetch a penny more than any other plate of *guacamole*, nor last a minute longer in the jaws of a hungry man. But it does give an added minim of nourishment to the spirit of maker and consumer. And it's fun! The craftsman's face lights up as he puts the added touch of design, or color, or drama into whatever he is working on. Unpaid? Isn't that pay enough? His face lights up too in reflection of the amusement or delight of each passer-by who stops to look at his product. And he takes pleasure and satisfaction in the anticipation of the pleasure and satisfaction which the lovingly elaborated object will give to the user. For sale? Of course. But still, for use. He has never mastered the pecuniary-acquisitive power of abstraction that divorces all of the qualities inherent in the uses of an object from its public existence and reduces them all to a single abstract, colorless, purely quantitative attribute, namely price-fetching power or exchange-value. "Queer," these Mexicans!

And he does seem "queer"—if we don't stop to realize how much "queerer," humanly speaking, are the ways and evaluations we take for granted under the inverted, anti-human values placed upon men and things by a pecuniary, acquisitive economy.

Elizabeth Morrow spies an inexpensive and lovely chair in Cuernavaca. She orders a dozen from the proud craftsman, and to her astonishment the price goes up: more than twelve times as much for a dozen as for one!

"But in my country they give us a reduction for buying in quantity."

"Ah, but *Señora*, think of the monotony of making twelve chairs all exactly alike!" Her "crushing" argument has been met by a still more crushing rejoinder.

A foreign business man in Mexico, bachelor, who does his own household shopping, goes to the market for eggs.

"How do you sell them?"

"Eight centavos a piece."

"Give me a peso's worth," thinking to get thirteen for a peso. He gets twelve!

"It should be cheaper, *Señora*, when I buy in quantity, and you're charging me more than if I bought them one at a time."

"*Si Señor*, any one who can afford to buy a whole peso's worth of eggs at once can afford to pay a little more for each egg."

Queer? But logically speaking, humanly speaking, any way but capitalistically speaking, unanswerable.

A TRIUMPH OF MECHANICS

Pre-industrial ways, when they get tangled up in machinery, often have their comical aspects. There is the famous case of the National Theater or Palace of Fine Arts, design of an Italian architect, product of the pseudo-Europeanizing tendencies of Porfirian days, and undoubtedly one of the two or three ugliest—and costliest—buildings of its size in the world. Built of Carrara marble with a dome of rainbow hues, a huge, oversized, overweighted, pin-cushion and candy-box structure whose massive external bulk surrounds a diminutive interior theater; it is much too heavy for the filled-in lake-ground on which Mexico City rests, and it has been sinking steadily into the earth ever since its walls were first raised. Millions in misapplied and often "diverted" funds have been sunk into the construction and support of this amazing monstrosity. Endless tons of concrete have been injected into the voracious underground caverns of the subterranean lake bed, but the building continues to sink. When it got so far below the general street level of the center of Mexico City that it was in danger of losing its "impressiveness," a new idea struck the engineers and architects: they simply lowered the level of the surrounding streets and made the sidewalks descend into a sort of depression where the building had sunk deepest. A veritable triumph of modern mechanical science! If the monster doesn't keep on sinking!

THE ADVANCE OF THE MACHINES

The entanglement of machine and pre-machine cultures has its tragic aspects as well. In the very shadow of the great textile factories of Mexico City, as in countless villages throughout the land, can be found pre-conquest hand looms at work. Rivera has painted a hand weaver and spinner at work in the village of Milpa Alta, close suburb of Mexico City.[4] In these pictures one can see the same primitive loom with warp fastened to post or tree and held taut by a belt around the waist, the

[4] Plates 89-91.

40

same wooden "sword" to beat down the weft, the same simple bobbin dancing in a baked clay bowl, the same movements and crouching posture and use of hands and naked foot, the same picture that Cortés saw when he wrote his glowing descriptions of the indigenous weavers' products to his king, or that the native artists painted in the ancient codices over three centuries ago. The materials may differ, wool having been unknown before the conquest, and the patterns may have altered somewhat, but their essential composition and color and the mode of their production remains unchanged through the centuries.

Yet, as the story of the introduction of power-looms into other pre-industrial lands repeats itself here, these hand weavers are doomed to a pitiful and tragic extinction. Will the plastic sense, the instinct of workmanship, the love of color, the honesty of materials, the wool that is truly wool and the colors that come out brighter and fresher after each washing, will these things be preserved? That too depends, like the fate of the human elements involved, upon the question of under what auspices and circumstances the machine is introduced and made dominant in Mexico. Certainly, the possibilities of preserving these values is not excluded. The plastic sense still alive among this folk has been caught up and given new and more complex expression by its greatest artists. A humanized (read, *socialized*) machine would have great artists designing its patterns, but not in servile and inappropriate copy of the patterns natural to handicraft and unnatural to the machine; rather, this continuous, living plastic sense would be applied to the laws and possibilities inherent in the nature of the machine product. This product such a society could multiply and distribute on a scale undreamed of under the poverty and productivity limitations of ancient handicraft.

THE BURDEN OF BACKWARDNESS

Certainly, pre-machine civilization in a machine age is not the Eden that the writings of nostalgic tourist-refugees from the ills of machine capitalism would make it. Like all pre-capitalist lands, Mexico is largely at the mercy of its machine-equipped and mechanism-armed giant industrial neighbor. Only the stubbornness of the Mexican mountains combined with the stubbornness of the Mexican people has thus far prevented complete absorption and subjection. A sensitive observer coming from Havana with its squalor and its casino-luxury, its servility to American control and its degradation of the native spirit to the dregs of an unhappy "Americanization," feels a positive sense of relief when he disembarks at Vera Cruz, and meets up even at the docks with representatives of a people who have succeeded in resisting the forces that have overwhelmed Cuba. Here is a people that, like reeds, bend before the overpowering winds but do not break: they have known how to adopt and adapt, to yield for a time to superior force but not be overwhelmed. Despite landing parties and punitive expeditions, despite servile native imitators and crusading foreign missionaries, despite investments and pillagings and "representations" and "good-will expeditions," they have succeeded in remaining indubitably and completely themselves.

Further, as in all pre-capitalist lands in process of transition, there are aspects of the national life where all the disadvantages of the old combine with all the disadvantages of the new, while the old has lost its positive features and the new has not realized as yet its favorable potentialities. Nowhere can exploitation be as merciless as in a land where the decaying remnants of feudal serfdom are mated to the first raw beginnings of capitalist accumulation. Fortunately, thanks to the superior resistant powers of this people, there are fewer such spots in the fabric of national life here than in Central America and the Caribbean and northern South American lands. But the lives of the henequen peons, of the woodcutters in the hardwood forests of Quintana Roo, of the banana harvesters of the empire of the United Fruit Company, of the workers in some of the more remote and less organized mines, are far from the tropical idyll that "picturesque" travelogues would make them.

THE SHADOW OF POVERTY

Over the Mexican "land of plenty," with its varied and rich natural resources, its mineral wealth that four centuries of Spanish, English and American rapacity have been unable to exhaust, its "lovely climate" and "quaint picturesqueness" and magnificent buildings "decaying with such charm," hangs the omnipresent shadow of poverty: of poverty and undernourishment, of illiteracy and ignorance, of degrading toil and landlessness, of poor sanitation, of staggering infant mortality and a monumental death rate from the ravages of easily preventable diseases.

According to Alberto Pani, cabinet minister under various governments, Mexico City's mortality rate is nearly two and one-half times greater than that of the average European city of similar size, nearly three times that of corresponding cities in the United States, and even greater than the notoriously high death rates of cities like Madras and Cairo. This in the nation's capital with its modern drug stores and doctors and hospitals, its all-year-round spring climate, its clean streets and generally excellent sewage and water systems. But even in Mexico City these things are the prerogatives of the well-to-do. The beautiful "City of Palaces," despite the recent improvement of large areas, still has a vast acreage of overcrowded slums, of mud huts with no windows nor ventilation nor (strange paradox in this land of tropic sun!) any sunlight. There are six, eight, ten and more people, of both sexes and all ages and conditions of health, together with dogs, cats, often chickens and pigs, all crowded into the single, unventilated, unlighted room of these huts, sleeping on straw mats on unboarded mud floors. There are acres of land with no sewage nor running water system, where precious water has to be carried great distances by the occupants, sometimes from doubtful sources: the only sign of urban "progress" is that the graceful water pitcher on the head has yielded to a yoke of shiny ten-gallon gasoline cans. In these huts animals can mingle freely with humans because the human way of living is physically indistinguishable from that of the animal.

With poverty goes insufficient food, illiteracy, ignorance of elementary hygiene, belief in the curative powers of witches, charms, amulets, crosses, talismans and prayers to saints or supernatural powers, fear of *el aigre*, the terrible god of the air. With poverty go long hours in the rain and damp, lack of money for firewood, insufficient clothes, inadequate and ill-balanced diets, food given children of tender age that would knock out many a foreigner of maturer years, use of semi-waste and spoiled foods because they are cheaper, lack of money for medicines or doctors, widespread alcoholism and lack of elementary cleanliness. Further allies of disease in such quarters are omnipresent lice, bedbugs, fleas, roaches, flies and rats.

Outside of Mexico City, if the water supply permits, the cleanliness is much greater. In fact, where water runs freely (and often even where it is scarce and precious), the spotless, sun-bleached, white pyjama-like clothes of the men and the brilliant, bright-clean *huipiles* and *faldas* of the women make the foreigner in his "European" clothes feel uncomfortably dirty.

But in most parts of the country water is scarce—often the sole supply of a village is a stagnant pool or a spillway from the monopolized water-supply of the local landowner [5]—and is likely to be contaminated with animal and human excrement. Fifty to seventy percent of the babies die during the first few years of intestinal disorders, infection by contaminated water, ill-selected and insufficient food, weaning on *pulque* and beans and *tacos*, and the prevalence of sanitary practices that spread infection. Those that survive must perforce be strong; if early illness has not weakened and maimed them, they have a splendid appearance of health and a real immunity under conditions that would be lethal to an unadapted stranger.

Add to this malaria in the tropical lowlands where the cost of a round of quinine for his family is more than a day-laborer's earnings; and the fairly wide prevalence of venereal disease which according to some authorities was brought to the new world by the *conquistadores* and most certainly was spread by them with amazing rapidity among the indigenous women who were the spoils of their conquest,[6] and one wonders at the many bright-eyed, clear-skinned children and healthy, firm-bodied, graceful men and women.

AN HISTORIC QUESTION MARK

The machine is a bearer of progress. In the long run it is the hope of Mexico, as it is of the rest of humanity. Immediately, it may bring to the country a sewer system, more nearly bacteria-free water, irrigation, a necessarily more literate and more class conscious worker. It may also bring fresh slums, piling the new upon the old; smoke pollution of Mexico's health-giving sun and mountain air which alone explain why

[5] Plate 6. This typical landscape was painted at San Juan Ixtayoán in the State of Mexico, where the village water supply for both animals and men is a stagnant overflow from the landowner's dam.

[6] There seems to be ample evidence that syphilis was a pre-conquest disease as well, as shown by the existence of venerated images marked with syphilitic stigmata and of the dog-faced, syphilitic god, Nanahuatzín. But there can be no doubt that this disease assumed new virulence and more universal dissemination after the Conquest.

In 1926, Dr. Bernardo J. Gastelum, for many years head of the Health Department, told the Pan-American health conference that 60 percent of Mexico's inhabitants suffer from syphilis!

health conditions are not worse than they are; speed-up; more merciless and destructive exploitation; relatively unknown forms of nervous disease; the early throwing of used-up men and women onto the industrial scrap heap; the mass production of ugliness in place of the slow, handicraft production of beauty; and a new and peculiar form of poverty, super-poverty in the midst of super-plenty. We are before the same historic question mark that has presented itself twice before in the considerations of this chapter. It all depends on who owns and who introduces the machine. Introduction of machinery after a social revolution, as another backward land, the Soviet Union, has shown, is quite a different thing from introduction by a raw and nascent capitalism, aided, abetted and overawed by a dominating foreign finance-capital. Rivera is on the side of the machine, for he feels it will create, organize, unite, and develop the consciousness of the class in whom he sees the hope of Mexico's future, the proletariat, and because he believes that under the leadership of the working class, the Mexican masses can take over the control of their destinies and begin the planned and humanized development of an industrial civilization in Mexico. Hence, side by side with his portrayal of the ancient handicrafts (pottery, weaving, dyeing) and agriculture—to the beauty of which this keen-visioned painter is certainly not blind—he has painted mining (primitive and advanced), steel-making, the tractor, and the esthetic beauties and human possibilities of modern machinery in his visions of Mexico's future.[7]

[7] See the murals of the Court of Labor of the Ministry of Education, plates 104 to 109. Also the crowned tractor in the ballad series from the third floor of the same building, plate 143; the industrialized land, plates 120, 152; the vision of "good government" in the Agricultural School at Chapingo, plates 165 and 166, and of the Mexico of Tomorrow on the left wall of the National Palace Stairway, plates 228 and 241. This view finds further expression in the marvelous painting of American machine industry in Detroit, reproduced in *Portrait of America.*

45

IV. DEATH AND LAUGHTER

One of the most vivid and distinguishing features of Mexico's slowly disappearing folk life is the fiesta. Where it exists not as a tourist spectacle, but in its traditional form, it is a truly collective expression. In its celebration the entire village, every man, woman and child, takes an active part. The costs are met collectively, or by the conferring of an honorary succession on selected individuals from year to year. The principal participants in the dramatic performances that are involved in some of them are often chosen by democratic election. The fiesta belongs to the *pueblo*, a word signifying both village and people at once. No two villages have the same local fiesta: they come at different dates, are devoted to differing patron saints or secular occasions or traditions, have dissimilar origins and ceremonials and observances. Only this do they possess in common: that the whole village is atingle for weeks before its fiesta and that corporate solidarity and folk joyousness reach their culminating point in the two or three days or week of its celebration.

The fiesta is a work of folk art to which all the arts of the folk contribute: music and dance and song, costume and color and bodily strength and grace, drama and lore and humor and imagination. In the accompanying *puestos* or fairs, all the local and regional handicrafts offer their products. It is a carnival, but not like those of the European cities which have become commercialized, formalized and vulgarized. It is a carnival in the ancient sense: a moment of unreserved play in the midst of serious labor, of complete release from the petty individual cares that separate man from man, of complete unity and communion. It is a respite from the tedium and burden of daily living, a collective joyousness that temporarily supplants mass suffering, a colorful moment of escape from inescapable reality, and a fulfillment of unfulfilled dreams. Hence in these dream-plays men can fly[1] who have hitherto been obliged to tread the solid earth; rain comes in abundance in lands where

---

[1] In the *fiesta del volador*, of pre-conquest origin and still celebrated in Papantla, Vera Cruz, on Corpus Cristi Day, four men fly in circles head down, suspended by cords from a newly erected pole dragged with much ceremony from a grove which was sacred in the ancient Indian faith. As described by Clavigero, the same fiesta, minus the superimposed Santiago and the "Dance of Moors and Spaniards," was being celebrated at the time of the Spaniards by men dressed like birds.

arid famine has so often held sway; the bandit triumphs over the general, allowing the oppressed people to taste the fruits of vicarious triumph over oppressive authority; the poor outlaw carries off the charming and aristocratic bride; the dead walk again among their forsaken loved ones and join them in feasting and drinking and play; the deer-god is propitiated and the chase will yield plenteous bounty and the crops will surely grow; the good saint or valiant hero is among us on horseback and will cure our cattle and diseases, make good our hurts and right our wrongs. Life which was hunger is replete with feasting, which was sorrow is full of gayety and laughter, which was drabness is illuminated with color and wonder and all our dreams come true.

FIESTAS IN RIVERA'S PAINTING

Rivera has caught many of these beautiful fiestas and dances and folk tales with his omnivorous eye, his pencil and his brush, and though they be eventually driven out of the disrupted villages and be destroyed, they will live as long as his canvases and his solid enduring cement and ground marble walls. He has devoted several canvases to the *Sandunga* (Tehuantepec Love Dance) and the rites of the Day of the Dead; his latest work at this writing is a series of four carnival panels in the Hotel Reforma; and the entire inner *patio* of the great double court of the Ministry of Education building has been turned into the "Court of the Fiestas" by Rivera's monumental brush.[2]

As you enter into the great *patio* your eye is caught by the massed flame of crimson banners on the opposite wall, where the four central panels and the space over the arches that divide them are devoted to one of the oldest and latest of folk festivals: the First of May.[3] Born of an ancient northern springtime holiday, celebrated in its time with green boughs, flowers, maypoles, dance and song and rites of fertility, traditionally accompanied by mock social revolution in the form of the crowning of some serf or peasant as a one-day lord or king (for are not fiestas ever the fulfillment of the people's dreams?), this dying rural celebration was manured afresh by the blood of the Chicago martyrs of 1886 and became the urban people's holiday *par excellence*, the day when all the workers of all the lands of the earth feel the might that is

[2] Plates 58, 59, 99-101, 122-135 and 242-249.
[3] Plates 128, 129.

potential in their solidarity. In many lands this is a day of fierce oppression and persecution and struggle, and the red banners are symbolically dyed afresh each First of May. But in Mexico, where recent governments, for reasons which will appear in a later chapter, have recognized Mayday as a legal holiday and provide theaters and speakers and military bands and actually give orders to the government employees to march in the parades, it is more fiesta than day of struggle.

As one's eye leaves the flaming banners and surging masses of the Mayday panels and wanders over the rest of the Court of the Fiestas, it is caught up by the whirl and swing of a Tehuantepec dance festival, the leap of a charger and clash of clubs and spin of firework pinwheels in two fiesta paintings by Amado de la Cueva,[4] a pagan dance of youths and little girls around a Maypole-like structure in a church, a flower festival thronging the canals of Santa Anita, the startling explosion of "Judas" effigies hanging in the air, the macabre dance of guitar-playing skeletons over a moving, stirring crowded market place, and the quieter contrast of a corn-harvest festival and the Day of the Dead in the country.[5] The whole court stirs, whirls, swings and dances in a great flow of form and color.

PAGAN FESTIVAL

Even the fiestas celebrated in front of or in the interior of churches but ill disguise, even unashamedly flaunt, their secular and pagan origin. The Church had to accept and attach itself to these ancient folk expressions by fastening to them movable feast days or some nearby or coincident saint's day if it was to get any attention at all in connection with them. In token of this Rivera has portrayed a sun and a moon at either

[4] In the whole huge three-storied double court of the Secretariat of Education there are three murals on the ground floor and a row of shields in one of the second-floor *patios* which are not the work of Diego Rivera. He had originally been commissioned to do half of the *patio* walls and various other members of the Union of Painters and Sculptors had been assigned the other half; but by the time he had finished his half, the other painters had finished only a few panels and shields. Rivera was then entrusted with finishing the entire job. The shields, which the other painters took an entire year to complete, remain, and Rivera preserved two out of three panels done by Charlot (which though they are in the present Court of the Fiestas have nothing to do with festive themes) and the two fiesta panels by Amado de la Cueva, while he destroyed only one panel done by Charlot which he felt could not be harmonized with the rest of the Court.

[5] Plates 122 to 135.

48

side of the portals of the church in the background of the *tianguis* or traditional market fair of Chalma.[6] The Sun and the Moon are older gods than the Lord of Chalma, who got into popular confidence and favor only by identifying himself with Ostotocteotl, the God of the Chalma caves, and by having his crucifix erect itself miraculously in the subterrean grotto and cast down the ancient idol that had reigned there. In most nature religions, as in ancient Mexican mythology, the lords of the heavens are the Sun and the Moon: the Sun being the masculine principle, the fertilizer and life-giver, and the Moon (or in some Mexican traditions the Earth) the feminine principle, the mother of gods and men. Hence the patron Indian Virgin of Mexico, the brown Virgin of Guadalupe who usurped the shrine of Tonantzín, the Mother of the Gods, at Tepeyac, is usually portrayed in Catholic iconography as standing on a crescent moon or having a horned moon as crest. Each twelfth day of December, fourteenth of the month of Atemutzli of the ancient Nahua calendar, this merged Virgin and Earth Mother, Snake Woman and Corn Goddess, still receives the immemorial tribute of the Indian masses offered in the immemorial way. In the courtyard and within the precincts of the great church, dancers wearing sandals, short bright-colored tunics, embroidered blouses and elaborate head-dresses of silver, beads, mirrors and feathers, and adorned with "snow-white flowers" of popped corn, with clinking tassels of shells, tiny cooking utensils, magic wind-pebbles of the wind-god Ehecatl, carved obsidian and claw-like bits of jade, swing slowly around in ancient pagan rhythms to the music of one-stringed violins and pre-conquest two-toned *teponaxtle* drums. In the center clog awkward, weird figures in odd head-dresses and skins of opossums, bears, leopards, coyotes, mountain lions, while the traditional Nahua jester, a black-faced venerable monkey-man called *huehue*, the old-old one, scurries around tripping up the dancers, swishing his lash at mockers and stray curs, solemnly and industriously adding his note of uproarious gayety to the most Catholic and most sacred of all Mexico's fiestas! [7] Certainly the good Father Sagahún was amply justified in his suspicion that the Indians came to that "little hill called Tepeyac, and now named Our Lady of Guadalupe [where] they had a

[6] Plates 132 and 133.
[7] See Carleton Beals: Guadalupe Hidalgo, in *Mexican Folkways*, Vol. I, No. 4, pp. 4-6.

temple dedicated to the mother of the gods, whom they called Tonantzín, which means 'our mother' . . . still to visit that Tonantzín from afar as of old, a devotion which is suspicious because in all parts of the country there are many churches of Our Lady, and they do not go to them, but continue to come from afar to their Tonantzín as formerly." [8]

Thus despite the number of candles and little silver arms and legs and hearts and even, oh pagan persistence! little silver animals, sold to serve as votive offerings to the saints, and despite the number of pence that flow into Peter's coffers on such occasions, even the most sacred of these folk fiestas are really secular and traditional and profane. Into the very gateways of the church the market overflows with its offerings of purely worldly delights and on the church steps or within the aisles and before the altar itself the *mariaches*, folk musicians, play their unconsecrated tunes for the dancers. One of the panels of the Court of the Fiestas [9] shows such a colorful dance performed annually in the church of Our Lord of Chalma with flower-crowned pole and crisscrossed ribbons held by dancing youths, while garlanded little girls in bright dresses hold flower arches for their little counter-dance and a *mariache* provides joyous music. It is clearly a survival of the sacred calendar fiesta, the center figure representing the Sun, the men representing the twenty days of the ancient ritual calendar month, and the little girls representing the planets or fixed stars. This colorful ceremony with its vari-colored ribbons and garlands and flower arches and bright raiment completely eclipses the images of the grim and tortured saints and the crucified Christ dimly visible in the background behind the barricade of bright candles. A Mexican fiesta, whether secular or pseudo-religious, is a time of rejoicing: there is enough of sorrow and persecution and suffering in their daily life.

THE FESTIVAL OF THE FLOWERS

So, as if by a touch of intensifying contrapuntal irony, it is on *el Viernes de Dolores*, the Friday of Sorrows, that the ancient, joyous, carnivalesque Indian spring flower festival takes place. Rivera has painted

[8] Sagahún: *Historia de las cosas de Nueva España*, Mexico, 1831, Book XI, chap. XII.
[9] Plate 131.

the festival as celebrated at Santa Anita and Xochimilco, source of the flowers and fresh vegetables which supply the markets of the Capital, and sacred to the ancient god of flowers and festivals, Xochitl.[10] In the capital itself this pleasant festival takes the form of parades of flower-decked autos, trucks and floats, and flower-laden and flower-adorned pedestrians. All day long and far into the night the passers-by pelt each other, not with choking eye- ear- and mouth-filling confetti, but with fresh colorful fragrant flowers. An engaging way of commemorating the "Friday of Sorrows."

THE KILLING OF JUDAS

And on the Saturday of Glory there is the noisy, hilarious burning in effigy, or rather exploding, of the huge firework-lined puppets or Judases. This festival came to Mexico from Christian Spain, but its origin too is pagan, with roots in a most ancient festival of death and resurrection, the burning of last year's grain. In fact, the whole Easter festival of Christendom, like the Jewish Passover, is rooted in the natural "miracle" of the death of the old plants, the burial of their seed and the springing up of the new which is still the old, the most significant agricultural rite in the life of man.

But as in the case of the Friday of Sorrows, so the succeeding Saturday of Glory bears the peculiar imprint of the Mexican folk. A closer inspection of the faces and clothes of the Judases reveals that the Mexicans are burning Judases of their own: Judas is a uniformed *gendarme*, a federal soldier, a general, a politician, a landowner, a reactionary leader—anyone who has earned the hatred of the people. Once more, one of the deepest of the dreams of the masses is being realized: vengeance on the tyrant and oppressor too powerful to be reached, except in dreams.[11] The Saturday before Easter has thus become a revolutionary fiesta, and where the people are largely illiterate, the authorities have learned to fear this potent "subversive propaganda." Hence in the time of the dictatorship of Santa Anna we find a police

[10] Plate 130 for the Fiesta at Santa Anita. For a painting of the flower-god, Xochitl, see plate 116.
[11] "The makers of these puppets . . . because of their peculiar psychology make up always figures that represent persons of the epoch, but those persons are always the ones who at the moment have earned the hatred of the popular classes." Ignacio B. del Castillo, in *Excelsior*, April, 1923.

51

decree censoring this holy festival of vengeance against the betrayer of the Lord: "Nor shall there be burned," reads the police order of 1853, "those figures commonly called Judases, if they have any dress or sign with which to ridicule any social class or person." And in the time of Maximilian, the resentment of the people being greater, this most Christian festival was prohibited altogether: "On the next Saturday of Glory no fireworks of any kind shall be burned in this capital, nor shall there be any sale of effigies known as 'Judases.'" [12] It appears that Rivera has but been following the custom of the folk, a little clarified in social consciousness, in making his Judases represent a bourgeois politician, a general and a priest—capitalism, militarism, clericalism.[13] Is not painting itself a kind of fiesta speaking with tremendous directness and power to an illiterate, or even to a literate people?

THE BANDIT "SAINT"

In fiesta as in popular ballad, the folk celebrates its favorite heroes. The old Saxons, smarting impotent under the Norman yoke, took vicarious vengeance in the triumphs of the outlaw Robin Hood and his merry men over fat gold-chained clerics and the boasting sheriff of Nottinghamshire. The medieval folk rejoiced in the exploits of Renard the Fox, who with only his wits to help him outwitted Baron Bear and Judge Wolf and King Lion. In old Russia the popular dreams of folk vengeance and folk justice clustered around the hero-deeds of Stenka Razin. The *picaros* of Spain were plebeian heroes and their adventures and victories a powerful form of social criticism. And in Mexico, where revolutionists are proclaimed bandits (and bandits, forced into outlawry by tyranny and intolerable conditions, easily turn revolutionary when there is a movement powerful enough to enlist their support and enlarge their vision), the outlaw is the hero of countless folk ballads and has even attained to the dignity of celebration in one of the country's biggest and most colorful fiestas.

Each Spring at carnival time at Huejotzingo on the old royal highway between Mexico City and Puebla, Augustín Lorenzo,[14] who was

[12] José D. J. Domínguez: "Los Judas in México," *Mexican Folkways*, Vol. V, No. 2, pp. 90-104.
[13] Plate 127.
[14] As this work was being written Rivera was adding four more to his series of fiesta paintings in the form of four carnival scenes in the banquet and dance

52

shot by the French more than a half century ago, rides again, holds up the mail coach express and despoils it of its stores of silver, carries off the fair and noble lady and does battle afresh with the French, the *Húngaros* (Maximilian used an Austrian guard) and, strange echo of the Spanish heritage, with the Turks!

Certainly, those who insist that Mexican fiestas are essentially religious outpourings of the primitive fervor of the folk and dedicated to some holy *santo* will be hard put to it to explain away this people's saint. The little village of Huejotzingo, sad and dreary-looking all the rest of the year, is transformed beyond recognition at carnival time: here are crowds from all the neighboring villages, gaily colored booths laden with food and drink and toys and local handicraft products, brilliant and fantastic uniforms of French "Zouaves," "Sappers," "Apaches," "Zacapanztles," "Tarahumares," "Hungarians" and "Turks," booted and spurred and gorgeously apparelled "Generals" and Outlaws," a mail coach laden with gold and silver, a noble lady carried off by an outlaw and appearing not altogether loath, rockets and pinwheels, exploding rifles, music, color, dancing, feasting, laughter and pageantry, a five-day enactment of a folk ballad come to life—all the stuff of poetry and drama in a people's dreams.

The carnival belongs to the entire village and the entire village gives itself up wholeheartedly to the celebration, as do neighboring villages for miles around. Frances Toor relates that when she witnessed it in 1929 as many as a thousand men took part as "soldiers," no doubt with an

hall of the Hotel Reforma. It is these carnival panels which, to conceal the social satire involved, were recently altered at the orders of Alberto Pani, owner of the Hotel Reforma. When Rivera protested they were removed altogether and mirrors were substituted. The frescoes are reproduced here in their original form prior to their mutilation. Two portray a carnival at Yautepec, Morelos. On closer inspection its figures in gay animal masks turn out to be a festive "Portrait of Mexico," its tourists and "distinguished" visitor-writers, its generals and clerics and labor leaders and "gold shirts" and political figures of various sorts. The other two are not so charged with double meaning, but portray the festival at Huejotzingo celebrating the exploits of Augustín Lorenzo here described and an accompanying Indian war-dance presided over by General Huichilobos in Mexican uniform, a dim folk memory of the fiesta to Huitzilopochtli, the ancient Aztec God of War, merged with the celebration of the heroic struggle of the Indian mountain tribes against the French. The four panels, together with their details, are reproduced as plates 242 to 249. A glance at the beautiful composition and movement and festive dream-quality of the figure of Augustín Lorenzo will convince the reader that the hero of Huejotzingo has captured the imagination of Diego Rivera no less completely than it has that of the Mexican folk.

53

incredible number of generals and a woeful lack of privates or even lesser officers (but then do not the traditional popular armies of recent Mexican history reveal similar folk-fiesta characteristics?).

On the Saturday of the fiesta the little plaza of Huejotzingo is occupied solemnly by the General-In-Chief, his Zouaves, Hungarians, Turks. Then at three in the afternoon the plaza is attacked and taken by the brave outlaw and his men. After which the outlaws hold up all the shops, demanding "the day's sales" and receiving food and drink, and the evening and the whole next day are given over to parades, dances, barbecues and festivities. On Monday the General-In-Chief leading his variegated host has somehow shaken off his captivity and reappears in the plaza. Another battle follows; then the robbing of the coach by the outlaw band, and the carrying off of the fair and noble lady. The bandit is pursued up Vulture Canyon where he is surprised celebrating his triumph with feasting and a wedding ceremony. It is his turn to be taken prisoner, but the next day he and his band reappear and the scene is enacted all over again on a still more impressive scale. At night, all the vari-colored bands parade together in festive firelight amity, and Wednesday is given over to more parades and feasting and a grand finale of fireworks in the evening, after which the village folds its colorful wings and settles down to its poor and gray monotony for another year.

Who is this Augustín Lorenzo who lives on in the folk imagination and receives tribute more brilliant than that accorded any saintly martyr? Legend and fact have gotten inextricably mixed, but the researches of Delfino C. Moreno in the village and surrounding hills where once the bandit rode and fought seem to demonstrate that he was indeed the leader of the *Plateados* ("Silver Bandits") who fought a brilliant guerrilla war against the French invaders, robbed their treasures, blocked their supplies and harassed their lines of communications, until he was defeated and killed by the French counter-guerrilla band under Colonel Dupin.

And the lady? It was the affair of the lady as much as the heroic resistance against the French that immortalized the name of Augustín Lorenzo. For the brave outlaw conceived the audacious scheme of holding up the royal coach and abducting none other than Carlotta, Empress of Mexico, Maximilian's bride! And, if we are to trust a *corrido* or popular ballad still sung in the neighborhood, his band surprised and

54

nearly routed her powerful military escort and he actually had his hands upon the door of her coach before the troops rallied and drove off the daring band.

In the fiesta, as in reality, Augustín Lorenzo is eventually defeated and killed; but that does not make him any less a hero. Defeat and sudden and violent death are the fate of virtually all of Mexico's folk heroes, in fact as well as in fiesta and *corrido*. A brave death seems as necessary to a popular hero as martyrdom to a saint: it is his consummation and consecration and guarantee of immortality. A tragic end lingers in the imagination: who would find Ophelia memorable without it, or how long would the Christ tale have lived in the folk memory were it not for the immortalizing ending of the crucifixion? Moreover, the Mexican folk does not believe a man knows how to live unless he knows how to die. Indeed, this valiant and death-friendly people devote to death itself the most colorful of all their fiestas.

FESTIVE DEATH

The attitude of a people or an age towards death is a reflex of their attitude towards life. The Mexican masses take death simply and naturally, as they do sex, as they do life as a whole. A Mexican dies silently, phlegmatically, and, to the best of his ability, heroically. His ballad heroes never evade an ambush though they have warning, face death like men, die with their boots on, their faces towards the enemy and their guns speaking to the last, though it be one against an entire detachment. Senator Field Jurado walked into such a trap after being warned of the exact place and time of his assassination by Carleton Beals, who had overheard the plans. The authors of this work were within three meters of Deputy and Governor-Elect Manlio Fabio Altamirano when an assassin discharged seven bullets into him at close range from an automatic: he was armed as usual but unguarded and had taken no extra precautions though he had been warned a few hours earlier that assassins had been dispatched from Vera Cruz to get him.[15] Villa died in ambush, Zapata by treachery, Madero at the hand of one of his generals and Obregon by an assassin's bullet at a banquet. It is not only in ballads that men die thus in Mexico.

The pre-conquest Indian also knew how to die a hero's death. The

[15] Plate 102.

55

tales of the conquerors give eloquent testimony to it in their accounts of the siege of Mexico. Their magnificent sculptures and frescoes depicting human sacrifice and their nobly carved sacrificial stones are mute and gruesome witnesses. In certain ceremonial sacrifices the prospective victim actually lived joyously for an entire year knowing it was to end with his death, and was given special raiment, flowers and jewels, beautiful maidens as brides to attend him, and honors beyond measure as a hero and god-substitute, the living incorporation of the god to whom he was to be sacrificed. At the end of the year, amid flowers and dances and music and incense, he proudly ascended the steps of the pyramid to the sacrificial altar where he met his exalted doom. According to the ancient Nahua (Aztec) faith, for a man to die on the field of battle or for a woman to die in childbirth was to have lived greatly and greatly died, and to merit not sorrow but pride and rejoicing on the part of those left behind, and a blessed existence as attendants upon the Sun in the world beyond the grave.

Today the attitude towards death is not far different from what it was in ancient times. The tremendously high death rate, the toll of guerrilla warfare and frequent revolution, the ready use of the pistol in certain circles to settle a "controversy," the tranquil and natural preparation for death among the very aged and the seemingly inevitable loss in every family of the majority of the very young, have made death a familiar visitor in the average Mexican household. In a world where life is valued lightly, its end is taken lightly too. The Mexican people give little thought to death, except to exalt a valiant death as one of the noblest acts of living. This nominally Catholic people (exception being made of the women of the urban middle class) does not live as a rule in the shadow of the fear of death and is little concerned with the sufferings and joys of a supposed life beyond the grave. Life is not viewed as a mere preparatory school for eternity, but is taken at its own value; and death is not thought of as a beginning of something but as an end.

When villagers tell tales and legends of the dead, they show no preoccupation with Heaven and Hell, but concern themselves with survivals of the pre-conquest tradition of the five-year journey of the departed shade in the underworld, an underworld more nearly comparable to the ancient Grecian Hades than to the Catholic Paradise or Purgatory

56

and Inferno. For the purposes of this shadowy journey, in many regions a dog is slain and buried with the deceased to guide his soul through the perils and difficulties of the lower world and ferry him over the river that marks its boundaries. Food and money are often included in the coffin, and even those who all their life went barefoot are likely, with unconscious irony, to be sandalled in death, for the way is long and hard. Often the best clothes and favorite trinkets of the deceased are buried with him lest he return for them later. Indeed, in so far as there is any vivid belief in an after-life, it is precisely of this sort: a simple extension of the life already lived. The dead like and require the same things as the living, and linger near the haunts of their days of life, savoring dimly of its pursuits and pleasures and memories with the bloodless, joyless, sorrowless life of shades.

But when the Day of the Dead rolls round, that is a time for rejoicing among shades and men, for the dead return to the bosoms of their families and partake of the pleasures of a communal meal once more. All Saints' Day and the day or two following are a species of "visiting days" in which the dead are allowed to return home and visit the living and then the living return the compliment by visiting the dead in their cemetery abodes.

This courteous and loving exchange of visits is truly a festive occasion with scarce a trace of melancholy about it: in the country among the more Indian folk it is an occasion of suppressed and quiet holiday festiveness; in the City among the predominantly *mestizo* people it has aspects of carnivalesque hilarity which give a new meaning to the death's head grin.

On November first, the day of the little dead, affectionately termed *difuntitos chiquitos* (little-tiny little-dead), the table is set with all sorts of dainties, fruits in season, little cakes baked in the form of animals (the old totemic gods?) and of skeletons, which cakes are known as *pan de muertos* (bread of the dead), lighted candles, festoons of the yellow *zempasuchitl*, the traditional Nahua "flower of the dead," and all the favorite flowers and fruits and even toys and possessions of the deceased.[16] The dead are invited to partake of the *ofrendas* (offerings) and then the rest feast with them (in some regions the *ofrendas* are left for visitors),

[16] See plates 99 to 101 and plates 125 and 126 in which Rivera has painted the festivities of city and country, of home and market place and cemetery.

the whole ceremony having an air of childlike earnestness and subdued joy. The next day, that of the *difuntos mayores* or adult dead, all Mexico goes to the cemetery. They go mostly on foot, though in the cities, where distances are great, auto, truck, burro or cart may also be used. They carry with them great baskets and bundles of food and dainties and flowers and jars and bottles and skins of *pulque, tequila* and other strong drinks, even braziers to make hot dishes at the graveside.

The approaches to the cemeteries become country fairs, where flowers, fruit, food, drinks and toys are sold. The cemeteries themselves are turned into crowded and animated picnic grounds. Whole families sit upon the graves, perhaps cry or pray a while if the death was recent, offer the dead food and drink and sweetmeats and toys and flowers, partake themselves of the offerings in fraternal communion with the dead, strum upon guitars, sing folk songs plaintive and gay, sometimes quarrel a little as the strong drink goes to their heads, and when twilight settles over the cemeteries take their leave of the deceased. Dragging sleepy children after them, they stream out in all directions to their homes.

In the cities, the evening too has its appointed festivities: all urban Mexico goes to the theater, and all theater-goers see the same play! Every regular theater abandons its program to give the play; the movie houses give a cinematographic version of it, or introduce live actors for the occasion; new theaters are hastily constructed of wood or canvas to take care of the entire city population, and all are crowded to the doors. The play deemed appropriate to mark the closing of the Day of the Dead is *Don Juan Tenorio*. It is not Don Juan's manifestation of dynamic masculine energy carried to the ultimate, not his deflowering of virgins and deceiving of nuns nor his proud formula for the wooing, winning and abandoning of coy maidens each in a period of three days, that have made this Spanish tragedy of cape and sword traditional for the solemn closing of this "religious" festival. It is the closing scene, his visit to the private graveyard devoted to all his outraged and murdered dead, his heroic attitude face to face with death, his macabre banquet with a tombstone effigy of one of his victims, and his reckless acceptance of an invitation to return the compliment by dining with the latter in his grave, that have made the play an inseparable part of the urban ritual for this fiesta.

58

DEATH IN THE MARKET PLACE

The Day of the Dead in the country has about it an air of suppressed gayety and solemn excitement: there is feasting and drinking, there is the reuniting with the dead in communal family festivity, in many places there are even illuminated plazas, enlarged markets, band concerts, and here and there villages where at midnight bands of young men and boys go from house to house eating and drinking and singing at each "to wake the dead." But in the city the festival becomes gay, grinning, sardonic. Here men not only meet death fearlessly and on friendly terms; they seem to exchange uproarious jokes with death, rub elbows with him familiarly, slap him on the back. Death and sex the peasant finds natural and familiar, but the urban Mexican finds them both irresistibly comical as well. He sees his death's head grin at him, and he grins back. In fact the whole city is agrin with death's heads for days before the event: skeletons in store windows, skulls on billboards, dead men in caricature, little toy funerals in candy, silver skull stickpins with weird ruby eyes, skeletons that pop out of boxes, that have stretchable spiral legs, that move their lower jaws rhythmically when touched or jiggled. Children crow and clap their hands at presents of little coffins, candy and cake death's heads and corpses. Sweethearts give each other skull rings and pins. Friends and enemies mail each other premature epitaphs in ironic verse illustrated like comic valentines with appropriately dressed skeletons. Broadsheet ballad vendors abandon their usual songs and stock in trade of outlaw and revolution and train wreck and murder ballads, to hawk pink and yellow and orange and purple paper broadsheets known as *calaveras* (skulls) bearing woodcuts of skeletons dressed in the uniforms of generals, the robes of priests, the overalls of workingmen, the *calzones, sarapes* and *sombreros* of peasants, the *charro* outfits of parading landowners, the high hats and cutaways of capitalists and diplomats, the uniforms of soldiers, the modish dresses of elegant *damas*, the flapper clothes of the *pelona*, the ample skirts and *rebozos* of servant girls, all with appropriate ironical epitaphs to match. The skeletons ride horseback, reach for money, wield brooms, fire guns, make speeches, all the things grotesque and serious that go to make up the human comedy in Mexico. The epitaphs make mocking comment on life, private and public, under the pretense of commenting on death; and they laugh at

59

death even while laughing at life. Their crude doggerel is ironical, irreverent, unblinkingly realistic. Like the *Judases* and the *corridos*, they are often a weapon of political satire, and always a deadly thrust at hypocrisy and pretense. That inimitable and even untranslatable product of the comic spirit of the urban mestizo Mexican, the *vacilada*, nowhere finds richer expression than when it turns its irony, wit and realism upon death, that ultimate jest that life plays upon each living being.

It is this spirit that animates Rivera's panel depicting the Day of the Dead as it expresses itself in the market place in Mexico City. The panel communicates admirably the traffic in gay and festive *memento mori*, the milling, eager, excited, hungry, thirsty, dressed-up throng of rich and poor, jesting and jostling each other in carnival spirit. In the middle foreground is a recognizable portrait of the mammoth, open-eyed painter himself, seeing and recording everything with those wide, bulging eyes and with that gargantuan appetite for sensation and perception that characterizes him. At his side is his ever open-mouthed former wife Guadalupe; next to him, with only hat and glasses showing, is the painter Jean Charlot; and, in black hat and veil, the latter's pious Catholic mother.

Associated with death in its fair is hunger of life: sidewalk stands sell *pulque* and soft drinks and *tacos* and edible funerals and skeletons; in the background, life-sized, brightly painted *calaveras* dance like dead men hanging in the wind, strumming on guitars their own death music; and in the remoter upper background, just around the corner from the great market of death, is the flesh market of the Hotel *Paraíso* (Paradise) with all the external signs of a common brothel: feasting and drinking and eroticism and laughter and death in close and intimate juxtaposition. Such is the most characteristic, the most distinctive and the most colorful of all Mexico's fiestas. Death and laughter, where else are they found in such intimate union?

V. BEFORE THE
SPANIARDS CAME

The time and manner of the appearance of the first men on Mexican soil is still wrapped in impenetrable mystery. One ancient legend declares them to have descended from a race of giants; and archaeologists once actually found "proof" of this in giant bones, which turned out to be the remains of prehistoric animals! Another legend, of Aztec origin, records that seven Mexican tribes, of which the Aztecs were one, issued forth from seven caverns out of the bowels of the earth. Perhaps this is a dim memory of the time when the ancestors of the Aztecs were cave dwellers living by hunting and fishing (there are still cave dwellers in certain regions and among that "lower race" in the great cities, the very poor); perhaps it is only a version of the wide-spread tradition of the earth-mother who gave birth to the first men.

Anthropologists would have it, on slender evidence (which prevails because the material for possible refutation is slenderer still), that the Indians of North and South America are of mongoloid origin, and that they migrated from Asia to the New World over a once continuous land bridge, over an ice cap, or in primitive canoes or coracles via the Aleutian Islands and Alaska.

Be that as it may, long before the domestication of plants or animals or the working of metals, a race of copper-colored men, neither white, nor yellow, nor black, but closer to a reddish brown, had spread all over the two American continents, had developed an elaborate diversity of culture on the foundations of a few basic common features, and had originated all that was characteristic of this culture and economy, here in the new world itself. From Asia they may have inherited their biologic structure and their somewhat mongoloid features, but when they invented agriculture, it was an American plant they domesticated, the *Teocentli* (Mexican Fodder Grass), which became the subsequent Indian corn or maize.

THE CONQUEST OF CORN

Corn is more than a food: it is *the* food, the very foundation of pre-conquest economy and culture. Rivera paints it again and again:

61

in overflowing voluptuous abundance held caressingly by great hands in the murals of the Health Building, in reassuring promise of plenty in all his pictures of a better organized future society, in decorated and tender gayety in his harvest festival portrayals, as a god in his wood carvings in Chapingo and as a goddess on the stairway of the Education building. Beans are important in the Mexican diet, and chile peppers are also, but there is no bean god or pepper god—only corn (which is now god now goddess) and the *pulque* plant, have attained to the dignity of divinity.

IRRIGATION, THE CIVILIZER

The earliest records of cultivated plants, and the earliest cradles of sedentary civilizations, are in Mesopotamia, Egypt, Mexico and Peru, all lands in which irrigation was needed and practiced to make agriculture possible. The battle to domesticate plants, to force nature to yield dependably and steadily where it did not yield freely, the struggle for a steady water supply—this was the first important enterprise that enlisted the cooperative efforts of man on a wider scale than those of the hunting pack. Great cooperative struggles with nature developed great social organizations, for in transforming nature man transformed his own nature and started on the long march from savagery to civilization.

The highest civilizations achieved independently on this continent, the Tarascan (around the lake region of Michoacan and Jalisco), the Mixtecan-Zapotecan (in the highland watershed of Oaxaca), the Mexican (in the lake region of Central Mexico) and the Mayan (facing the problem of beating back the jungle and securing a subterranean water-supply in Yucatán) all arose from such collective efforts. The most imposing of these enterprises was the Mexican, and it produced the most advanced and wide-spread social organization.

THE MAYA CULTURE

The ruins of the once mighty Egyptian empire are impressive because they stand alone in the midst of great expanses of desert waste. The remains of Yucatán and the Mayan-Quiché region of Central America are no less impressive because the explorer comes upon them, mysterious, imposing, unsuspected, in the midst of trackless jungle growth, where the only modern works of man are mere grass and reed huts. Mute

62

witnesses of vanished glory and ruined majesty, they possess an endless fascination and give impulse to mystic and far-winged speculation. Only shadowy legends and undeciphered hieroglyphs and the trammels of unwonted sobriety have set limits to these fantasies. Yet, slowly the evidence accumulates (see the work of Spinden, Mendizabal *et al.*) that this great civilization was not the first on this continent, nor the most tenacious, nor the most capable of ultimate development, nor did it any longer exist when the Spaniards came to interrupt the promising course of development of indigenous culture.

In the partisan struggles between the admirers of Mayan and Aztec or Mexican civilizations, Rivera is an "Aztec" (with certain reservations in favor of the freer artistic propensities of the Tarascans). Archaeological, botanical and historical evidence alike point with increasing strength to the Mexican highlands of the *Mesa Central* as being the cradle not merely of the civilization of the Mexican region, but even of the two American continents. It was from here that maize culture and irrigation, and then the attendant characteristic arts of sedentary peoples (such as pottery and weaving) and the social and intellectual structures made possible by greater leisure and a surer food supply, spread slowly over America. Spinden and his confreres have traced the obscured footsteps of this archaic civilization on its march northward along the highlands, southward in a more or less continuous road through the mountains of central and upper South America to a second magnificent center in Peru, and downward from the semi-arid plateaus to the jungle land below. Only gradually was highland corn adapted to the hot humid climate of the lower slopes. Only later, in the early centuries of the Christian era, did the Maya-Quiché civilization flourish and put its peculiar, super-luxuriant jungle stamp upon the derivative culture it had gotten from the uplands. Thereafter there was much give and take as the two sister civilizations weakened and flourished and weakened again, and now struggled with each other, now reinforced each other, but the younger Mayan culture was less vigorous and did not long survive. The weight of the jungle, perhaps a fresh cycle of heat and dampness in the great continental climatic tidal waves,[1] the superior might of the uplands, and that nemesis of youthful civilizations, violent class struggle against a prematurely senile and top-heavy social structure, prevailed over the

[1] See Ellsworth Huntington, *Civilization and Climate* (Yale, 1915), pp. 238-243.

63

precious and precocious elaborateness of Mayan life. When the Spaniards came, their great epoch had ended, the jungle had long reconquered its domains, and ruin, dispersion and rebarbarization had set in.

THE VALLEY OF MEXICO

The main theater in which the drama of Mexican history was enacted is the Valley of Mexico. It is a great bowl, situated near the exact center of Mexico, of which the "floor" or bottom is 7500 feet above the level of the sea, and of which the rim rises many thousands of feet higher, so that nowhere can one leave the valley without ascending at least above the ten-thousand-foot line.

The rains and snows that fall upon its mountain slopes find no outlet, but run down into the highland valley of Mexico to form the great salt and sweet-water lakes on the partially dried beds of which Mexico City now stands.

In the long series of migrations of Mexican, i.e., Nahuatl-speaking tribes, in quest of land and in search of plunder from the accumulated wealth of preceding waves of migration, Anáhuac, the "Valley of Waters," was ever the coveted prize.

THE TOLTECS

Among the most important of these Nahuatl invaders of this fertile valley were the Toltecs. Their name, although originally perhaps derived from their capital city, came to mean the builder-people, the constructors, the craftsmen. Sometime shortly after 500 A. D. they worked their way from the northwest into the Valley of Mexico, subduing and subjugating the previous inhabitants and beating off (for a time) subsequent waves of invasion. They established their great centers of construction and civilization at Tula, Tulancingo, Teotihuacán, Cuauhnahuac (Cuernavaca), Tultitlán and Cholula.

The imposing pyramids of Teotihuacán and Cholula are eloquent testimony to the right of this people to call themselves the master-builders. The great pyramid of the Sun at Teotihuacán has a base of forty thousand square meters, a much greater area than is covered by the somewhat higher but less massive Egyptian pyramid of Cheops. In its ruins were found the well preserved remains of overwhelmingly forceful sculpture and lovely frescoes and painted, illuminated, glazed, en-

64

graved, stamped, and cloisonné-encrusted pottery. The sacred city of Cholula, replete with pyramid-crowned temples, was even more impressive, and the Catholic Church has had to accept its lingering consecration and cover all its pyramid temples with countless churches dedicated to new gods and saints. The largest of its pyramids, that of Quetzalcoatl, covers more than twice as much ground as that of Cheops, its base averaging more than one thousand feet on a side and its probable height being over 200 feet above the level of the plateau.

QUETZALCOATL

Quetzalcoatl ("feathered serpent," from *Quetzalli*, Mexican bird of paradise of bright plumage used in feather work, and *coatl*, serpent) was the tribal god of the Toltecs; but thanks to the great area over which they ruled and their wide civilizing influence, this tribal leader and deity, like the great constructions and intellectual systems attributed to him, has left his mark on all the major civilizations of Mexico and has entered, in one form or another, into all of their complicated pantheons.

To Rivera, he seems to be the most attractive of the pre-conquest deities (no doubt in his capacity as civilizer and creator of the arts and crafts) and is the only one of the ancient legendary semi-historical figures to enter into his painting. He appears in the great pre-conquest mural on the right wall of the National Palace stairway, not once but three times: at his birth, issuing forth in his most familiar form as a feathered serpent from the flames of a fiery volcano; as priest-king-teacher while he lived among men; and, defeated, as he departs in his serpent boat out to sea, promising to return some day to renew the golden age.[2]

Like all the figures in the Mexican pantheon, Quetzalcoatl is an extremely complicated, many-sided figure, subject to innumerable and often contradictory traditions of different ages and regions, superimposed upon each other like the successive layers of his own pyramid-temples.

Most of the deities of the thickly populated Mexican pantheon, Quetzalcoatl among them, seem to have originated in the early nomadic-hunting stage through the deification of a tribal leader, as a tribal god. Huitzilipochtli, the famous Aztec god of war, was originally the tribal god of the Aztecs, and Quetzalcoatl, identified with Hueman, the wise priest-leader of their wanderings, was the tribal god of the Toltecs.

[2] Plate 220.

Deification of a tribal leader served the treble purpose of giving sanctity to tribal solidarity and blood-kinship; giving the tribe confidence in itself and its own destiny; and preserving, by rendering them sacred, the procedures and techniques of their wise men or priests at a time when the feeble beginnings of civilization were in danger of being lost again unless they were zealously preserved. In this capacity Quetzalcoatl is teacher, civilizer, law-giver, inventor of agriculture, inventor of astronomy and author of an improved calendar so necessary to primitive agriculture, which plants and waters and reaps, not by weather-bureau report and the rules of age-old experience, but by mysteriously and divinely appointed times and sacred procedures. He was also the inventor of feather-mosaic, stone-cutting, jewel-making, metal-working and other arts and crafts contributing to the nascent beautification of life as leisure and civilization developed.

Reports the Song of Quetzalcoatl, as translated by Hubert Cornyn:

> *And his people, they the Toltecs,*
> *Wondrous skilled in all the trades were,*
> *All the arts and artifices. . . .*
> *Fashioned they the sacred emeralds,*
> *Smelted they both gold and silver*
> *Other arts and trades they mastered. . . .*
> *He, the master workman, taught them*
> *All their trades and artifices.*

THE GOLDEN AGE

While he lived among the Toltecs they enjoyed the morning splendors of a golden age: the people possessed wealth untold, gold and emeralds were used for the walls of palaces, the prized chocolate stolen by him from heaven grew in abundance, the land was covered with giant cornstalks with ears so big that it took two arms to embrace one, and with thick forests filled with gay flowers and birds of brilliant plumage and lovely song, and cotton grew of itself in the fields, springing up already tinted in all the resplendent colors of ancient weaving. But alas, this golden age was too good to last. His enemies, three necromancers, headed by his rival twin-god Tezcatlipoca ("Smoking Mirror," the moon god), persuaded him to drink of a potion (according to some versions

66

pulque) which was to restore his lost youth, whereat he was intoxicated and overcome by shame and a great desire to return to the "red land" of his fathers from whence this bearded, white-complexioned hero-teacher had come on his mission of culture. The Toltec civilization was destroyed by pestilence, famine, and hostile tribes. (Tezcatlipoca as a tribal god of the Mexicans is thus the symbol of a historical event, the overthrow of the Toltec regime by a hostile and probably formerly subject people and Quetzalcoatl becomes the banner of a decaying aristocracy in a primitive tribal class struggle.)

Quetzalcoatl, defeated by his rival, went sadly away, stopping at Cholula to teach his cult, reappearing among the Zapotecans, among the Mayans as Kukulkan or Gucumatz (exact translation in the respective Maya-Quiché dialects of "feathered-serpent"), where he built cities and palaces, and then after twenty years of wandering, fashioned himself a boat of serpents and sailed sadly out to sea.

> *Outward, onward, ever moving*
> *O'er the far-extending waters*
> *Went the serpent-fashioned vessel*
> *Till at last from sight it vanished. . . .*

THE FEATHERED SERPENT

As tribal deities the primitive gods usually possessed animal forms, doubtless a kind of totemism, hence Quetzalcoatl is the feathered serpent. But the serpent cult was widespread throughout America and indeed much of the world, for the serpent is also the god of the ripple of wind and water, the god of motion which is life, and of water which quickens the plants in the ground, and of fire with which man alters the earth-substances, the metals, to his uses. And indeed, we find all these attributes clustered around the "precious serpent," Quetzalcoatl. For, as the nomadic tribes mastered agriculture, building construction and metallurgy, or conquered peoples of already settled civilizations, then the gods of the heavens and of agriculture became important and the old tribal gods were identified with the nearest of the newly found ones. Quetzalcoatl is also known as Ehécatl, the god of the air, and becomes a god of agriculture and of the calendar, and his legend grows into a planetary myth, for he is now Venus, the "precious twin," the bright morning

67

and evening star (so important in the calculations of the Aztec calendar), in strange rivalry with his gloomy twin brother, Smoking Mirror or Night Wind, Tezcatlipoca, the fearful god of the moon and of fate. As such, he comes from the "red land" of the sunset, and vanishes again into the "red land" of the dawn.

And finally, as the departing hero-ruler who will come again some day to restore the golden age, he is the incorporation of man's dream of a better world, which he ever places in the nostalgic past, ever seeks in the longed-for future, since in the present he knows it not.

Quetzalcoatl was born in the year *Ce ácatl* ("One Reed" of the Nahua calendar) and in another year *Ce ácatl* he would come again. By a rare coincidence it was in precisely such a year that Cortés set foot on Mexican soil, and the superstitious Moctezuma, already disheartened by evil omens and a succession of natural misfortunes, saw in the white-complexioned and bearded Cortés who came from beyond the sea the fulfillment of the ancient prophecy, a belief which helped to paralyze his resistance. But alas, it was no golden age that the bearded conqueror of the pale skin brought to Mexico!

THE AZTEC EMPIRE

The key to the history of ancient Mexico is found in three factors: the developing culture and productive forces of the indigenous peoples; the consequent development of class divisions and primitive class struggles which again and again tore a nascent society apart (driving it backward because the conditions for a forward drive to a higher social organization were as yet lacking); and the struggle for the desirable lands by still savage tribes who repeatedly overwhelmed the already settled societies that had been weakened by internal struggles. For thousands of years this drama had been repeating itself on a gradually higher scale. Civilization after civilization rose and fell, torn by internal contradictions and overwhelmed by external attack, by still classless savage tribes.

Historians generally give too much importance to the superior fighting powers of the savages in a purely personal sense, matched with the "debilitating effects of refinement and settled life," and not enough importance to the superior fighting powers of the savages by virtue of their tribal unity and solidarity as against the class-struggle—divided and internally weakened civilization. Again and again subjugated tribes com-

68

bined with fresh invaders, or became themselves the conquerors of their conquerors.

Yet, with many relapses, the tide of civilization rose slowly higher and higher. Superior productive techniques, fire, agriculture, pottery, arts and crafts, once learned were never wholly forgotten. Again and again savage conquerors were in turn conquered by the richer life and higher civilization of the vanquished. They poured in fresh blood and unity, temporarily resolved the class contradictions by the re-injection of their more primitive democracy, and disseminated and further developed the culture they had taken over. In the New World as in the Old, great empires frequently developed thus.

The last and the greatest of these was the Aztec "empire" which Cortés encountered and which provided the principal opposition to Spanish conquest of the New World. Whether it in turn would have been destroyed by internal contradictions and fresh invasion from without, whether it could have overcome the natural handicap of lack of domesticable beasts of burden on the American continent with consequent difficulty of far-flung communication, or whether it possessed the requisite degree of development to extend and improve its semi-feudal culture until it should embrace and unify the whole Mexican and Central American region, shall ever remain matters of conjecture, for the Spaniards interrupted this development and merged it with a European feudal civilization.

The seven Nahuatl tribes (literally "the tribes who express themselves clearly") of Aztec tradition developed the great culture which amazed the Spaniards in a matter of a mere two hundred years. Their earlier state as a savage hunting nomadic people may be judged from their own naive account in the *Chronicles of Quautitlan* concerning their early King Tactli:

. . . he was a king unacquainted with the sowing of grain for food; neither did he know how to make shelters for his subjects. He wore only a simple garb. The people ate only birds, serpents, rabbits and deer: as yet they had no houses and came and went in all directions.

Dimly we can trace the wanderings of this obscure tribe of half-naked, nomadic, cave-dwelling barbarians until some time around 1325 (only two centuries before the arrival of Cortés) when they erupted into the

Valley of Mexico and founded what was to be the historic city of Tenochtitlán (now Mexico City) in the shape of a few miserable reed huts on a swampy little island in the middle of the Lake of Texcoco.

Far from being the vigorous conquerors of an effete people, they were themselves conquered, and accepted into the valley only on terms of vassalage to the already settled and more cultured Nahuatl tribes that had preceded them. Under the guidance of the prophecy of their deified tribal leader and war-god Huitzilopochtli, they looked for a cactus (tenoch) on which was perched an eagle devouring a serpent, and the prophecy discretely led them to this uninhabited and undesirable island in the center of the lake where they were at least safe from attack. In transforming this bit of swamp into a broad and fertile land built up out of *chinampas* or artificially constructed island-rafts of reed and lake-bottom mud, traversed by ditches and connected by great causeways and aqueducts to the mainland shores of the lake, the Aztecs transformed themselves into a great and cultured people.

When Bernal Diaz, soldier and chronicler of the Conquest, first beheld Tenochtitlán two centuries after its foundation, he could write:

It is like the enchantments they tell of in the Legend of Amadis. Are not the things we see a dream . . .?

Gazing on such wonderful sights we did not know what to say or whether what appeared before us was real, for on one side of the land there were great cities and on the lake ever so many more, and the lake itself was crowded with canoes, and in the causeway were many bridges at intervals, and in front of us stood the great city of Mexico. . . . I stood looking at it and thought that never in the world would there be discovered other lands such as these. . ."

Such was the transformation which in two hundred years this naked and savage hunting and hunted tribe had wrought in themselves and in their environment.

AZTEC SOCIAL ORGANIZATION

Aztec organization began as a tribal one: membership in the tribe was based not on birth in a certain territory but on blood kinship; basic property (the region, the land, the woods, the water supply, the public works) was held in common. The elders of the clans formed a sort of council of wisdom and derived their authority from age and experience. Leaders were chosen by the council of elders on a democratic basis for the great collective enterprises of the chase, of war, and, as agriculture developed, for the direction of agricultural enterprise, which was also in the beginning carried on in common.

THE PRIESTHOOD

Primitive lore or wisdom was not experimental but traditional, ritual and ceremonial in its nature. As production and social life became more complicated a special class grew up as the professional repositories of this wisdom, as the interpreters of the will of the gods of grain and fertility and rain and the seasons, as the masters of the intricate and sacred knowledge of the calendar and the ways of the sun and the stars, as the experts in cajoling or compelling the deified earth and elements to obey the will of man. Thus magic, religion and science were one, and the masters of this unitary and complicated knowledge became a special and gradually self-perpetuating theocratic caste requiring careful selection and a prolonged period of training, and possessing great prerogatives, taxing duties, and enormous authority. The buildings in which they served the gods and learned their will, became the most important and imposing buildings in the community. Within the civic center of Tenochtitlán the wide *Zócalo* or *Plaza de Armas* of today would be lost. According to Sagahún, it possessed twenty-five temple pyramids, five oratories, fasting houses, sacrificial and penitential stones, seven skull racks, two ball courts (even games had their social-religious aspect), a well, three bathing places, a dancing court, nine priest houses, a reception temple or "jail" for the captive gods of conquered nations, arsenals, great open spaces for the congregation of the multitude and many other edifices. And overtowering them all was the great pyramid of the two gods, Tlaloc and Huitzilopochtli; rising terrace on terrace and surmounted by the two temples, each three stories high. The impressive Cathedral of Mexico City today occupies but a small part of what was once the temple ground.

THE RISE OF A FEUDAL ARISTOCRACY

The great pyramid bore on its summit the temples of two gods: Tlaloc, the god of rain, an agricultural deity; and Huitzilopochtli, the

7 1

god of war. Militarism and agriculture—their union has ever proved the basis of feudal life.

When the Aztecs entered the Valley of Mexico, they had to fight for the right to remain; then they were tolerated as the military auxiliary vassals of older tribes, and at last went into the "fighting business" on their own account. By 1440 they had entered into a league of conquest with Texcoco and Tlacopan (Tacuba) on the basis of a division of the spoils of war between the great Texcoco and Tenochtitlán, two-fifths falling to each, and the lesser Tlacopan to receive the remaining fifth. Soon these three cities dominated the Valley of Mexico and began spreading their power far and wide under the increasing domination of the Aztecs over their partners, till in the time of Moctezuma II, the Mexican standard had been carried to Tehuantepec and far off Guatemala and Nicaragua, westward to the Pacific, northward through the highlands of northern Mexico, eastward to Vera Cruz and Tampico and even into the difficult and distant regions of Chiapas and Yucatán. The capital city of this great conquering people grew steadily in size and importance, became an administrative-military-religious and commercial center of perhaps two hundred thousand inhabitants, the magnificent "city of palaces," the city of stone and adobe houses, of great public buildings and pyramids and temples and bridges and aqueducts and canals and causeways which so astonished the Spaniards who had hitherto in the Caribbean dealt only with semi-naked savages living in miserable villages of huts of reed.

But as the years of war were prolonged, engagement of the entire populace permanently in arms became impossible. A specialization, a division of labor, took place. Greater and greater grew the separation between those who went continually into battle and became skilled in warfare, and those who remained in agriculture and handicraft and cared for the supplies of army and community. Ever more exalted was Huitzilopochtli among the gods, and ever more exalted his warriors among men. War became a ceremonial to bring him captives for the sacrifices; a means of securing slaves and additional lands for tillage; and a means of securing tribute in the shape of blankets and copper axes and lowland fruits and feathers and chocolate and all the things lacking to the growing life of the Valley of Mexico. The war chiefs returned laden with spoils and honors and authority, possessors of conquered lands and conquered

72

tillers of the soil and slaves. Great office, military, administrative or religious, continued to be elective, but the election became ever more nominal and tended to fall ever more and more automatically on a succession of brothers or nephews within a few powerful families. The ancient clans, now settled in *calpollis* or clan territories or quarters of the Great City, continued to administer local agriculture and religious matters in a semi-communal manner, but the agricultural products produced by vassals of the war leaders on conquered land or sent as tribute by subject tribes, outweighed the clan products in importance.

Much ink has been spilt in the war between the followers of Morgan and Bandelier, who profess to see in the social organization of the Aztecs tribal democracy and primitive communism, and opposing writers, who take literally the reports of the feudal-imperialist-minded Spanish conquerors who could see only a completely feudal organization. Actually tribal democracy and primitive communism were in full decay and there was a growing caste system of priests and warriors under ever more powerful military-theocratic leaders. The advocates of either view can find much evidence in Mexican society, for it was well advanced in transition from the one type of social organization to the other at the moment of the Spanish invasion.

Rivera has portrayed the structure of pre-conquest society at the moment of the arrival of the Spaniards with that gift for dramatic synthesis in which his monumental painting is unique. On the right wall of the National Palace stairway [3] he has painted with tender sympathy the pre-conquest artists and craftsmen: musicians with their rattles, conches, flutes, and insistent forceful percussion instruments, the hand-operated drum and the two-toned *teponaxtle* beaten upon with sticks like modern drums and *marimbas;* primitive agriculturists scraping the ground with a sharpened stick and inserting the seeds of the precious corn; weavers making cotton and cactus-fiber cloth (sheep, and hence wool were unknown) dyed and woven and embroidered into beautiful patterns; potters painting and molding clay vessels; jewellers making the precious ornaments of gold and silver and jade and turquoise and obsidian that were melted down and torn apart in such abundance by the gold-hungry and esthetically unappreciative conquerors; a painter at work on the conventionalized but deeply pleasing designs of hieroglyphs on parch-

[3] Plate 220.

ment; stone-cutters using stone hammers and untempered bronze or copper chisels to compel the refractory granite to reveal the magnificent sculptural forms which their imagination saw in the brute material—a society where the arts and crafts were loved, respected, sanctified, and inextricably interwoven with all the common uses of life and all the trends of daily living. As one watches these dreamy-eyed Mexicans at their creative tasks, one gets a feeling of the pleasure their portrayer takes in the employment of his own craftsman's skill, and an inkling of the pleasure and pride that was once inherent in productive labor, and that may some day inhere in it again.

Such is the idyllic right-hand side of the great mural picture of pre-conquest civilization. But the other half of the wall completes the story. Here the primitive delight in newly discovered arts and crafts and pursuits in which use and beauty and the exercise of the productive powers of man are united, yields to the gloomier aspects of later indigenous culture. The landscape is dominated by great pyramid temples, symbols of the growing theocratic power of the priestly caste whose functions are changing from direction of technique to domination of social life. Up the sides of an uncompleted temple-pyramid toil straining slaves bent under the head-strap burden of huge blocks of stone for the construction of the upper reaches of the temple. About the idols and the priestly figures are grouped sacrifice-offerings of corn and other products, and visible at the base is the skull-rack, fearful symbol of human sacrifice. Overseeing the labors (degrading toil as against the loving labor of the free artist-craftsmen on the other side) are the figures of the military aristocracy: a knight of the eagle (the eagle and the tiger were the two dominant military orders) provided with a lash-like serpent-scepter, backed by a warrior armed (since steel weapons were unknown) with a "sword" of grooved wood into which sharp obsidian stone knife-blades have been set with resin.

In the foreground is a scene of the incipient class struggles which were waging in Mexico at the time of the Conquest. An orator is stirring up the once free craftsmen and agriculturists to resist the growing weight of theocratic-feudal-military oppression, and subjugated tribes are seeking to throw off the Aztec yoke of tribute in kind, and in human beings to be used for slavery and sacrifice.

It was these internal and external revolts of mixed class-tribal character, far more than the superiority of Spanish steel over Mexican stone weapons or of horses and burros and mules over human beasts of burden and of gunpowder-hurled projectiles over hand-wielded slings and spears and javelins, that determined the victory of the Spaniards over the Aztec defenders of Mexico.

VI. THE CONQUEST

The conquest of New Spain by Cortés and his tiny band is one of the most amazing exploits in history. It is impossible not to admire the energy and heroism that burned the ships on the beach at Vera Cruz to release the sailors for war and still the longings to return; that sustained a little army of five hundred-odd soldiers in their drive from the water's edge up precipitous mountain walls through often deeply hostile and populous nations and tribes into the very heart of the unknown Mexican land; that renewed the hopeless-seeming struggle again and again when many had been killed, every man in the company wounded in one or more places and when the decimated forces had been driven from the great fortified city of Tenochtitlán in precipitous retreat; that plotted and planned and schemed and betrayed and fought and plundered and bribed and cajoled and tortured and battered and hacked and burned its way at last to incredible victory. The energy was the energy of great social forces that beget great men: it was the accumulated energy of Spain's seven centuries of struggle to drive out the Moor and achieve national unification; it was the boundless predatory energy of world trade and world empire, of a Europe in transformation; it was the energy of that once tiny and self-contained medieval world that suddenly overflowed its boundaries and expanded to all the ends of the earth.

A bearded Franciscan friar in the Church of the Virgin of the Remedies once showed the writer a tiny flaxen-haired doll less than twelve inches high and confided: "This image of the Virgin conquered Mexico. How else do you think a few hundred men could conquer a nation of millions?"

And indeed, the Conquest seems a miracle:

> . . . *When we saw so many cities and villages built in the water,* wrote Bernal Diaz del Castillo, *and other great towns on dry land . . . great towers and temples and buildings rising from the water . . . the lake itself crowded with canoes, and in the causeway many bridges at intervals, and in front of us stood the great City of Mexico, and we—we did not number even four hundred soldiers. . . . What men have there been in the world that have shown such daring?*

76

MOTIVES THAT MADE THE "MIRACLE"

In Europe an old order was dying and a new one was in travail of birth. With irresistible explosive force the rising capitalist order, still in its mercantile infancy, was unifying the nations of Europe and expanding them over all the seven seas. Geography and navigation suddenly became sciences; navigators became heroes, and merchants, princes. Static, somnolent, locally circumscribed feudal Europe was shaken to its foundations: the stir and pageantry of the Crusades was followed by the clash of arms in national, religious and commercial wars, the search for new routes to the Indies and Cathay, and the conquest of a hitherto unknown world. The new order used the fantastic dreams, the romantic chivalry, the wonder and credulity of medievalism, in the service of navigation, colonial conquest and the quest for the never-to-be-sufficient gold. Nascent capitalism provided the underlying driving forces, but unconsciously moribund feudalism provided the pageantry and romance, the ideology and conceptions of themselves and their tasks, for navigators, explorers, conquerors, colonizers and Christianizers of the unknown lands beyond the seas.[1]

GOLD HUNGER

There was no limit to Europe's new-found hunger for gold, no peril that hardy spirits would not brave to seek this precious yellow metal. It had ceased to be a mere shining and malleable earth serviceable for works of art and use: it had become the mediator between all objects of wealth and commerce, the price of all things of the flesh and the spirit, from the love of women and the consciences of kings to the mitigation of the pangs of Purgatory and the evasion of the tortures of Hell. Ancient sculptures and plates and goblets of gold were melted down in Europe as Cortés ruthlessly melted down the precious works of the goldsmith's art presented to him by the Aztec chieftain, Moctezuma. It was brute gold, unformed except perhaps to stamp upon it some guarantee of its weight and fineness, that was the aspiration of the age and the source of all power over men and things.

[1] This peculiar mixture of motives and views is synthesized in Bernal Diaz's report of the words of Cortés when winning over the followers of Narváez to his hand: "He promised to make them rich and give them office, and as they came to seek a livelihood, and were in a country where they could do service to God and His Majesty, and enrich themselves, now was their chance."

The ambitions of adventurers like Cortés and Columbus knew no limits either. Columbus delayed his famous voyage, the realization of his whole life's dream, for several years till his fantastic price was met: the title of admiral, nobility for himself and his family, vice-royalty over all new found lands, the right to nominate candidates for all royal official appointments in the conquered domains, one-tenth of all the pearls and precious stones and gold and silver and (a touch of the rising commercial spirit) one-tenth of all the profits from the sale of spices and merchandise to be gained by his voyage. The dream of the great captain, Hernán Cortés, spread its wings as wide; Captain General, Governor and Viceroy of New Spain, one-fifth of all the gold to be found in regions replete with the yellow metal, ownership of lands and mines and Indians without number, a position scarcely subordinate to that of the King of Spain, then the greatest monarch in Europe, and a bright name in the pages of history—such was the dynamic force of the dream that drove Cortés from Spain to Cuba, from Cuba to Yucatán and Vera Cruz and then up into the center of the Mexican land.

TALE OF TREACHERY

"At that time," writes Bernal Diaz of his captain, "he was very poor and much in debt." By bribery, a promise never fulfilled to give Governor Velázquez's secretary and accountant each one-third of all the spoil of gold, silver and jewels which might fall to his share, he won from the suspicious and reluctant Governor of Cuba the appointment of Captain General. He recruited his men among the impecunious gentlemen-adventurers in Cuba by a promise, also evaded later, "that whatever person might wish to go in his company to the newly discovered lands to conquer them and to settle there, should receive his share of the gold, silver and riches which might be gained, and an *encomienda* of Indians (i.e., a "trusteeship" over their labor and their souls) after the country had been pacified. . . ." Yet all the while he had a secret agreement with the Governor not to settle at all, merely to trade a bit, seize some slaves, acquire some gold, and return to Cuba. With characteristic medley of the feudal and the capitalist, they took cheap beads and trinkets, a priest "so that our voyage should proceed on right principles," an overseer to guard the King's fifth of any treasure they might acquire, and

78

instructions to "make war on the natives and load the vessels with Indians, as slaves, with which to pay him (Governor Velázquez) for his bark."[2]

New Spain was born in treachery and greed, each many times compounded, and Judas has been a symbolic participant in Mexican history from that day to this. Through corruption of the Governor's trusted agents Hernán Cortés had gotten his appointment as Captain General. No sooner had he sailed for Trinidad than the Governor sent instructions there to have him "detained or taken prisoner." But with the aid of "that solvent of hardness, presents of gold from our store to some, and promises to others, he bought them (the Governor's emissaries and Trinidad officials) over to his side. . . ." Next he got his men to make him their independent chieftain by revealing the Governor's (and his own) duplicity, in providing originally that there were to be no conquests nor permanent settlements; and in good time cheated his own men, who had braved every hardship and were even then facing imminent peril with him, out of their share of the gold looted from Moctezuma's treasury that he might bribe therewith the King of Spain ("impress him" would be the more delicate expression) into confirming his treachery to the Governor of Cuba. He even cheated his men out of their share of their Indian women captives under pretext of preserving for the King the "royal fifth," so that the most beautiful ones might go to him and his captains.[3]

To the Indians who gave Cortés a naive and hospitable welcome, he offered assurances that he had come but to trade, to purchase gold which was the only medicine for a strange affliction of the heart from which

[2] From Bernal Diaz's account of the instructions and equipment of the voyage of Hernández de Córdoba which preceded that of Cortés.

[3] Says the generally admiring Bernal Diaz: "When they had all been brought together and had been marked with the branding iron . . . when we were not expecting it, they set aside the Royal fifth, and then they took another fifth for Cortés, and . . . they took away and hid the best-looking Indian women, and there was not a good-looking one left, and when it came to dividing them, they allotted to us the old and ugly women, and there was a great deal of grumbling about it against Cortés."

It is noteworthy that these Christian gentlemen scrupled at first to take concubines until they had been baptised. "These damsels," Cortés told the chiefs in Cempoala and Tabasco, "must become Christians before we can receive them." But as the spoils of war increased, the tenderness of their scruples diminished, and rape without benefit of baptism became the order of the day.

Rivera has painted the branding of slaves and the seizing and raping of women captives in the Conquest scenes in Cuernavaca and the National Palace murals. (Plates 199 and 222-224.)

the Spaniards suffered, and to admire their great chieftain and be his friend. He rewarded Moctezuma's generous hospitality by imprisoning him in his own palace. When he learned that the Aztecs had enemies, he played one Indian tribe against another (the enormity of this uncomprehended treachery of the Indians against their own future and the freedom of their land, they at least could not conceive) and systematically he deceived each tribe as to his relations with the other.

His men too, who followed him through every danger, constantly lent themselves to plots against their Captain. When he was separated for a few days from his company, all the gentlemen therein "played the game" of who should take the Captain's place. In Vera Cruz, partisans of Diego Velázquez organized a conspiracy against Cortés, but one of their own number betrayed it—treachery twice compounded. Cortés retaliated by ordering two hung for the crime of loyalty to his and their overlord, sighing unctiously the while: "Would that I did not know how to write, so as not to have to sign away men's lives. . . ." And he had the pilot's feet cut off, remembering with characteristic foresight that he might yet have need of his hands.

Even while the little band of four hundred men was in Mexico City, surrounded by a hostile population of perhaps two hundred thousand and battling for their very lives, Governor Velázquez sent an army of 1400 soldiers under Narváez to attack Cortés and to inform Moctezuma that his captor was a traitor to the great king he claimed to represent. But Cortés dispatched Father Bartolomé de Olmedo to the camp of the opposing Spaniards, and the friar, under cover of the privileges of his sacred office "very secretly distributed ingots and chains of gold (and promises) to those whom Cortés had named, and he got together and won over the chief persons in Narváez's camp." So well did the holy friar do his work that when Cortés engaged in a surprise attack, Narváez was almost the only man who fought in earnest. He lost an eye in the brief and unequal battle while his 1400 troops, his ninety crossbowmen, seventy musketeers and eighty horses passed over to swell the ranks of the resourceful conqueror. Thus was provided the first pattern for so many military *cuartelazos* that have succeeded each other with monotonous regularity in the history of Mexico, colonial, independent and "revolutionary"; a phenomenon so common that the shrewd General Obregón was once moved to declare: "There is no Mexican general that

can withstand a *cañonazo* (bombardment) of fifty thousand pesos."
Without taking into account this military tradition of the general who
is on the side of the greatest number of pesos and the "civil servant"
whose only requisite qualification is a razor-keen sense of the exact
moment to jump on to the next bandwagon (a moment too soon or a
moment too late may alike be fatal), much of subsequent Mexican history
is a meaningless jumble.

THE GREAT CAPTAIN [4]

Into the explanation of any particular historical event there enter a
multiplicity of factors, individual and social, things "accidental" from
the standpoint of underlying social forces and things "lawful" from the
standpoint of historical law. Undoubtedly Cortés was a military genius:
he possessed the requisite daring and hardihood, vastness of conception
coupled with careful attention to detail, a readiness to endanger himself
and others at decisive moments, a propensity to avoid force where guile
might do, a boundless confidence in the star of his own fortune and a
calculating determination not to tempt fate by neglect. Blunders he made
on occasion that very nearly proved fatal; but on the whole his skill
in using the antagonisms latent and patent within Mexican society, his
use to advantage of every weakness psychological, technical or social of
his opponents, and his magnificent and ruthless plan for the siege and
destruction of Tenochtitlán, stamp him as one of the great captains of
history. Had he failed to discover one of the plots of some of his
own men to assassinate him, or had he died of his repeated wounds, or
had the Tlaxcalans lost faith in him after his forced and panicky retreat
from Mexico City, Cortés would have been defeated and his little band
exterminated. Yet it is impossible to believe that Spain would not have
conquered Mexico, as it did all the gold-bearing regions and much of
the rest of the New World.

The Mexicans on the other hand were peculiarly unfortunate in their
leadership at the moment. Moctezuma was a great ruler in the sense that
his predecessors and his captains and the bravery and organization of his
people had extended his sway over much of Mexico. But he was a
vacillating and superstitious ruler and in the face of these bearded white
men from beyond the seas in whom he thought he beheld emissaries of

[4] Portrayals of Cortés may be seen in plates 201, 209, 210, 212, 213, 222.

Quetzalcoatl, emissaries themselves divine, he was weak as water. Signs and portents and the teachings of his faith and the prophecies of his priests told him they had come to rule over him. How was he to receive the divine emissaries of the morning star? He sent them gifts and more gifts and at last put all his treasures into their hands, hoping thereby to satisfy their greed and persuade them to return to their great lord beyond the seas. But how could he understand the boundlessness of the appetite for gold of these men from another world, an appetite formed by another social order? It was a strange hunger that grew by feeding, and every present he made of gold or jewels or precious stones but increased the determination of Cortés to press on.[5]

When Cortés arrived in his capital and rewarded the courtesy and hospitality of Moctezuma by making him a prisoner and hostage in his own palace, he himself stayed the wrath of his people, weepingly swore fealty to the King of Spain, surrendered his treasures as tribute, permitted the Spaniards to burn alive the faithful Cuauhpopoca whose sole crime consisted in giving battle under Moctezuma's own orders to a lieutenant of Cortés, and handed over to the conqueror the Indian chieftains who tried to free him.

But again we are forced to conclude that had the brave Cuitlahuac or the fearless and brilliant Cuauhtemoc been at the head of the Aztecs from the first, still Spain would have conquered in the end.

THE MIGHT OF SPAIN

Spain was at that moment the mightiest country in Europe and Europe the mightiest continent of the earth. The historical forces that were shaping nascent capitalism with its great fleets ("houses that move upon the surface of the waters," Moctezuma's messengers reported to him) and its commerce, its cannons and its gunpowder, its greed for gold and endless appetite for empire, and its surplus floating population released by the breakdown of feudalism, provided an enormous expansive force. During the brief half-century when the center of the mercantile earth had shifted from Italy to the gateway of the Mediterranean, Spain conquered the two Americas and the Philippines and lorded it over the

[5] Plate 210 shows Cortés, with doña Marina (Malinche) known as "the tongue of the conqueror," receiving the first ambassadors with presents from Moctezuma on the beach at Vera Cruz. It was these mollifying presents that inflamed his mad determination to penetrate into the country.

82

seven seas and left the permanent impress of its culture and its language upon the greater part of the New World. It had just completed seven centuries of warfare with the Moors and of struggle for national unification. In 1492 it captured Granada, the last Moorish stronghold in Spain, and in 1492 it sent the great navigator Columbus overseas. A century later the center of trade and empire had shifted: it would have proved powerless then to conquer, as it proved powerless to administer decently, and in the end to hold, its American dominions; but at that moment it was at the very zenith of its powers. Its king was indeed, as Cortés told Moctezuma, the mightiest king on earth; and its people, because of their historical position at the moment, possessed the energy to give battle all over Europe and extend their culture and power in magnificent if predatory enterprises (it is impossible not to admire the eagle though it be a bird of prey!) all over the New World.

A CLASH OF CULTURES

In the conflict of cultures that ensued, the Europeans possessed certain decisive advantages: domesticated animals which provided horses, mules, burros for war and communication, and a superior, concentrated energy-providing meat and milk diet; superior technique in the extraction and working of metals, which provided a steel sword against an obsidian-blade-edged wooden club; a superior method of hurling projectiles—cannon, musket and cross-bow against sling, spear, javelin-thrower and bow-and-arrow; and a greater degree of political unity and density of population. To this we might add a greater ruthlessness in war—the Aztecs sought to take their opponents alive for sacrifice purposes and regarded war as a ceremonial and religious rite as well as a source of sacrificial victims. Thanks to the solemn rules of the game as the Mexicans played it, Cortés and his captains, several times surrounded and seized, could be rescued again. And we might add, too, a superior subtlety and craftiness on the part of the Spaniards: this was not a racial trait, for the Indian used strategy according to his lights, but rather a product of feudal-clerical medieval subtlety which has come down to us under the names "Scholastic" and "Byzantine," upon which had been superimposed the mental traits developed by commerce and monetary economy which gave the Europeans a superior capacity for mental complication and

8 3

abstraction from real objects and acts and immediate elements of experience.

It is too customary in occidental thought to take it for granted that that culture is superior which wins out when two civilizations clash. Yet superiority in war does not necessarily mean superiority in all the arts of peace. Indeed, in certain significant ways, the culture of the conquering Europeans was definitely inferior to the culture of Mexico and Peru which it overthrew and destroyed. In the arts Europe and the United States are only now becoming aware of the wonders of a once magnificent architecture, sculpture and painting, and of the pitiful and decadent remnants of pottery, weaving and jewel-making. In the sciences we may instance the marvellous progress of Mexican instrumentless astronomy, with its elaborate calendar based on careful calculation and observation of the path of the sun and the moon and the planet Venus, which provided an intellectually and esthetically satisfying system of four simultaneous and correlated calendars with a calculated solar year more accurate than the Julian calendar of the conquerors. And what shall we say in the presence of a time sense that created legends dealing with periods of time (mythical of course) as high as 1,841,639,800 days and which even possessed a name for a time period of over 460 billion days!

Their hieroglyphic writing was in transition to a phonetic symbolism and in mathematics they had invented a sign for zero and a local place value for written numbers, two prime requisites for higher mathematics, prior to their invention in Europe. That they had not proceeded from thence to the development of a higher mathematics was due to the fact that they lacked the mechanical stimulus (deep mining, pumping, navigation and ballistics) which might have made it necessary and possible.

Not lack of mechanical ability and constructive energy (their pyramids and temples and aqueducts and dikes and floating islands and bridges bear witness to that) but lack of domesticable draught animals and the corresponding road and wagon was the real secret of their inferiority in the decisive field of mechanics, as it was of their retardation in the achievement of economic and political unity over a wide area. Just as the New World possessed only one domesticable cereal, maize or corn, and lacked Eurasia's wheat and rice and barley and rye, so it possessed almost no domesticable animals (neither ox nor pig nor burro nor horse) except the llama of the Andes and possibly the bison of the

84

still savage northern plains, and the dog and the turkey which were used for food. Hence communication over a distance was difficult with man as the only beast of burden, great empires were hard to construct and hold together, and an elaborate geographical division of labor with consequent economic-political unity scarcely attainable. On the other hand, a plenitude of wild game prolonged the stage of hunting and nomadism, while a plenitude of surface metals in the virgin state (copper, gold, silver and natural bronze) rendered mining relatively unnecessary. In time, had the settled Southern culture extended to the bison plains (its sphere of control was even then moving northward) the domestication of that animal might have ensued, thereby lifting the indigenous civilization to new social levels. Already on the basis of human burden-bearers, human runners or messengers and exclusive use of foot soldiers, a great empire had been built up, commerce and a merchant class developed, the rudiments of a money economy and division of labor over a wide area had come into being: a blend of tribalism with a feudal and elementary mercantile superstructure in great cities had produced the great Aztec "empire," the course of whose further development the Conquest suddenly interrupted.

SPAIN'S INDIAN ALLIES

Just as England conquered India and Italy Ethiopia because national unity possesses a decisive advantage over localism and internal division, so the decisive factor in Cortés's conquest of Mexico was the internal division and antagonisms within the not fully consolidated Aztec "empire." Indeed, Cortés was about to turn back to Cuba from the beach of Vera Cruz when a visit from the discontented Cempoala Indians chafing under Moctezuma's yoke suggested to him the audacious scheme that was to make him the master of Mexico. It was the Cempoala Indians who served as his first guides and auxiliary troops. It was Malintzin (the Spaniards called her Malinche or doña Marina),[6] the beautiful and intelligent Indian girl given as a present to Cortés by a Tabascan chief, who, giving herself body and soul to the conqueror, became his translator and councillor in strategy and interpreter of the psychology and

[6] Malintzin is portrayed at the side of Cortés in plates 210, 211 and 212 and in plate 225 with the son of their illicit union (Cortés was already married) Martín Cortés later a leader of the colonial ruling class.

strategy of his opponents. And it was the Tlaxcalans, blood brothers and traditional enemies of the Aztecs, who provided the vanguard and shock troops and burden bearers and providers and multitudes (Cortés estimated their contingent at over one hundred thousand warriors) for the siege and destruction of Tenochtitlán.[7]

THE SIEGE OF TENOCHTITLÁN

The Spaniards passed through the Mexican countryside like a lava torrent. From tribes that submitted they demanded food and guides and auxiliary troops, women and gold. Those who resisted they overwhelmed with fire and sword, pillage and rape and enslavement. Even among the Tlaxcalans, who became their most faithful allies, there was at first a divided opinion. War was feebly tried, but the Spaniards came preceded by the fame of their prowess and audacity, by the mystic prestige of their rumored divinity, by the paralyzing terror of the thunder and lightning that issued forth from the monstrous mouths of their brass cannon, by the incredible wonder of their horsemen, for to the Indians horse and rider seemed to be a single being.[8] After brief and half-hearted resistance the warlike Tlaxcalans, who had never yielded to the Aztec power, now submitted to the spell of their own superstitions and the shortsighted hope that with such mighty allies they might shake off forever the menace of the hated Aztec yoke. The alliance there consummated they faithfully upheld in adversity as in good fortune. It fulfilled all their expectations as to the destruction of the rival Aztec empire but at a fearful price they could not then foresee.

Backed by the Tlaxcalan hosts Cortés became more reckless, and, passing through Aztec Cholula on his way to Mexico City, he for the first time engaged in an attack unprovoked by previous resistance, mercilessly slaughtering unarmed nobles and warriors who had come a little sullenly to provision him and see him off. In Tenochtitlán, after they had long inhabited the palaces of Moctezuma with the chieftain as hostage, another such act of wanton savagery occurred. This time, Cortés was absent from the city for his war with Narváez, and his lieutenant Pedro

[7] Plate 211 shows Cortés making his pact with the Tlaxcalans. He is facing Maxicatzin who headed the pro-alliance party; behind him stands the dissatisfied Xicotenga who headed the tendency favoring war to the death with the Spaniards.

[8] The reader will note the prominence and dramatic force given horsemen and cannon in plates 222 and 223.

de Alvarado [9] chose the solemn moment of the fiesta of Tezcatlipoca when the Mexican nobility, unarmed and in holiday attire, were dancing in religious dance in the great temple court, to fall upon them with ruthless fury and attempt to exterminate them all. Over four hundred unarmed nobles died in the slaughter, but the Aztec warriors rallied and the Spaniards were thrown into flight.

Now the patience and the blind obedience of the Mexicans to the weak Moctezuma were alike exhausted: a revolt broke out under the leadership of Cuitlahuac [10] which even the return of Cortés with his newly won reinforcements was powerless to check. The Spaniards and their Tlaxcalan allies were put to flight, a flight so panicky that the Spaniards even flung away their precious burdens of gold. Those who escaped with their lives were all of them wounded, and only lack of ruthlessness on the part of the Aztecs, who failed to follow up the fleeing foe beyond the limits of their city's environs, saved the remnants of the "conquering" band.

After recovery in Tlaxcala, Cortés began the merciless siege of Tenochtitlán aided by one hundred thousand Tlaxcalan troops and reinforcements from Cuba. The aqueducts conducting fresh water to the city from Chapultepec were cut. Launches patrolled the lake and cut off the supply of food. Suburb by suburb the environs were taken, their male inhabitants put to the sword, their women and children branded with a white hot iron which burned in the letter G for *guerra* (war) and taken into slavery, the buildings razed to the ground till not a stone was left standing upon another. Eighty-six frightful days the siege lasted, while inside the city hunger and thirst and a plague of virulent small pox, unwittingly introduced by the Spaniards, and other forms of pestilence, did their work. The brave Cuitlahuac was carried off by small pox in a few days, and the eighteen-year old Cuauhtemoc (Falling Eagle) took command.[11] The epic of the defense he conducted deserves to go down in history alongside of Thermopylae, the defense of Jerusalem against the Roman legions, the defense of Paris by the Communards or of Irún by the Spanish workers' militia in the civil war that is waging as this is

[9] Plate 224 shows Pedro de Alvarado at lower right with a branding iron in his hand.

[10] Cuitlahuac is shown in plate 222, lower right, full face.

[11] Plate 222 shows Cuauhtemoc in the center with the insignia of the falling eagle at his left.

being written. Each day, each building and ditch, each backward step, represented an epic of heroism. "I was at a loss," wrote Cortés, impressed despite himself, "how to free ourselves from the dangers and hardships we were enduring without totally destroying their city, for it is the most beautiful city in the world." And totally destroy it he did: "The plan was," he continues, "to demolish every house on each side of the street as we penetrated into the city, and not to advance a step until all was levelled to the ground and what had been water was dry land. . . ."

Even unarmed non-combatants, women and children and feeble old men, Cortés testifies, were fallen upon with ruthless fury as they wandered about in search of food, and bit by bit the various quarters of the city were reduced to smoking ruins, filled-in canals, and heaps of pestilential dead.

"They did not have anywhere to walk," writes Bernal Diaz, "except on top of their dead and on the roofs that remained to them, and for this cause they did not find arrows, nor lances, nor stones." Yet still the enfeebled remnant of brave warriors held out.[12]

At last the day came when the brave Cuauhtemoc was captured in battle and brought before Cortés. Then he spoke the epitaph on himself and his heroic leadership in these simple words:

Sir Malinche (a nickname for Cortés), I have done what I was obliged to do in defense of my city, and can do no more; therefore I come by force and a prisoner before thy person and power. Take thou the dagger which thou hast in thy belt, and kill me now with it.

His life was spared a little longer so that he might be tortured to extract information as to the whereabouts of a supposed hidden treasure, but no word could they force out of him. Then Cortés sought to use him as an instrument of pacification and government, but fearing the rallying power of his person, had him treacherously assassinated in violation of the pact of peace they had made.[13] His statue stands today on the Paseo de la Reforma in Mexico City, and he is an inspiration to every Mexican who loves freedom and admires heroism shown in its defense.

[12] Plate 212 shows the siege of Tenochtitlán.
[13] Plates 213 and 214 show the torture and death of Cuauhtemoc.

But there is nowhere in Mexico any statue to his opponent, the conqueror Cortés.[14]

[14] The Cuernavaca murals, plates 195 to 219, are devoted principally to the Conquest.

On the vast center wall of the National Palace stairway (plates 222 to 227) Rivera has painted an epitomé of all of Mexican history from Cortés to Calles. The foundations of the present Mexican social structure having been laid by the Conquest, the entire lower foreground is taken up with the dramatic scenes of that event. An Aztec army in battle array was a thing of barbaric splendor and blazing color. Black and white and the diminutive pages of a book cannot hope to reproduce the imposing construction, the truly epic proportions, the stir and color and movement of the National Palace fresco, in my judgment the greatest work of mural art on our continent.

VII. NEW SPAIN

Tenochtitlán at last was left a heap of smoking ruins. Its canals were filled in with the débris of destroyed palaces and temples, its gods overthrown and hacked to pieces or buried deep in the earth. With holy zeal the manuscript repositories of the defeated culture were consigned to the flames, the gold and silver jewels melted down into ingots, the fierce and beautiful sculptures defaced beyond recognition, the stones of the temple embedded in the masonry of the new cathedral, and over the scene of ruin and desolation was planted the cross of Christ and the banner of his omnipotent and Christian Majesty, Charles the First of Spain.[1]

The completeness and brutality of the defeat, the death of all the leaders except the most cowardly and venial, the breaking of body and spirit by torture, hunger, disease and humiliation, caused the spiritual conquest to come easily after the military one. The sword had proved stronger than the *macquauitl*, the image on the cross mightier than the idols on the pyramid's peak, the flood tide of European civilization had overwhelmed the young springs of nascent Indian culture. There was no recourse left for the bewildered, leaderless and disheartened people but to feign humility (a feigned humility and super-courtliness of address have become second nature since) and to obey.

In the five days that I was in that monastery, writes Friar Motolinia, *another priest and I baptized by count fourteen thousand two hundred and some odd annointing all with holy oils, which was no small task for us.*

And Father Juan Díaz, first priest in Tlaxcala (land of Cortés's allies), has left behind the claim that together with two other mighty laborers with the spirits of men, he baptized "one million one hundred thousand souls!"

So easy was the spiritual conquest of this broken-spirited people that the priests sought for some explanation of the mass miracle and Father

[1] In Cuernavaca and the National Palace frescoes Rivera has portrayed this work of cultural destruction. See plates 215 and 224.

Vetancourt found it in the formal ritual similarities between the two creeds attributable to the fact that "the devil had introduced things which he stole from our evangelic law," whereby his Satanic Majesty had overreached himself and actually facilitated the conversion of these countless souls.

The best of the priests sensed that all was not well: the conversion had been too easy, the European culture and civilization were already compromising, adulterating, absorbing elements native to this soil and the temperament of its people. They are worshipping at shrines, wrote Motolinia, "with the image showing and the idol hidden—behind hangings, or on the other side of the wall, or inside the altar. . . ." But the good father did not know the past history of his church. Rome had been won in similar fashion, and so had the pagan tribes of the North, by adopting and adapting their gods and their festivals and rites to the flexible body of original Hebrew-Christian doctrine. True, there was a great difference in degree; but basically in the conquering polity of the Church this was really nothing new, and most of the priests questioned not at all and continued to work their wonders of mass conversion without troubling themselves too much at the difficulties of language and alien mentality in the explanation of subtle medieval doctrine.

COLONIAL POLITY

Colonial polity was simple: stripped of all its trimmings it might be summed up in the formula: "Enrich thyself." Not that *conquistadores*, king, viceroys, clerics, great merchants and colonizers phrased it thus nakedly to their neighbors, to the natives, nor to the mirror of history in which they assumed their poses and viewed themselves. Conquest has ever clothed itself in shining if tenuous raiment of civilization, culture, faith, or some other altruistic purpose. Cortés, when wooing the followers of Narváez and speaking with the straightforwardness of a soldier to other soldiers had said: "You are in a country where you can do service to God and His Majesty and enrich yourselves." In these words lay the sum total of colonial polity, together with all of its decorative trimmings.

More clearly than in Europe, where the ownership of landed property had been complicated by many successive conquests and overgrown with a softening moss and ivy of legalism, the right of property in the New World was based solely and nakedly on force. The only legal raiment covering this nakedness lay in grants from the King and the Church, whose right to grant was itself based directly on force. Symbolic of the nature of the new dispensation are Cortés's first acts in founding his initial settlement, the Villa Rica de la Vera Cruz:

A pillory was placed in the plaza and a gallows set up outside the town . . . a church, a market place and arsenals and a fort, and all those things that are needed for a town. . . .

European civilization had established itself in the New World!

These *conquistadores* (conquerors by profession!) had not come to till the soil: they had come to get rich swiftly and boundlessly. To the feudal-gentlemanly distaste for any labor save the plying of the sword they added the insatiable voracity of nascent capitalism and the limitless visions of the Renaissance imagination. Their appetite had been whetted by marvellous tales, and these were seemingly confirmed by the light value set upon gold by the Indians. Could any people value gold so lightly unless their supply of it was plentiful as any most common thing? But when torture proved of no avail in securing this fancied treasure from the Indians, they set to work to extract, with forced labor, gold from the rivers and the hills.[2] And in regions where that did not succeed or did not suffice, they mined the conquered Indians themselves as if they were a surface or subsoil deposit of wealth to be gathered quickly and taken back to Spain.

So intense had been the fury of exploitation of the *conquistadores* in the Antilles that in a few short years they had wiped out the population of the islands and the lack had to be supplied by Negroes kidnapped in Africa, else the "island paradises" would have had to be abandoned or the conquerors would have had to go to work themselves! Now Cortés introduced the same *encomienda* (trustee) system into Mexico. In theory it was a system of feudal and paternal guardianship, the entrusting of the natives to the care and command of overlords who were to christianize them, defend them, and rule over them. In return for these favors, the entrusted people were to give their labor and obedience. Feudal exploitation is an improvement over chattel slavery, as chattel slavery is over the slaying of the conquered. But this was feudal exploitation without

[2] Plate 216 (Cuernavaca frescoes).

the protections of medieval custom, and chattel slavery without the restraining calculations involved in an initial cost in the purchase of the slaves.

Nor were the land and mine-owners always obliged, as they are in the case of serf, wage-worker and chattel slave, to permit the producer to keep part of his product for his own sustenance. Tribes were formed into *congregas* and were obliged to provide their maintenance in addition to working land and mines.

To nourish them, relates a chronicler, *they sent them to the mountains to gather and bring to the* congrega *the wild fruits, roots and herbs which they knew and with which they maintained themselves in the time of their liberty, denying to them the fruits and seeds which they themselves sowed and harvested. During the absence of the men on this expedition, the protectors remained with the women and children both to assure thereby the return of those sent and to prevent the insurrection and flight of all.*

It became a common practice to brand the slaves on the face with a heated iron that they might not so easily escape.

There were marked on their faces so many letters, wrote Father Motilinia, *besides the main brand of the King, that they had the entire face written upon, because of each who had bought and sold them they bore a letter.*[3]

PROTECTION BY CHURCH AND CROWN

Some limits had to be put on this insatiable fury or Mexico would have been depopulated as successfully as the Antilles. The Spanish King, as later the King of England, attempted to prescribe rules of exploitation which would preserve his newly won subjects and his own interests. In this he was aided by the various bureaucratic agencies at his command, visitors, viceroys, inspectors, auditors, and churchmen.

There were enlightened priests in the first post-conquest missions to reach New Spain while the Church was yet subordinate to the Crown and had not developed its own wealth nor become, as later, the chief

[3] Plates 199 and 224.

exploiter of the colony. Friar Bartolomé de las Casas [4] had seen with his own eyes the wiping out of whole villages of Christian souls by Christian masters in the Antilles. He pled with the *encomenderos* for moderation and with the Crown for restrictive laws; he met threats of violence with threats of anathema, and preached, exhorted, thundered and fought until his death. His struggle was linked up with a factional feud within the Church itself between his own Franciscan order and the Dominicans who looked with favor on the *encomienda* system. Archbishop Zumarraga [5] held an *encomienda*, and the majority of the upper churchmen, themselves beneficiaries, were active defenders of the institution.

But there were other enlightened churchmen in that early day. Pedro de Gante, Fray Motolinia, and Vasco de Quiroga sought to teach selected Indians the gospels, the Spanish tongue, and new arts and crafts; they aimed to give them an education, not, to be sure, such as might set them free or make them the equals of the whites, but at least "to prepare them for their station in life." And if men like Father Landa were consumed with a fanatic fury to burn all manuscripts and obliterate all traces of indigenous culture, it is to priests like Father Sagahún that we owe such knowledge of indigenous tongues and cultures and institutions as have come down to us. And ironically enough, so thorough was the job of the fanatical Father Landa and so elaborate his explanations of his actions in consigning to the flames the Mayan manuscripts of Yucatan, that it is chiefly from his report of the "horrible examples" which moved him to burn them, that we glean our knowledge of the culture of the Mayan peninsula.

[4] Las Casas is portrayed defending the Indians in plate 217 (Cuernavaca) and in plate 223 (National Palace—figure on extreme right facing Cortés and holding aloft a cross). Motolinia is shown instructing the Indians in plate 203. Plate 222 shows Bernardino de Sagahún (at right, pen in hand), Vasco de Quiroga (holding an ear of corn) and Pedro de Gante (extreme right). Balancing him, at the same level on the extreme left, is the sinister figure of the Inquisitor General. All of these, as in the case of all historical figures painted by Rivera, are the product of much historical research both in the realm of occurrences and in contemporary iconography of the period in question.

Motolinia explained to the *encomenderos* the motives of the clerical defense of the Indians in these terms:

"If we did not defend the Indians you would have no one to serve you. If we favor them it is to conserve them. If you exterminate them, who then will serve you?"

[5] Archbishop Zumarraga is shown in plate 225 facing the flames in which native manuscripts are being burned.

94

As the English colonists were infuriated by the king's protective proclamation on behalf of the Indians in 1763, so the Spanish colonists were moved to resist the interference with their "rights" on the part of the King of Spain. Indeed, the first attempt of the colonists to secure their independence from the mother country arose almost at the beginning of the existence of New Spain, on precisely this issue. It was a conspiracy of the *encomenderos* led by Martín Cortés, son of the Conqueror by the Indian woman Malinche, and while it was checked, the protest was sufficient to nullify and reduce almost to dead letter the more or less enlightened and humane restrictions of the Crown. Thus the gradual strengthening of Church and King came as a blessing to the hapless Indians. It was only later, after these two institutions had grown powerful indeed that they in turn became the chief exploiters of the colony.

DEVELOPMENT OF THE RACIAL "CASTES"

The difference in treatment of the Indians by English and Spaniards has wrongfully been attributed to Anglo-Saxon "pride of race" and a supposed lack thereof in Spain. Yet the Indian half-breeds and mulatto population of present-day America are living testimony to the mythical nature of this "pride of race" of the Saxon; while on the other hand there was no more race-proud people in Europe at the moment of the conquest than the Spaniards. Their preoccupation with purity of blood in the face of the Moorish and Jewish infusions yields nothing in zeal or absurdity to the Nazi theories of today. Even in Mexico the Spaniard and the *criollo* or native-born Mexican of "pure" Spanish blood, had enormous privileges as compared with those whose blood was mixed or pure Indian. For entrance into posts of privilege, for qualification as teachers, and even for entrance into the institutions of higher learning as students, one had to present evidence of such "purity of blood," not only free from Indian or Negro admixture, but also "without trace of Judaism or heresy."

The English found Indians living in nomadic savagery who proved in the main "unassimilable" to sedentary, mercantile European civilization; it was easier to drive them off or exterminate them than to force them to settle down to a life of feudal serfdom adulterated with chattel slavery. But the Spaniard encountered peoples of settled culture already in the process of developing their own urban life, commerce, serfdom and

95

slavery, and readily "incorporated them into European civilization." The Spanish conquerors even found it desirable in consolidating their rule to intermarry, legally or extra-legally, with daughters of Aztec nobles and princes, thus creating a tiny *mestizo* upper class of which Martín Cortés, son of the Conqueror by Malinche, and Leonor Cortés Moctezuma, daughter of Hernán Cortés and doña Isabel Moctezuma, are conspicuous examples. However, with such rare exceptions, even the most aristocratic *mestizo* came to be considered a sort of social outcast or pariah, far below Spaniard or *criollo* in rank and privileges. As to the bulk of the *mestizos*, they were scorned as illegitimate children and disowned by Spaniards and Indians alike, wandering homeless and neglected in the half-world of social unrecognition.

As things stabilized in New Spain and the fury of the conquest gave way to the implacable coldness of systematic exploitation, a complicated race-caste-class system developed. By the end of the eighteenth century, there were perhaps seventy thousand Spaniards in the Colony; born in the Peninsula of Old Spain, they had migrated with royal and church approval and favor but at great personal cost, and in the New World they occupied all the leading ecclesiastical and governmental positions and mercantile monopolies, with the avowed intention of realizing substantially on the investment of the journey and returning in a few years to the Peninsula to enjoy the fortune they had extracted from Mexico. These were popularly known as the *gachupines*, the "men with the spurs," and there was no native-born inhabitant of Mexico who did not either envy or hate them. Next in order of rank were a million and half or so of *criollos*, native-born Mexicans of Spanish parentage on both sides. They too were well off, the provincial land-owning and lesser merchant class, the lesser bureaucracy of church and state and the provincial aristocracy. They were a revolutionary factor in so far as they wished to drive out the *gachupines* and change their junior partnership into a sole ownership of the sources of colonial wealth, power and exploitation. They did not hesitate to make demagogic use of the grievances of the indigenous masses and the universal hatred toward the Spaniard, for the purposes of their climb to power; but at the slightest sign that the indigenous and *mestizo* lower layers were finding their own leadership, initiative and program, they were wont to flee in terror to the arms of reaction and contribute pitiless and treacherous fury to the crushing of

96

their allies. As the *mestizos* gradually worked their way up in the social hierarchy, they too played a similar role in their relation to the indigenous masses.

At the bottom of the social pyramid was a population of several million Indians. They paid tribute to the Crown, a system taken over from the Aztecs. They received as a rule no wages, nor had they the wageworker's right to change masters. They worked at forced labor, diaphanously veiled with legal procedure, in mines and fields and urban unskilled and heavy labors. Upon their bent backs rested all the weight of the imposing edifice of the colonial structure, a social pyramid beside which Cholula's or Cheops' weight sinks into insignificance.

INDIAN REVOLTS

Again and again during the long nightmare of three centuries of colonial rule (a nightmare which did not end with Independence), the Indians rose by villages and tribes and regions against the intolerable exploitation which kept them ragged, starved and subjected to subhuman indignities. The first revolts in the central region were repressed with such fury that the Indians there gradually lapsed into hopeless sullenness and wheedling servility. But the outer regions remained unsubdued and whole villages took to the barren hills as less unkind than the landowners, until *ir al monte* (take to the hills) became a tradition of national life, which it still remains.[6] When the *mestizo* and *criollo* found it desirable to cease to aid in the suppression of this revolutionary spirit and used it for their own purposes, independence was assured.

THE SPANISH CONTRIBUTION

We cannot close this brief survey of the colonial period without noting the positive contributions made by Spain to the development of Mexico. She gave her language and the heritage of her great literature, and (in Hispanified, Catholic-feudal form) the social values of European technique and economy and culture. She introduced cow and horse and burro and mule; cart and road and sailship; iron and steel and deep mining and chemistry and metallurgy; wheat and sugarcane and a more

[6] Rivera has portrayed leaders of Indian revolts in the Cuernavaca frescoes (plate 219) and in the group of fighters for independence in the National Palace mural (plates 222 and 226, the figure with armor and sword just below Morelos).

97

advanced agricultural technique; many new arts and crafts and the stream of Asiatic-European thought and culture to blend with and fructify the native civilization and to become dominant in the resultant Mexican culture and life. However cruelly and selfishly and at whatever irreparable price to many successions of suffering generations, Spain enormously accelerated the social evolution of Mexico towards completer feudalism and subsequent capitalist development. We cannot regard either of them as a blessing, but they are the valley of the shadow through which mankind must march in his journey from primitive communism, already agonizing in Ancient Mexico at the time of the Conquest, to a future classless society.

THE DECAY OF SPAIN

But Spain's power to colonize and contribute did not last long. The very discovery and colonization of America caused the shift of the center of world trade and destiny from the Mediterranean to northern Europe, to England, France and Holland. The expulsion of Jew and Moor accelerated the ruin of nascent capitalism in the Spanish peninsula. The great streams of gold and silver pumped out of America passed through Spain as through a sluice, leaving a sediment of high living costs and ruined local industries, and came to rest in the mercantile countries of the North. The gallant wars and epic expeditions impoverished the land. Reaction soon set in, and with it three centuries of slow and ignoble decay. All social progress and intellectual activity was paralyzed by the heavy weight of absolute monarchy rendered independent of popular pressure through the wealth of the Indies, by the burden of decadent militarism, and by the dead hand of the Inquisition and feudal-clerical retrogression. Thus the social structure transmitted by Old Spain to New represented a prematurely blasted mercantilism overwhelmed by a predatory and decaying feudalism, which not only pillaged the New World but soon strangled its further development as well.

Now the Church lost its humble role as servitor of the Spanish Crown and in both New Spain and Old it became in time the great monopolist of wealth and property, the master of economic and intellectual life and the blocker of progress in every field. Gone were the days of the "enlightened" priests, the apostles and teachers and defenders of the Indians. Now the King in turn had to try to defend the Indians against the limitless avarice of the clergy. Crown grants, private gifts of dying landowners who sought to pave with gold the way to Heaven, tithes, fees for birth, marriage and death, parish donations and offerings, and money-lending and financial speculation, all steadily piled up wealth for the Church. As early as 1644 the conservative *Ayuntamiento* (municipal council) of Mexico City petitioned the King against further ordination of priests and foundation of monasteries, and complained that the real property owned by the Church amounted to half the value of all the property in New Spain! The Church had grown too powerful, and the petition was denied.

It controlled all education, all printing and importing of books (even from the mother country!). From time to time the Inquisition in great *autos da fe* stamped out questioners, opponents, Jews, heretics, witches and conspirators. Rivera has painted the ritual sacrifice of the Aztecs and the *autos da fe* of the Inquisition side by side in the Cuernavaca frescoes, as if to say that human sacrifice to religion and to the glory of their respective gods was not a peculiar possession of the Aztecs.[7]

The closing years of the Colony found the soil exhausted, the forests laid waste, the natural aridity of the land aggravated into chronic drought and famine, the surface mines depleted of their wealth, the physique and spirit of the natives broken, their culture destroyed without having been replaced by another, industry and commerce hobbled and hamstrung by mercantile restrictions far more sweeping than those which had aroused the English colonies to revolution, Spain unable any longer to maintain steady naval and mercantile contact with her colonies and unwilling to permit ships of England, France or the United States to touch their shores. Education was decadent, thought stifled, the Indians in revolt, the *mestizos* and *criollos* openly hostile to the Spanish ruling strata. The land was monopolized by a few big landowners, and all the resources of the country concentrated, directly or by mortgage, and rendered sterile in the "dead hand" of the Church.

In America the English colonies had revolted and were now a free and growing nation. Europe was being shaken to its depths by the storms of the French Revolution. The decaying Spanish structure was cracked from top to bottom by the Napoleonic invasion, and the once great Spanish empire began to crumble and fall apart.

[7] Plates 195 and 204.

VIII. THE STRUGGLE FOR INDEPENDENCE

It has often been assumed that there is an automatic relation between oppression and revolution. Yet the English colonies, the freest in the New World, revolted first: the far less free Spanish colonies took another half century to secure their freedom. No less puzzling to the superficial view is the fact that shortly before New Spain revolted, she began to experience for the first time in her three centuries of existence a relative freedom for economic development. Under Charles III, and such enlightened viceroys as the second Count of Revillagigedo and royal investigators such as José de Galvez and the Count of Aranda, the Colony experienced such reforms as the expulsion of the Jesuits, the installation of a more efficient, honestly administered and moderate taxation system, a removal of some of the restrictions on commerce, and a mild boom in mining, industry, and even agriculture.

Far more essential to revolution than oppression (which may endure for centuries with only an occasional blind and hopeless flare-up of resistance) is the growth of conditions for the development of a new order, and with them the growth of the ideology and organization necessary for a successful struggle. In the beginning, the colonials (excepting of course the Indian masses) needed and appreciated their colonial status; a market for their raw materials and a source of manufactured goods; the source too of laws and officials and ideas and institutions; the means of protection against Indians and rival colonial powers. These things became oppressive only in proportion as the colonials outgrew them. Thus *growth*, economic, political, social, is the key to revolution and constitutes its underlying driving force, the force that in the long run makes it irresistible. And the English colonies, being freer to grow, sooner outgrew their colonial status and came to find the outgrown colonial structure absurd, oppressive and intolerable.

It was not merely that New Spain grew more slowly: its colonials had a much greater "Indian problem" than the English. The Indians never ceased to struggle blindly, hopelessly, fiercely, for freedom. But the fulfillment of their needs in practice would have carried Mexico beyond the limited horizon of bourgeois conceptions of freedom. The leading colonials feared the Indian, Negro and lower *mestizo* masses far more than they resented Spanish governmental exploitation and restriction. Even the antagonism between *criollos* and *gachupines* was but a minor squabble over the percentage division of the privileges and spoils of the exploitation of the Indians and the natural resources of the country. But the real forces of revolution were slowly maturing in the womb of time, near-ripe but not yet ripe, when the earth-shaking disturbances of the French Revolution caused an historical miscarriage in New Spain. The Spanish Empire suddenly fell apart, and the Mexican ruling class found it necessary to head the slowly rising revolutionary forces in order to head them off: else these forces would have overwhelmed them in their rising.

Therein is provided the key to the subsequent "maze" of Mexican history. The movement for independence was a fusion of two inherently antagonistic movements: the social revolution slowly germinating deep in the lower layers of Mexican society and a political movement for independence from above, the better to prevent that germination from reaching fruition.

PRELIMINARY RUMBLINGS

Even the stuffy intellectual atmosphere of the upper circles of the Colony felt the stirring of fresh breezes at the turning of the eighteenth century into the nineteenth: a passion for the classics (pitiful attenuated form in which the Age of Reason and its rejection of medievalism filtered into church-ridden New Spain!); the smuggling in of forbidden French literature (Father Hidalgo in his heresy trial was accused of reading French philosophers); Jesuit counter-propaganda against the absolute powers of a monarch who had hitherto rested his claims upon the sanction of Divine Right; royal challenge of the temporal power and wealth of the Church; reports by enlightened royal advisers suggesting the loosening of the colonial apron strings lest the growing child snap them altogether; news of Indian revolts in Durango and Yucatán, the conspiracy of the *machetes* in Mexico City; calculating proposals for the separation of New Spain from Old under a prince of the Spanish royal house; generous sporadic dreams of freedom even in the Municipal Council of Mexico City and within the very precincts of the viceroy's palace; warning from the enlightened Bishop of Michoacán that the opposition between "those who have everything and those who have nothing" was growing to the breaking point, aggravated by the fact that "there is no intermediate state," i.e. no middle class; radical agitation among theological students who have been reading prohibited French tracts; draft constitutions for "a perfect government" earnestly discussed article by article in conspirative house parties; elegant "French salons" where literary discussions take on an ever more philosophical and political turn—and at last, from one of these literary circles an open movement of insurrection that electrifies the country!

TWO STRONG WOMEN

If Padre Hidalgo is the "Father of Mexican Independence," the brave and strong-minded doña Josefa Ortíz de Dominguez,[1] wife of the Corregidor of Querétaro, has some claim to be called the "mother." It was in the brilliant provincial *tertulias* in her house that the movement captained by Ignacio Allende and Padre Hidalgo was born. At her home, one of the wealthiest and most distinguished in the province, foregathered Captain Allende of the royal guards, Mariano Abasola, Juan Aldama and a score of others, and when Hidalgo visited it in 1808 he came away with his half-formed dreams and incoherent resentments crystallized into definite plans for insurrection. And she it was who managed to give him warning when, as an official's wife, she was able to learn that those plans had been betrayed.

Another leading woman figure in the long list of heroines of the struggle for independence is Leona Vicario,[2] sweetheart of Andrés Quintana Roo, himself one of the outstanding propagandists of the revolution. A woman of great wealth, she purchased arms, secured supplies, suffered confiscation of her estate; when imprisoned she resisted torture without revealing the names of her confederates and escaped after an exciting jail delivery to take the field alongside of her husband. Almost alone of the original revolutionists of 1810, she survived the defeats, round-ups, executions, abjurations and betrayals of the long years of reverses, and

[1] Woman in profile facing right, plate 226. Behind her is Aldama, to her right Abasola and below them Captain Allende.
[2] Leona Vicario is the woman facing left in plate 222, next to her is Quintana Roo.

was still in the field to enter Mexico City on horseback with her fellow fighters when the revolution had won its deceptive triumph.

TWO POOR PRIESTS

The two outstanding leaders of the Independence movement were village *curas*, native-born poor priests. By virtue of their native birth they were ineligible for the highest posts in the Church, and by social position and close contact with the masses in poor rural churches they were predisposed to sympathy with the aspirations of the Indians and to antagonism to Spanish clerical hierarchy and colonial rule. Both met in the end the same fate, excommunication by their superiors, condemnation by the Inquisition for the crimes of heresy, apostasy and sedition, and deliverance to the secular arm of the Catholic state for execution by a firing squad with the solemn blessing and rejoicing of the hierarchy. The decree condemning Hidalgo charges him with

declaring war on God, on His holy religion and on the fatherland . . . alarming the people to sedition in the name of the most holy Mary of Guadalupe and that of our beloved and sworn King Ferdinand VII.

The decree of excommunication was ordered read and posted in all churches of the realm, and any attempt to remove it was a sufficient cause for "major excommunication and (lest the loss of eternity be not impressive enough) a fine of five hundred pesos."

And we declare to be guilty of the crime of aiding and abetting, continues the verdict of the Inquisition, *and subject to the same penalties, all persons, without exception, who approve your sedition, receive your proclamations, maintain your kind of aid or favor, and all those who, following revolutionary ideas and in whatever manner furthering and propagating them, for all are directed to overthrow of throne and altar, of which no doubt is left by the erroneous creed of which you are denounced and . . . your cruel procedures, very similar to those of the perfidious Luther in Germany.*

Each year on the night of September 15th, anniversary of the beginning of his revolt, the great cathedral of Mexico City is illuminated with floodlights in honor of Father Hidalgo. Thus does the Church, asserting its doctrinal continuity through the ages and depending upon the shortness of secular memory, claim credit for having supplied from its ranks the Father of the Revolution. With grand flexibility it adapts itself to the *fait accompli* and seeks credit and honor in the men and women whom it cast out at the time of their hour of service and struggle. And thus, despite its imposing façade of structural and doctrinal unity, does the omnipresent class struggle invade even the Church in decisive moments of history.

FATHER HIDALGO

Father Hidalgo had been in trouble with his superiors before. His learning and his progressive ideas had brought him under suspicion on more than one occasion. Aroused by the misery of his Indian charges, he had taught them new arts and crafts and aided them in the cultivation of the grape, the mulberry and the silk worm—a serious crime in the eyes of the colonial authorities, for the grape was forbidden in Mexico in benefit of the Spanish wine-growers, and silk culture was prohibited to aid the Spanish merchants engaged in the oriental trade. The government had sent men to uproot his vines and cut down his mulberries and undo the modest work of this village curate for the temporal redemption of his charges.[3]

Gradually his resentment at the thwarting of his simple efforts on behalf of his starving and miserable parishioners was fitted into the ampler framework of the generous vision and social views of the French philosophers, and when the little circle of enlightened conspirators of Querétaro drew him in, they soon recognized in Hidalgo an ideological leader and banner-bearer and partial shield against the terrors of the churchly condemnation that the revolutionary movement was sure to call down upon itself.

Their slowly maturing conspiracy, which had set its date for insurrection as December 8th, 1810, met with the inevitable betrayal early in September. Warned by messenger, the parish priest of Dolores met the emergency by proclaiming the independence of Mexico on the night of September 15th, since then sacred to Hidalgo's name and Mexico's freedom.

[3] Rivera has painted him with broken chains in his hands, symbolic of his proclamation of the abolition of slavery, and with the forbidden grapevine and mulberry plant at his feet. Plate 226, central figure.

My children, he said to a little group of his parishioners from the church steps in the early dawn of the next morning, *this day comes to us a new dispensation. Are you ready to receive it? Will you be free? Will you make the effort to recover from the hated Spaniards the lands stolen from your forefathers three hundred years ago?*

Here was a proclamation which guaranteed that his would be no mere movement for separation and a change of exploiters, but one for independence as a step in the process of social revolution. To the Indians his message came as a dazzling ray of light in the darkness of their century-old oppression. Only sixteen men followed him that dawn as he marched away from his church after imprisoning the Spanish priest there as the first step in his plan to arrest all *gachupines*, but in a few short weeks his following grew to fifty, to eighty, to one hundred thousand! A disorganized band, recruited in the main from those who had been forbidden by colonial law to learn the use or manufacture of arms; a band equipped almost wholly with staves, pikes, slings and *machetes;* but Celaya was soon his, then Guanajuato, then Valladolid. With brilliant comprehension of the psychology of his people, the attack he was to meet from the religious authorities, and the democratic implications that were hidden in her legend, he chose as his standard the parish banner bearing the image of the brown Virgin of Guadalupe, she who had refused to appear to an archbishop but had presented herself to a lowly Indian, she who was identified in the popular mind with Tonantzín, the pre-conquest Earth Mother. Another standard which he raised, whether as tactical maneuver or as token of his own illusions and the incompleteness of his program, was that of Ferdinand VII, whom Napoleon had deposed as lawful sovereign of Spain. As his arms met with their first brilliant successes, he began unfolding other points of his program: he proclaimed the liberation of all slaves; opened the jails crowded with humble folk whose chief crime had been their poverty; abolished that heritage of Aztec vassalage, the tribute on the Indian tribes; arrested Spaniards; confiscated their great estates; ordered the restitution of stolen Indian lands; laid plans for the calling of a constituent congress. The Congress would realize on paper that dream of the French philosophers, a "perfect government," which government would "exile poverty" from this poverty-striken, wealth-blessed land.

Crafts will be stimulated, proclaimed Hidalgo thinking of his uprooted vines and destroyed silk worms, *industry will come to life, we shall make free use of the intensely rich products of our fertile land, and in a few years, its inhabitants will enjoy the benefits which the Sovereign Author of Nature has poured over this vast continent.*

The astonished government put a price upon the curate's head, called the Church into action with the awful weapon of excommunication, rushed through fragments of Hidalgo's program as tardy and reluctant reforms, and sent its crack troops under Brigadier General Trujillo against him. In a hard-fought battle at Las Cruces the ill-organized, ill-armed but huge army of the revolution held the field and defeated the famous army of Spain!

Now was the moment, as Captain Ignacio Allende, the best military man among the revolutionists, urged, to advance on the defenseless City of Mexico, and the war would have been over. But Father Hidalgo hesitated: could he restrain his ill-disciplined Indian bands from looting the wealthy capital? Should he go so far from the field of his labors and influence? Should he not perfect his army and his government before he entered Mexico City? He withdrew; and that moment of hesitation proved fatal. An insurrection that does not keep the offensive is a lost insurrection. He gave the Government time to build a new army, to get reinforcements from Spain, to rally the *criollos* and well-to-do *mestizos* to its side against the infidel and against the terror of an Indian insurrection. The excommunication of Hidalgo and all who followed him began to have its effect, and the Virgin Mary now entered the lists on the side of Spain as well, in the shape of her incarnation in the Virgin of the Remedies, the same imperialist Virgin who had accompanied Cortés and accomplished the miracle of the conquest of the Indians three centuries before. Not content with using her as a banner, the viceroy laid his insignia of office at her feet, asked her to lead his troops and solemnly conferred upon her the title of *Generala*, generaless-in-chief of the royal forces!

At Aculco, and again near Guadalajara, Hidalgo's forces were defeated, and he was at last, too late, deprived of the military supremacy in favor of the more expert Captain Allende. But retreat had been costly to the disorganized and ill-trained insurrectionary army, and before it could

106

be reorganized in the protective mountain fastnesses, it was betrayed in ambuscade by one of its own officers, Lieutenant Colonel Ignacio Elizondo. Allende, Aldama and Jiménez were shot in the back as traitors, a peculiarly disgraceful way to die according to the Mexican military code, and their heads were exalted on pikes for the multitude to see. Hidalgo, being a priest, had first to be degraded, and was then handed over to the State for execution.

IGNACIO MORELOS

But the movement started by these men was never again to die out completely. Its scattered remnants took to the hills, that stout refuge of all Mexican revolutionary movements, and after a brief interregnum under the insignificant and uninspired leadership of Ignacio Lopez Rayón, it reached the greatest height it or any other movement for freedom was to attain on the American continent for more than a century to come, in the leadership and program of another poor priest, poorer and lowlier of origin and office than Hidalgo, Father José María Morelos.

Son of a poor carpenter of Valladolid (today renamed Morelia in his honor), Morelos was early orphaned and worked until nearly thirty as a mule-driver while he prepared himself in a then almost unheard-of manner for the priesthood by "working his way through college." His favorite teacher and leader in intellectual inquiry was none other than Father Hidalgo, who had been, for a time, rector of the College of San Nicolás in Valladolid. He had joined the revolt as soon as he learned of it and had received from his former teacher a commission of lieutenant, a blessing, and instructions to "raise troops in the South." At the very moment the insurrection was being defeated in the center of the country, he was winning his first victories in Guerrero, Morelos (also named after him) and Michoacán. He won to his support several idealistic landowners of wealth, the Galeana brothers and the Bravo family. They became his lieutenants as did another priest, the *cura* Matamoros, who turned out to be one of the most capable of the revolution's military leaders. Morelos and his lieutenants [4] held the field in the main with signal success from the close of 1810 till late in 1815, winning for much of that time

[4] Morelos is depicted next to Hidalgo in plate 226. To his right are Pedro Ascencio and Matamoros. Behind the banner to his left, above Hidalgo, is Nicolás Bravo.

most of the southern regions. But the capture and execution of his best lieutenants, Hermengildo Galeana and Matamoros, the weakening of his own forces by political intrigue and treachery (he was captured in the end by Matias Carranco, a lieutenant who had served under him and been bought over), the restoration of the Bourbon Ferdinand VII to the Spanish throne and the sending of important reinforcements to America, finally encompassed his downfall, degradation from the priesthood and execution.

But Morelos was more than a brilliant military leader and revolutionary hero. He was the greatest thinker that the whole independence movement in Latin America produced: and while comparisons are difficult, given the differences of medium, it is hard to think of a figure in our own Revolution to equal him in sweep and consistency of revolutionary program.

He proposed to strike out the name of Ferdinand VII, whose restoration Hidalgo had proclaimed as an illusory legal shield for his insurrection, and openly declared for complete Mexican independence. He called a Congress into being and voluntarily gave up his political command to it. This has few parallels in the history of Mexico! All Mexican histories comment on the fact that though huge sums passed through his hands not a centavo stuck to his fingers and he died penniless: this too has few parallels in a land where Obregón began as a mechanic and small rancher, Calles as a school teacher, and Cárdenas as a printer.

The Congress was the first authority capable of claiming the representation of the Nation and challenging on the field of legality the authority of the viceroy. Its theoretical temper is indicated by such proclamations as the following:

Sovereignty emanates directly from the people. Laws must extend to all alike, without exception or privileges. . . . Those which our Congress shall enact must be such as to moderate opulence and penury, and so augment the salary of the poor, that they may improve their habits and do away with ignorance, rapine and theft. . . . The people shall pay no tithes other than what their devotion may prompt them to give.

But the program of Morelos went far beyond the vision of the rest of the members of his Congress. In his proposals to them or instructions

108

to his officers, he advocated the abolition of slavery, race equality, abolition of caste discriminations, suppression of the sales tax, of tributes and
government monopolies, remission of debts, establishment of a popular
militia, the obligation of useful labor for all adults, the confiscation of the
property of all wealthy Spaniards, nobles and government officials in each
town taken and its use, half as a fund for revolutionary purposes and
half for division among the poorer residents of the town, the same
treatment for the accumulated church funds, the demolition of all royal
tax and record centers, the breaking up of all large landed estates and
the distribution of the land.

One looks in vain through the pages of New World history for a
figure of equal stature. Neither Shays nor Jefferson nor Paine in our own
history, nor the continental-visioned Bolivar in South America, nor even
the somewhat analogous program and leadership of Emiliano Zapata a
century later, offers a figure of comparable stature and horizon. Had the
revolution triumphed under his leadership and on his platform, and it
came very near to doing so, Mexico might have been spared a century
and more of turmoil and confusion, and would have taken first place as
the most advanced example of bourgeois democracy in the New World.
It is not hard to understand why the Inquisition upon his capture declared
this ex-muledriver priest "a heretic, disturber of the ecclesiastical hierarchy, profaner of the sacraments, schismatic, lascivious, a hypocrite,
irreconcilable enemy of Christianity, traitor to God, King and Pope." But
it is not so easy to understand his relative neglect in Mexico nor the
very ignorance among other Americans of the name of one of the greatest
figures in the history of these two continents.[5]

FRANCISCO JAVIER MINA

With Morelos dead the movement for independence seemed at an
end, and the viceroy actually stopped the sanguinary reprisals and
offered general amnesty as a measure of pacification. With the exception
of Vicente Guerrero, of whom we shall hear again, virtually all guerrilla
leaders submitted in the face of the ebbing revolutionary tide. The Colony seemed to be settling into slavish slumber once more, when Francisco

[5] Recently appreciation of Morelos's real stature as a social revolutionist has
begun to grow in Mexico. Rivera shows the importance he attaches to him by the
prominent position he assigns to him and by painting him both in the National
Palace and in the Cuernavaca frescoes. Plates 207, 222, and 226.

Javier Mina,[6] a sort of Spanish Thomas Paine, suddenly appeared on Mexican soil to stir up afresh the struggle for freedom. A Spaniard, he had fought for Spain against Napoleon; and when Ferdinand was restored to the throne, he had waged guerrilla warfare against absolutism and for a liberal constitution. Defeated and proscribed, he fled the country. In England he met revolutionaries from all over Latin America, among them the rebellious and eloquent Mexican friar Servando de Teresa y Mier. In them he began to recognize natural allies in a common fight against Spanish absolutism, anticipating by a full century Lenin's formulation of the theory of the relation between imperialist subjection abroad and autocracy at home. Aided by the English liberal, Lord Holland, and the American General Winfield Scott, Mina and Mier landed in Mexico and raised anew the fallen standard of the war for freedom, a "war on the Spanish tyrant and not on Spaniards."

The cry of all Spaniards, continued his initial proclamation, *is that America must win her independence from Spain. The slavery of the latter coincided with the conquest of the former. . . . Let America be separated, and the colossus of despotism will then be humbled, because through its independence, the King would no longer be independent of the Nation.*

Landing in April, 1817, he won some victories, but before the end of the year was captured and "shot in the back as a traitor"; Mexico lost a true friend with that execution and Spain one of its greatest citizens, whom it has not yet known how to honor.

ANTI-CLIMAX: FREEDOM ON A SILVER PLATTER

The giants had all been killed off, and now the stage was to be occupied by strutting pygmies. Ten years of heroic tragedy were cruelly parodied in a few months of unheroic farce. Adventurer, embezzler, sanguinary general of reaction, hero of a double treachery, to the Spanish government he had so bloodily served and to the cause of Mexican

[6] To the right of the skull and cross bones banner in plate 226. The three banners there visible represent three divergent tendencies, the royal-conservative banner of Iturbide on the left, the Virgin of Guadalupe banner of Hidalgo in the center, and the red and black banner of the radical left, bearing the slogan, *Doliente de Amos*, on the right.

liberty in whose name he suddenly professed to act, for ten years a general, then commander-in-chief of the royal forces, then by the technique of the barracks switch, the *cuartelazo, generalísimo* of the forces of emancipation, and once more by *cuartelazo* Emperor of a "free" Mexico—such was the protagonist of anti-climax, Mexico's "emancipator," Augustín de Iturbide.

As a leader of the royalist forces in the field he had distinguished himself for his merciless and brutal execution of prisoners, women as well as men, non-combatants as well as participants. We can judge the human qualities of this man by his message to his superior on April 17th, 1813, beginning with the famous words: "I have signalized with abundant blood Good Friday, 1813, in the history of this place. . . ." Or from the fact that in 1816 his shameless plunder and embezzlement of funds caused him to be put on trial by his Government and retired for a time to private life, the charges finally being hushed up only because he was able to terrorize all but one of the witnesses and because too many notable personages of the Colony were implicated. It was this honor-stained and blood-stained hero that the most reactionary forces in Mexico suddenly chose to become the leader in the cause of Mexican independence!

The explanation of this precipitate change of heart on the part of the ruling layers of Mexican society is to be found in the growth of the democratic and liberal movement in Spain itself. In March, 1820, Spanish troops about to embark for service against an insurrection in Buenos Aires mutinied in Spain and forced Ferdinand VII to restore the liberal constitution which had been drafted in his absence in 1812. Terrified by the visions of liberalism coming from the mother country to her loyal colonies beyond the seas, the Church hierarchy and wealthy Mexican conservatives suddenly lost their loyalty: no longer did they see in revolt against Spain an act of treason to "God, King and Pope." Not an abstract loyalty to constituted authority but a loyalty to their own property and privilege and the ancient colonial order was the real driving force of their actions. Mexico City now became a complicated web of intrigues and conspiracies: high churchmen, leaders of the Masonic order, rich Spanish merchants, big landowners, the very viceroy himself, became spinners of rival plots for palace counter-revolutions. So confused and tangled are the strands of the many conspiracies that they defy untanglement to this day. But increasingly the forces of law and order and privilege turned to the discredited and sanguinary figure of Iturbide as a fit instrument for their plot against social progress.

Of the genuine revolutionists only Vicente Guerrero and Pedro Ascencio and the romantic Guadalupe Victoria were still in the field at the head of small guerrilla bands. The viceroy, Apodaca, himself secretly plotting on behalf of Ferdinand (who was expected to flee from Spain and liberalism and make himself King in Mexico), raised an imposing army and put it under Iturbide to wipe out Vicente Guerrero.[7] But in place of going into battle, Iturbide proposed a parley to the justifiably suspicious revolutionary. It took a long time to convince Guerrero that this was not a trap, but at last they met at Iguala and he was persuaded by the astute Iturbide to enter into an agreement known as the Plan of the Three Guarantees. It tendered the crown to Ferdinand, but left subtly open the possibilities of a choice of another sovereign; it proclaimed the separation of Mexico from Spain, the union of all Mexicans (oppressors and oppressed in a common national front); and the safeguarding of all the privileges, exemption and possessions of the Church: Liberty, Union and Religion, such was the slogan of the "Three Guarantees." The viceroy,. who had dreamed of turning the trick himself, was thus double-crossed by his own general; the rest of the royal commanders switched with astonishing celerity, the viceroy was made a virtual prisoner, and in a few months the hero of this amazing intrigue entered the capital in triumph, proclaiming to the bewildered inhabitants of the land: "Now ye know how freedom is won; to you falls the task of achieving your own happiness."

Iturbide proceeded to name a provisional government of thirty-eight men, known for their conservatism, aristocratic personal position and bitter opposition to independence. These named him president of a Regency of five, and as their first, second, third and fourth revolutionary acts voted him hereditary honors, the title of *Generalísimo* and Supreme Highness, an annual salary of 125,000 pesos for life and other honors and tributes. He tried calling a semblance of a "Congress" but it did not prove subservient enough: he drove it out with armed forces, arranged a street riot by a nondescript hired rabble after a fashion later made

[7] Holding the banner on the left, next to Emperor Iturbide, in plate 226.

famous by Louis Napoleon in Paris, and had himself proclaimed Augustin I, Emperor of Mexico.[8]

Thus were the brilliant social visions of Hidalgo and Morelos and the sacrifice and heroism and high dreams of countless martyrs, reduced to the dust and ashes of an illusory independence. Mexico started on its separate existence under the triple curse of churchly, feudal and aristocratic-monarchical domination. Independence as a political preliminary to social change was converted into independence as a preventive of social change. Mexico was "free," but its people more enslaved than ever. Spanish control was ended, but all the evils of the colonial system were intact. There had been a change in the ruling class (for the very Spaniards who plotted the *coup d'état* along with leading *criollos* were soon betrayed and exiled), but no change in the ruling system. The Crown had acted as a restraining power upon the Church and royal absolutism had challenged the absoluteness of the power of the landowner over his property and his serfs; now the clergy and the landowners had even that feeble restraint removed. The bourgeois-democratic revolution had ended in a cruel caricature of itself—an aristocratic, conservative, clerical-feudal counter-revolution parading in the external trappings of its opposite.

The achievement of independence through treachery, intrigue, a purely military coup, a personal dictatorship and the cynical abuse of revolutionary phrases for purely personal and anti-revolutionary ends, set a precedent which has left its mark on all the subsequent history of Mexico. The tradition there initiated has become a chronic disease. It has since cost Mexico an added century of turmoil and struggle. Yet the masses had been aroused by the promise implicit in their own activity, and though betrayed, and subsequently a hundred times betrayed again, they were never to be fully quieted. Thenceforth they could only be ruled by naked force, or by force adulterated with trivial concessions and deceptive demagogy. And in the great revolution known as the *Reforma* and in the movement initiated in 1910 they were to surge forward with renewed hope and vigor and march far along the road of their aspirations. But at the time of this writing, after more than a century of tears and blood and treachery, the program of Hidalgo and Morelos is not yet completely fulfilled.

[8] The crowned figure on the left in plate 226.

113

IX. "MEXICAN MAZE"

During the first century of independence the presidential palace was occupied by over forty presidents. One of them, Díaz, was the ruler of Mexico for over thirty of those years. Another, Santa Anna, bobbed in and out of the presidency more than a half dozen times. Juárez carried the title with him while he fled before foreign invasion and conservative conspiracy and even into alien lands. Most of the rest of them were in office only fragments of terms, sometimes only a few months, a few days, even a few hours; shadows that scarcely darkened the doors of the presidential palace as they passed through into repudiation, assassination or oblivion. To the dizzying list of presidents, as hard for the Mexican schoolboy to memorize as the names of the bones of the body for the medical student, we must add two emperors, a "perpetual dictator," three regencies and two provisional governments.

Almost all of these seventy-five changes of administration were preceded, accompanied or followed (or all three at once) by armed insurrections, military "pronouncements," and even in a few instances, by genuine popular uprisings. And with nearly all the insurrections and changes of administration go new "plans," constitutions, or basic alterations in the theoretically prevailing political structure of the country. Sometimes the government was renovated and transformed as frequently as three times in a single year. None of these constitutions has ever been fully carried out in actual life. Few have even reached the stage of being taken seriously or of being acknowledged all over the country. Yet the bewildering rhythm of changes of men and structures gets somewhat slower toward the end of the period, and two constitutions, those of 1857 and 1917, represent a continuity of governmental theory and have attained a stability and practical meaning and widespread acceptance not accorded to the earlier documents. However, even these remain largely on paper, while after 1910 insurrections succeed each other once more at accelerated speed, though all acknowledge the same document as their inspiration.

Mexican historians have despaired of giving meaning to this mad dance of men and documents. Carlos Pereyra, one of the most philosophical of them, sums it all up in the hopeless phrase: *Todo esto nada*

114

dice y nada enseña. (All this says nothing and teaches nothing.) And the foreign commentator has all too often contented himself with a few pharisaical phrases about Mexican anarchy, racial incapacity for self-government, or some other convenient myth or verbal evasion. Yet history cannot thus abdicate its tasks and continue to maintain its scientific pretensions. It must seek the guide lines of underlying causality in the apparently chaotic and meaningless whirl of Mexican movements, men and measures.

ELEMENTS OF THE KALEIDOSCOPE PATTERN

After Independence Mexico continued to possess an essentially colonial economy and colonial social structure. Mining and agriculture continued to be conducted by large landowners, largest of which was the Church, on a feudal basis. Industry too remained in the stage of handicraft and medieval guild organization, and was beyond imagination feeble and rachitic. For capital, Mexico depended upon the tied-up wealth of the Church, on the mines which because of constant civil war were seldom in operation, and on foreign investment. For manufactured goods she depended on foreign industry, and on foreign markets for the absorption of her minerals, dyestuffs, woods, and surplus agricultural products. Mexico was a living demonstration of the emptiness of political independence without economic independence, of political "freedom" unaccompanied by social revolution.

The Mexican ruling class was the old colonial ruling class—with the gradual elimination (not completed for half a century) of Spanish elements, and their gradual displacement by well-to-do *criollos* and *mestizos.* Except for this one change, every attempt was made to keep the old clerical-military-feudal-conquistador system intact. The dominant classes even attempted to continue the colonial restrictions on trade with England and the United States, for these were Protestant countries, bourgeois countries, democratic countries, three abominations in conservative Catholic eyes. They rightly feared the smuggling in of institutions and ideas along with goods: the introduction of new economic forms and relations and conceptions which would ultimately undermine and destroy the "old régime" of Mexican feudal colonialism. It was not nationalism and patriotism which made them oppose Anglo-American influence and intercourse. nationalism and patriotism are post-feudal, bourgeois developments. On the contrary, they feared Mexican independence as a menace to their privileges; they fought it till Spain itself became a source of liberal infection; then they set up native monarchy first under Iturbide, then under Santa Anna. But they never gave up the idea of getting some foreign Catholic prince to rule over Mexico as a Spanish or French protectorate or colony. Thus one of the elements of constant unrest was the plotting of the conservative forces to reverse the current of history, and the operation, now open, now covert, of the contrary and antagonistic forces of English-American and French-Spanish intervention. Even the hyphens are misleading simplifiers of the picture, for sometimes Spain and France opposed each other, and after Juárez the main mischief was caused by the counter-pulls of British and American interests at the expense of Mexican stability.

MEXICAN MILITARISM

The heirs of the headstrong *conquistadores* and of the later colonial military apparatus are the generals, colonels and captains that make up the Mexican military caste. Their ranks were supplied from Mexico's best families. Freedom from royal restraint removed the only check upon them, and the successive mutinies, barracks switches, military *pronunciamentos* and bids for wealth and power enabled sub-lieutenants who knew how to pick a winning *jefe* to advance to a brigadier generalship within a year or even a few months of disorder.

At the very outset of the period of independence, out of 8,308 soldiers in Mexico City, 1,802 were officials ranging from sub-lieutenant upward! And 3,161 were classified as petty officers or musicians. That made about two soldiers of the line for every officer! In the course of the endless series of civil wars and insurrections, the number of rank and file soldiers grew and diminished, generally by forced levy offset by hunger, pestilence and desertion; but the number of officers and the rank of each represented an almost continuous triumphal progress. Rare indeed have been the civilian presidents of Mexico, and rarer still those who have dreamed of curbing the military or putting an end to its control of government. The few who tried it did not outlast the promulgation of their decrees.

The "glorious army" was far better adapted to its peculiar brand of civil strife than to foreign defense. Its budget was much greater, thanks to the innumerable officers' salaries, than that of the American army of the forties, but so little of it was devoted to feeding or clothing the army, paying the salaries of the rank and file or providing equipment and munitions that it proved impotent despite the reckless bravery of its soldiers. The Mexican soldiers had been recruited by levy (kidnapping), were barefoot, ragged, accompanied by their women and children, equipped with ancient weapons, short of bullets and powder, backed by short-range, antiquated, often useless artillery, without tents or means of transport, and well trained, in the words of General Arista, only in "the tactics of not eating." Corrupt generals resold supplies in the brief intervals of peace to accumulate personal fortunes, and during the war with the United States there are several cases of the sale of cannon as old metal in the face of the enemy, so as to have ready cash to pay or feed the troops. The very mules for transporting cannon were generally far from the area of battle in the hour of need, because influential contractors who rented them at fabulous prices were not minded to have the animals' lives endangered by service under fire.

Worse than the lack of equipment of the soldiers, was the inefficiency of the officers. Generals like Santa Anna showed a positive genius for selecting the most indefensible places and the most inappropriate moments for giving battle. And worse even than their inefficiency was the disloyalty of most of the professional military leaders: the only loyalty they recognized was loyalty to the cause of their own personal advancement. So practiced were they in engineering military *pronunciamentos* and in judging the most profitable moment to switch when others had started an insurrection, that the chances were more than even that an officer sent to crush a *cuartelazo* would end by joining it. Even during the war with the United States, when the very existence of the country was at stake, Yucatán declared its neutrality and dickered for foreign annexation; General Paredes left Mexico City with six thousand men for the Texan border only to start a reactionary coup (his fourth military attempt to capture the presidential chair!); the garrison of Mexico City drove out President Herrera; other reinforcing and rival revolts occurred in Oaxaca, Puebla, Sonora, Sinaloa, and Jalisco; General Salas started a second revolt in Mexico City on behalf of Santa Anna as soon as Paredes finally left for the front; the aristocratic regiments derisively known as the *polkos* started a third revolt in the capital when the American troops were already approaching it; and clergy and military maneuvered and intrigued and plotted and betrayed while the land was being dismembered and its very existence as an independent nation was in question. It is not to be wondered at that the army of the United States rolled over its opponents so easily. The only serious resistance it met was offered by young cadets and by an improvised popular militia in the Port of Vera Cruz and in the Valley of Mexico.[1]

As for the French invasion, it was actually invited and supported by the majority of the professional military leaders, the landowners, the clergy and the conservative classes generally! If the French were held off for a while, and continuously harassed till stubborn resistance and foreign difficulties forced their withdrawal, this was largely the work of improvised generals of civil, intellectual origin, popular volunteers and courageous irregular guerrilla bands.

Thus the regular army, like the pretorian guard in the decaying Roman Empire, was primarily an apparatus for swallowing the public treasury and making and unmaking rulers from among its own generals. More than that, it was one of the most important levers of the primitive accumulation of wealth. Its fat officers' salaries kept the State perpetually bankrupt; its method of provisioning by "living off the countryside" and requisitioning forced "loans" from actual or manufactured opponents, enabled its officers to seize any estates which pleased them and shoot as "traitors" any who resisted their demands; its military *fuero* or exemption from civil trial and responsibility made each general into a local, regional or national ruler; promotion, wealth and power were the by-products and real objectives of the vast majority of military insurrections; and in place of sustaining governments it made and unmade them to sustain itself and feed its voracious and insatiable appetites.

The question arises inevitably: how is it that the military, in place of being an instrument of governmental policy, class domination and national defense, becomes a relatively independent apparatus dominating society and replacing civil government? The answer to this, as to many another puzzle of Mexican politics, lies in the backwardness of Mexican economy and social development.

[1] The heroic defense of Chapultepec Heights by the military school cadets is shown in the upper part of plate 223.

With a few brief interruptions Mexico has been throughout its independent existence a nominal democratic-parliamentary-constitutional republic. But these institutions: the democratic republic as a governmental form; the written constitution as a limiting and prescribing instrument; equal citizenship and civil liberties as theoretical restrictions on power, place and privilege—all of these are products of the rise of the bourgeoisie to social-economic and political power. Yet in Mexico there was no developed bourgeoisie. A native capitalist class capable of ruling in its own name and creating institutions after its own image scarcely exists in Mexico even today, in the fourth decade of the twentieth century. Parliamentarism, developed by the European bourgeoisie when it already controlled the main forms of wealth and was seeking to control the purse strings of government, has never been in Mexico more than an empty imitative form, a hollow shell cast upon its shores from overseas. Not till 1894 was there ever once a balanced budget, and if this fails to astonish the politically literate reader, it is merely because he is once more getting used to the unbalanced budgets of the bourgeois order in the period of its incipient decay.

In 1937 all the members of both houses of the Mexican Congress publicly declare that their sole ambition is to find out what the president wants and then enact it into law. No accusation is more insultingly made nor more hotly denied than that some Congressman disagrees with the chief executive! They openly execute his will instead of his executing theirs. When in Mexico's history a Congress has resisted the desires and dictates of a president-general it has almost invariably been because it was already serving and planning to make some other general president. Or rather planning to sanction and give legal trappings to his anticipated ascent by military means to the presidential chair.

Elections, too, imply a certain maturity of bourgeois class relationships which have not obtained in Mexico. The reflex of the absolute power of the feudal landowner in his domain is the political power of the *cacique* or *jefe político*, and the baronial power of the general in the area he controls, subject only to the general overlordship of the *jefe máximo*, the big chief, in the presidency. While he controls the military-political apparatus, he either succeeds himself or names his successor:

elections are a meaningless ceremonial like the anointing of a king whose real royalty is acquired automatically by hereditary succession. Oppositions as a rule are not permitted, unless they are deliberately organized shadows as part of the show. The only real oppositions are rival generals, exaggeratedly loyal to the *jefe máximo* till they see a chance to displace him. Governors are imposed by regional generals or the general-in-chief who occupies the presidency. Members of Congress are named in the same fashion. Local government employees are sent to the voting places to do as ordered, and the military sees to it that no unexpected results can come to pass. Practically every election in the history of the country has been an act of violence poorly clad in *legal* forms; and practically every change of *jefe* has been an act of violence poorly clad in *revolutionary* forms. Hence the incredible lightness with which both legal forms and revolutionary phraseology are taken by men and movements in Mexican political life. Nowhere in the world is the word "revolution" more glibly used. It is not that revolutionary phrases have new or different meanings, but rather that, like worn-out coins, they have lost their imprint of meaning altogether.

THE CLERGY

Corresponding to the relative independence of the military was the relative independence of the clergy. They too rose above the level of a mere instrument of class rule to that of an independent vested interest on their own account. Long before the end of the Colony they had become so wealthy and powerful that even the Crown could not control them. In the closing years, first the Bourbons with the help of the papacy, then the *Cortes* of Cadiz, attempted to reform the clerical structure, cut down the number of religious orders, liberate some of the vast wealth rendered sterile by *mortmain*, the "dead hand" of the Church, abolish the ecclesiastical immunities and privileges and exemptions from civil law, retain the power to appoint clerics, reduce the tithes and fees which were monopolizing the wealth of the land and were making sacraments such as marriage an unattainable luxury for the poor. Further, the State sought to levy upon the vast wealth it had helped the Church accumulate so that it might be used in part for the purposes of government.

But the reactionary clerical-feudal revolution that brought about

120

independence as a means of checking the spread of European liberalism to Mexico, put an end to these inadequate attempts at control, and left the clergy, as it had left the military and the big landowners, more powerful than ever. After excommunicating the revolutionists of 1810 and even taking up arms to crush their movement, in the end it organized the coup of Iturbide to cheat the Revolution of its social fruits. To the Republic it denied the funds and the appointive power it had formerly grudgingly conceded to the King. According to its most accredited spokesman, the conservative historian and clerical leader Lucas Alamán, the Church owned, until the *Reforma* in the latter half of the nineteenth century, more than half of the country's wealth and resources, including lands, mines, mortgages, sugar mills and funds, and was the chief landowner, capitalist and banker in one. Land, once entering into its possession, could never again be divided, deeded, inherited, sold, or enter into economic circulation; while every pious death and all lives, pious and impious alike, increased its store of possessions. In no country of the modern world has the word *mortmain* had more literal and sinister economic meaning. The clergy monopolized education and dominated literature, censorship, the press, and the thoughts of the inhabitants. Its leaders received incomes that dwarfed into insignificance those of presidents and generals. The luxurious living of members of orders vowed to poverty was too notorious to occasion surprise or scandal, and even the diversion of funds to the illegitimate families of ecclesiastics was taken as a matter of course. We find more indignation aroused among the pious by the refusal of the sacrament of marriage and the refusal of holy burial to the poor, except at prohibitive fees. When marriage often cost more than a half year's income of a peon, it is not surprising that whole rural regions got out of the habit of marrying and that even today there are many parts of the country where the majority of the poor live together without benefit of clergy.

When in 1833 the first timid attempts at reform were made by Gómez Farías, the Church promptly organized a revolt under the slogan of *Religión y fueros* ("Religion and Privileges") and overthrew the existing administration. The program of the clerical party for the dictatorship of Santa Anna is stated in a letter from its theoretical leader, Lucas Alamán, to the Dictator, in the following terms:

. . . to preserve the Catholic religion . . . to maintain the ecclesiastical properties . . . prevent the circulation of impious books. . . . We are against the representative system through election, and against everything that may be called popular election. . . . In your hands, General, lies the happiness of your country and the opportunity to cover yourself with glory and benedictions.

SANTA ANNA AND THE CLERICAL DICTATORSHIP

A man of limited attainments and limitless conceit, of bounded horizon and boundless ambitions, an ardent soldier but an incredibly bad general, an agile politician without a trace of statesmanship, an inglorious thirster for glory and impotent reacher for infinite power, Santa Anna [2] is the prototypical incarnation of the socio-economic backwardness, clerical-military-feudal domination, personalism and phrase-juggling which we have been analyzing. Mexican history seems to have made him to order to illustrate the forces that were shaping it.

Santa Anna began his career as a royalist commander, vanquisher and executor of ill-armed revolutionaries fighting for independence. He switched with Iturbide, and that master adventurer rewarded his apt disciple by successive promotions from lieutenant to brigadier general, all within six months. But Santa Anna was not satisfied, for there was still a military superior in the Vera Cruz region where he was stationed, the Captain General. In a retreat that suspiciously resembled treason, he abandoned his chief officer in the face of a Spanish attack. When he added to this the defalcation of regimental funds, the Emperor Iturbide began to comprehend that he had in Santa Anna a man after his own heart and a potentially dangerous rival. When the master attempted to remove the disciple with these flattering and deceptive words, "I await you in Mexico City to make your fortune for you," Santa Anna proclaimed himself a republican, rechristened his regiment *el ejército libertador* (the army of liberation) and joined forces with Vicente Guerrero and Nicolás Bravo in a revolt against his chief and benefactor. He was defeated, and, besieged in Vera Cruz, he was preparing to leave the country. But suddenly the besieging generals switched sides and

[2] Plate 227 shows Santa Anna in military uniform, presidential ribbon and medals on his breast, surrounded by the high dignitaries of the Church who supported and manipulated his dictatorship.

122

Iturbide was forced into exile! Thereafter the shadow of Antonio López de Santa Anna darkened the land for more than two decades while he proceeded to play hide-and-seek with principles and presidency; now centralist, now federalist; now conservative, now liberal; now republican, now monarchical dictator; seizing the presidency, resigning in the face of mounting disapproval and difficulties, only to seize it again as soon as his successor had left himself open to conservative-clerical or popular-liberal or foreign attack. He was not above organizing revolutions against his own vice-president or even his own presidency when he found it convenient to nullify some liberal law restricting the clergy, or when he could arrange that the revolting generals would seize him and oblige him, all reluctant and unwilling, to assume more dictatorial powers. He realized that place and power were in the hands of the clerical reaction, so while he played with the other side, he gravitated steadily in their direction. His three attempts at the establishment of an absolute dictatorship were undertaken under their tutelage.

Santa Anna's reputation as a military hero was based upon one fortunate victory and an even more auspicious defeat, in which he lost a leg. With the aid of these two achievements he got himself recalled to power in every national emergency, only to lose and sign away Texas, lose half the territory of Mexico in the war with the United States, and sell an additional piece (the Gadsden Purchase) in order to provide himself and his favorites with some additional swift-winged millions. His famous "victory" was won at Tampico in 1829 over an ill-advised, ill-equipped and ill-supported Spanish invasion of reconquest. His opponent had burned his own ships after landing in Vera Cruz, in ridiculous imitation of the exploit of Cortés, and then, after repulsing Santa Anna, had been forced to surrender because he had cut his own line of communications with Cuba! But Santa Anna was forever after "the Hero of Tampico."

In Texas, after a campaign notable for military blunders against an insurrection which his own political blunders had provoked, he was captured by Houston together with his entire army in 1836, and to save his life, signed away the state. His defeat moved him to tell his captor: "You were not born to a common destiny: you have conquered the Napoleon of the West!"

He returned to Mexico in disgrace, but two years later in the comic opera *Guerra de los Pasteles* (Pastry War) he managed to redeem his reputation when he lost his leg and the Port of Vera Cruz to the French. They had landed a military force in an effort to collect some claims, among which were those for the damages done to a French pastry-baker's shop in the course of a riot. But they found it impossible with their limited forces to attempt to occupy the whole country, and so, though victorious, they withdrew. The redeemed hero and his leg were each of them accorded a separate triumph on their return to the capital. The leg was buried with military and clerical honors and an elaborate monument constructed over it to commemorate its heroism.

This new wave of popularity enabled him to get the presidency again in 1839. But he soon abandoned it in the face of difficulties, seized it by military force in 1841, was overthrown and exiled in 1845, returned in time to lose the war with the United States in 1847, seized the presidency by insurrection in 1852, and after dissipating the $10,000,000 received from the unpopular Mesilla Valley sale (the Gadsden treaty), in 1853 had himself proclaimed "Perpetual Dictator" and "Most Serene Highness" with the right to name his own successor. This he accomplished with the aid of the Church. The motives of the Clergy become clear in the proclamation of the Metropolitan Diocese:

A thousand times blessed the man who with so skillful a hand has known how to return to God His legitimate inheritance. His memory will be held in eternal thankfulness throughout the ages and his crown will be precious and unforgettable for all eternity. . . .

But alas for the vanity of even ecclesiastical prophecies, his "perpetual dictatorship" lasted only two years and in 1854 he was overthrown by a liberal revolt; his heroic leg, guiltless of all his more recent crimes, was disinterred and dragged through the streets in derision, and the self-styled "Napoleon of the West" passed forever from the stage of military and political history.

THE REFORMA

A nation cannot lose half of its territory ingloriously through the crippling effect of its own social structure and the incompetence and treachery of its ruling class, without being stirred to its very foundations. The United States, under the domination of its expansionist slaveocracy, had taken first Texas and then California and the Rocky Mountain region, and Mexico had been rendered incapable of effective resistance by its own internal dissension. While the invading armies were advancing upon the center of the country, rival generals had continued to consume munitions, money and man-power in their struggles for personal domination. The Church, tax-exempt and monopolist of the major share of the wealth of the land, stubbornly refused to contribute funds to its defense. When an attempt was made by the liberal Vice-President Gómez Farías (acting as President) to force them to contribute, the clergy resorted as they had in the past to anathema, conspiracy and the fomenting of reactionary insurrections. For the latter purpose it did not hesitate to part with a fund of several millions of pesos!

Aroused by this callousness and treachery, the liberals took on new definiteness of program and acquired for the first time significant mass support. Hitherto liberalism had shown all the weakness and vagaries of an isolated sect. It had been a shadowy movement, full of amorphous and imitative enthusiasms, now imitating French revolutionary doctrine, now admiring the practices of American democracy. It had been taken in by calculating generals fighting for Federalism versus Centralism. It had organized under Yankee influence the York Rite Masons against the more conservative Scottish Rite Masons, whose Mexican branches were of Spanish military origin. It had fought for the republic against the monarchy, for "progress," for free trade, for a free press, and, hesitantly and timidly, for the reduction of the power of the generals and the clergy. But its champions had been isolated provincial intellectuals, un-class-conscious forerunners and champions of a social class scarcely yet existent in Mexico. The Mexican bourgeoisie, what little there was of it, was far too feeble, too undeveloped, too timid and ignorant of its own historic destiny, to recognize in these liberal intellectuals and their generous and vague enthusiasms the ideological image of itself, or to give driving force and coherence to their program. The forces of reaction possessed the formidable apparatus of the Church and the Military, and deep roots in the feudal structure of the land. But the forces of "progress" had to depend on declassed liberal provincial landowners, occasional dissentient elements in the lower clergy, provincial lawyers, doctors, poets and philosophers, on isolated individuals whose social vision reached uncertainly beyond the limited horizon of their time and place and class. Such elements were notoriously unreliable and susceptible to vacillation, self-deception and betrayal.

But now the intransigeance of the Church was beginning to create an intransigeance in its opponents, and the incompetence, callousness and repeated treachery of the professional military leaders was beginning to undermine their prestige. New provincial intellectuals arose, stubborn as flint, concentrated on definite objectives, clear as to their goal, unafraid of struggle, ready to raise military forces of their own and learn the science of military strategy and tactics through the hard lessons of repeated defeats, and to reform their forces again and again in the shelter of the mighty fortifications of Mexico's volcanic hills.

These men were convinced that militarism and clericalism were the curse of the Mexican nation; these twin evils were preventing social stability, retarding economic development, hindering the working of the country's rich natural resources, maintaining mass misery and ignorance and political and budgetary bankruptcy. Mining, agriculture, industry, education, social life, political institutions, they pointed out, were actually at a lower level even than in colonial times. From this the conservatives deduced the moral that Mexico must take the road back and become a colony of some foreign monarch once more. But the liberals rejected the organized backwardness of the Colony as they did the disorganized backwardness of the period of Independence. Had not the same twin evils beset the one period as the other? These evils they were resolved to cut at their roots: the hitherto moderate liberals were becoming radicals in the strict sense of the word.

They proposed now to subject the generals and clergy to civil government, to substitute the "rule of institutions for the rule of persons," and to release the tied-up wealth of the land into circulation for rational exploitation and capitalist economic development. Without being fully conscious of it, they were fighting for the prerequisites necessary for the growth of capitalism and the industrialization of Mexico. Inevitably connected with their program, though they did not yet see it, was a drive to break up the great estates, not only of the Church but of the landowners as well, for this was the economic base of the feudal reaction. They also made war upon the communal landownership of "civil corporations," i.e. the Indian village communal *ejidos*, along with their struggle against the communal landownership of the monasteries. For

126

this unhistorical-minded radicals of a later date have severely condemned them, yet it too was a logical part of their program. They wanted to create individual private property in the form of small land parcels in the village as a concomitant part of capitalist individualism. Capitalism requires that land be an object of purchase and sale and rental, and that the tiller of the soil be at least formally a wage worker. They could not foresee that capitalism in its imminent development is the enemy of private property and concentrates small land parcels inevitably into larger estates at one pole while it develops a landless agricultural proletariat at the other. And if they had, some of them would not have opposed it, while others would have proposed to forbid the workings of economic law by means of the prescriptions of statute law. It remained for the present century to catch up with the vision of Morelos and grapple with the new problems that the church and land reforms of the mid-nineteenth created.

MEN AND MEASURES OF THE REFORMA

The War of the *Reforma* seemed to begin like any other insurrection in the revolt-scarred history of Mexico. Santa Anna had met the discontent and intellectual ferment which followed the war with the United States by establishing an absolute dictatorship. He abolished the shadowy freedom of the press, jailed or exiled all liberal leaders, established a nobility and the pomp and glitter of a royal court, as far as a ruined economy, a debt-crammed treasury, and crown jewels borrowed by force from the National Pawnshop, would permit. He surrounded himself with clerical advisers and put Lucas Alamán, theoretician and leader of the Catholic party, at the head of his cabinet. His "perpetual" dictatorship lasted, as we have seen, almost two years: then the usual discontented officers started the usual uprising with the usual vague "Plan" (the Plan of Ayutla) for an ideological banner. But this time the leader of the revolt was an old-time liberal general who had acquired new civilian advisers and supporters, and a new stubbornness. Old General Juan Álvarez was the *cacique*, boss, of the southern region of Guerrero and Morelos—like many another regional boss except that his rule was based very largely on popularity among the Indians of the Southland, and he was reputed to be full-blooded Indian himself. He received the support of the usual ambitious and unscrupulous officers, but he also received the support of the moderate liberal Ignacio Comonfort,[3] commanding officer at Acapulco, and of the popular masses and intellectual leaders of the entire South. As the civil leadership and social aims of the revolt became increasingly prominent, more and more of the old-line army officers rallied to the clerical reaction; but the new civilian leaders undertook the tasks of actual leadership in the field and by dint of many defeats acquired the necessary military capacities. When they were defeated, they did not scurry for the opposing bandwagon: they went into the hills, gathered new forces, and began again. And in victory and defeat they continued issuing new decrees of social reformation and continuous propaganda for their cause.

The *pronunciamento*, known as the Plan of Ayutla of 1854, seemed to come to as easy a flash-in-the-pan victory as its predecessors, and before long Juan Álvarez was in the presidency with Ignacio Comonfort as Minister of War, Benito Juárez [4] as Minister of Justice, Miguel Lerdo de Tejada in Fomento (roughly corresponding to our Ministry of the Interior), Melchor Ocampo in Foreign Relations and Guillermo Prieto in the Treasury. None of these were mere figure-heads for a military government, and with the exception of Comonfort, none of them were generals: they were the *élite* of the new young liberal movement. And they, together with others whom they rallied around them, were to be the political and intellectual leaders of the nation through a revolution which shaded off into guerrilla warfare, then flared up again into three years of the fiercest civil war in the history of the nation, then degenerated into guerrilla warfare once more, only to be converted into a five-year struggle against foreign intervention and alien empire invited by the desperate forces of clerical and military reaction. In the end the liberals were to be victorious, and though they did not succeed in rooting out completely the evils they had fought, yet they did succeed in altering materially the rhythm and pattern of Mexican history and laying the foundations for the industrialization of the land.

They met too the usual attempts at betrayal. The generals of Mexico City, when they saw Santa Anna toppling, pronounced themselves in

[3] The bearded figure directly above the high hat in plate 227.

[4] Benito Juárez is shown in plate 227, holding in his hand the Constitution of 1857. He is surrounded by the chief figures of the *Reforma:* above to his right, Altamirano, to his left, Ignacio Ramírez, and further left, Melchor Ocampo.

favor of the Plan of Ayutla and tried to name one of their number provisional president. But for once the southern provinces refused to accept the leadership of the Capital. Juan Álvarez retired under conservative pressure in favor of Ignacio Comonfort, and that moderate liberal, terrified by the fury of the opposition and played upon by the clergy, tried to temporize and then connived at a plot against his own government, the "Plan of Tacubaya." But the liberal movement shook him off, and Benito Juárez advanced from the Ministry of Justice to the Presidency.

The last military man was gone from the government; it carried on under the leadership of lawyers, journalists and poets. Ignacio Ramírez, who held various cabinet posts under Juárez and followed his fortunes through prison, persecution and exile; Ignacio Altamirano, who went from teaching and writing to the field of battle; Guillermo Prieto, Minister of the Treasury, are three of the most distinguished names in Mexican literature. Riva Palacio was an important historian. Miguel Lerdo de Tejada, Arriaga, Mata, Guzmán, Iglesias, De la Fuente, and a dozen others, were the nation's intellectual leaders. It was these men who drew up the Reform Laws, drafted the Constitution of 1857, led the popular party through the War of the *Reforma*, rallied the country against the French intervention, and carried on while the army was reformed under the new leadership of such men as Ignacio Zarazoga, González Ortega, Mariano Escobedo, Santos Degollado, Miguel Negrete and Leandro Valle.[5] There is no period in the country's history which shows a greater collection of figures of the first rank. And the rallying center and real leader of them all was the bronze-faced, strong-featured Indian of lowly origin, Benito Juárez of Oaxaca.

BENITO JUÁREZ

Though Juárez, Altamirano, probably Álvarez, and a number of others were full-blooded Indians, yet it must not be thought that the *Reforma* was a movement of the Indians for their own "redemption." It was rather a movement for which Indians formed the popular driving force and military reserves, led by provincial intellectuals, representative of the nascent petty-bourgeoisie, and predominantly *mestizo* in racial

[5] In plate 224 the four uppermost faces of the first arch are, from left to right: top row, Miguel Negrete and Ignacio Zaragoza; lower row, Mariano Escobedo and Benito Juárez.

complexion. It sought to emancipate the Indian masses from superstition and tribute to the Church, but it served to "free" them from their communal property as well. It laid the foundations for their ultimate emancipation, but only through the long and grievous detour of incorporation into capitalist civilization.

Benito Juárez was an "assimilated" Indian. As a lad he spoke no Spanish, but he was given an opportunity for a Spanish-language training and school education by a powerful local protector. He outshone his classmates, rose rapidly in local and provincial circles, became a lawyer, a political leader (the old distinctions between indigenous, *mestizo* and *criollo* were beginning to lose their significance as they were their economic-class basis), and then Governor of Oaxaca. Here he attracted something approximating national attention by taking over a bankrupt and debt-buried state treasury and leaving office penniless himself but with a fifty thousand peso surplus in the possession of the State. This tradition of honesty in office he followed throughout his stormy career, and not one of the men who surrounded him achieved a fortune through his connection with the nation's presidency. This is well-nigh unique in the history of Mexico.

Imprisoned by Santa Anna, whose dictatorship he opposed, he fled to the United States, reentering the country to participate in the revolt based on the Plan of Ayutla. As Chief Justice of the Supreme Court in the Álvarez and Comonfort governments, he drafted the famous Ley Juárez which provided for the subjection of clergy and military to civil law. This, together with the Ley Lerdo providing for the sale of all church property not actually used for purposes of worship (not at all a confiscatory measure, for the proceeds were to go to the Church!), initiated the Reformation and aroused the furious, reckless, two-decade-long resistance of the Church and its conservative adherents.

The continued and open plotting of the Church drove the reformers to the reluctant realization that they must undermine its immense economic power if they were ever to have peace and an opportunity to reorganize the country on the new basis. Only then were the Reform laws extended to the partial confiscation of the wealth that was being used to finance rebellion and intervention, to the establishment of a Civil Register of births, deaths and marriages, the abolition of monastic orders and public religious processions (so often utilized as political demonstrations and the starting point of riots), the secularization of education, the prohibition of priestly intervention in the control of politics, and other measures which tended toward the complete separation of church and state, not basically different from the laws characterizing such modern Catholic countries as France. The Reform Laws were given a systematic foundation in the famous Constitution of 1857, the first to acquire any lasting validity in the history of Mexico. Once adopted, it was to be many times challenged, and to remain largely unenforced, but it was never again to be fully repudiated by the whole nation as previous constitutions had been. It remained the acknowledged governmental basis till 1917, when a new constitution was drafted which is in essence a modification of the social features of the old, not a rejection of its basic structure.

When the Constitution was adopted, the fury of the hierarchy knew no bounds. Pope Pius IX declared: ". . . we lift our pontifical voice . . . to condemn, reprove, and declare null and void the said decrees." The Archbishop of Mexico ordered that any government official who swore loyalty to the Constitution, as required by law in taking office, was to be denied the sacraments until he publicly retracted his oath. Governor Manuel Álvarez was assassinated in Colima after taking the oath and they refused to inter his body until his relatives had permitted it to be publicly whipped in penance and had contributed two thousand pesos to the Church. The Bishop of Michoacán declared that no Catholic could accept the articles providing for free education, free speech, free press, freedom of assembly, abolition of titles of nobility, the theory of popular sovereignty and a half-dozen other provisions.

The great wealth of the Church was now employed freely to buy generals, equip guerrilla bands, and finance revolts throughout the country. The liberals carried on their propaganda in the press, but the bulk of the nation (over 90%) were illiterate, and far more easily reached in the pulpit. A fury of civil war swept the land such as it had never known before. Juárez and his associates were hunted from village to village; Melchor Ocampo was slaughtered in the peace of his home; Juárez even fled the country at a Pacific port, only to cross Panama and reappear at Vera Cruz. But through it all he never ceased to issue decrees, attempt to reorganize the structure of government, and carry on the fight. Here was a man who did not know when he was licked: he was as stubborn as his native volcanic rock. But his opponents were no less stubborn. When at last it looked as if he was consolidating his power, generals like Márquez, Miramón, Mejía and Zuluaga took to the hills and, aided by the Church, organized guerrilla bands. And when that proved insufficient, the conservatives sent emissaries abroad to invite an army of foreign troops and an alien prince to take over the land. Juárez for his part did not scruple to use the aid of the United States. He did not offer up Mexico's sovereignty as did his opponents, but he did propose sweeping concessions of perpetual transport through the Isthmus of Tehuantepec with the right to protect the route with American troops. Fortunately, the Senate of the United States, fearing slave-expansion, and not yet an agency of imperialism, rejected the McLane-Ocampo Treaty. But the negotiations of the conservatives with France and Spain for the surrender of Mexican sovereignty were so successful that they plunged the country into another frightful and devastating war to retain its independence.

MAXIMILIAN AND THE EMPIRE

While the reaction had been trying to borrow its poetry from the past with the trappings of throne and nobility and landed estate and medieval church, the impoverished succession of shadow governments since the inception of the Republic had been borrowing hard cash against the country's future. The foreign debt, begun with Iturbide, was swollen by non-payment, by the borrowings of every successive government, by accrued interest, by "forced loans" from foreign residents, by claims for damages from every insurrection, by the costs of a top-heavy military apparatus, by the purchase of munitions at inflated prices on the part of governments which never lived long enough to receive them, much less to pay the bill.

Especial demands were made upon Juárez for the borrowings of his opponent, the counter-president, General Miramón, including a "forced loan" (seizure) of British funds, and a loan from the Swiss banker Jecker for a face value of 16,800,000 pesos on which Miramón was supposed to receive only 15,000,000 (a heavy enough discount), but on which Jecker paid only a million and a half and then went bankrupt. A relative of Napoleon's took over the Jecker claim for the full amount, the bankrupt was made a French citizen, and the adventurer Napoleon prepared to attempt to occupy the country on the basis of this disreputable claim!

132

At the same time Spain, which was also being worked on by the clerical conservatives, presented a bill for claims.

Juárez, seeking to restore peace and economic order on his war-weary country, offered to yield to the bullying, to recognize the English and Spanish and part of the French claims, but to suspend interest payment for two years in order to accumulate funds for the purpose of meeting the debt. The response of the foreign claimants was the appearance of a French, a British and a Spanish fleet, with expeditionary forces, in the harbor of Vera Cruz.

France was the driving force in this united intervention. Its real purposes ran far beyond the collection of its outrageously inflated claims. Mexico looked "easy." The United States had carved off half of it, and there was gold in the other half. Conservatives and clericals from Mexico had long been tugging at Napoleon III's not unwilling ear, begging him to march in and set up some relative as King. That anachronistic adventurer dreamt of reestablishing the ancient empire of New France which his illustrious uncle had bartered away. He saw himself strengthening the "prestige of the Latin race," checking the expansion of Anglo-Saxon America, conciliating Austria which he had just despoiled in Italy and would recompense by putting an Austrian on Mexico's throne, running his itching fingers through great heaps of gold rumored to lie buried in Sonora, fulfilling the Napoleonic dream of empire on which he had ridden into power and which was now riding him into adventures which would soon encompass his downfall.

England, which seemed to see no further than collecting interest at the cannon's mouth, and Spain, which had also been plied by conservative-clerical Mexican propaganda, lent themselves to the strange adventure. Austria gladly supplied an unwanted prince who was too popular and too restive at home, and on bad terms with his brother, the Emperor. And to make things perfect, the United States, which might have protested, was torn in two by the opening of its own great Civil War.

When England woke up to the meaning of the invasion, it accepted Juárez's assurances of payment and withdrew. Spain, with a change of administration, underwent a change of heart; and the French, accompanied by the plotters of reaction, began their advance into the country alone.

There were *Te Deums* in the churches, but no cheering multitudes flanked the line of march. In place of the uprisings the conservatives had promised them, there was a sudden unification of the populace behind Benito Juárez. The haughty Count Lorencez had already written "I am master of Mexico," when the hastily gathered government troops made a stand behind the defenses of Puebla under General Ignacio Zaragoza and to the Count's astonishment, the amazement of Mexico and the admiration of Europe, the Mexican troops remained in possession of the field!

Now Napoleon realized with alarm that the honor of France, or rather of its Emperor, was at stake. Great war credits were raised, a huge army sent, and the whole power of France was put behind what had hitherto seemed an insignificant filibustering expedition. Slowly the reinforced, well-equipped French army advanced through all the main centers of the country. But they had to fight for every inch of the way, and Juárez and his generals, Zaragoza, González Ortega, Escobedo, Negrete, Porfirio Díaz, Riva Palacio, Ramón Corona, and innumerable nameless leaders of heroic guerrilla bands, never ceased their resistance. Márquez, Mejía, Miramón and other conservative generals and the whole clerical apparatus put themselves at the disposition of the French, but they had lost their power to rally the masses. There were the usual treacheries, too, of bandwagon generals who are, on principle, on the winning side. But this was a new Mexico with a new stubbornness, headed by a man who didn't have "sense" enough to know when he was beaten. The French invaders with their conservative and clerical allies, though they held the centers of the exhausted country for half a decade, were never able to control more than the ground under their feet and within the range of their guns.

Juárez, his noble dreams of reconstructing a modern Mexico shattered once more, fled with his perambulating government to the hills. No sooner had he left the capital than a *junta* of notables, including the commanders of the city garrison, declared:

We the undersigned have agreed . . . to accept with pleasure and gratitude the generous intervention which the Emperor of the French offers to the Mexican people. . . . And a little later: *The Mexican Nation adopts as its form of government a moderate hereditary monarchy with a Catholic prince. . . . The imperial crown of Mexico is offered to His Imperial and Royal Highness, Prince Ferdinand Maximilian, Archduke of Austria, for himself and his descendants.*

Maximilian had his misgivings, and within the limits of his romantic and royalist mental horizon, good intentions; but he willingly let himself be persuaded by a "Napoleon plebiscite," signed a ruinous treaty to recognize the Jecker and other claims and to pay out of a non-existent Mexican treasury all the fantastic costs of the huge expedition. He and his wife Carlota took ship to America full of dreams of establishing pomp and splendor and courtly life and dynastic glory in the New World. Alas for their dreams! The cold, bayonet-produced reception at Vera Cruz caused the young princess to burst into tears, and they found the French command already engaged in bitter controversy with the clergy over their impossible fiscal and political demands. The devout Empress of Mexico was soon to write to Eugenia, Empress of France:

The conservatives think themselves to be temporal subjects of the Pope and are animals enough, pardon the word, to believe that religion consists in tithes and the power of possession. . . . The clerical party would with pleasure abandon its place of honor and its cross, but not its income.

Slowly the net of inevitable tragedy closed around the visionary Emperor and his ambitious Queen. The clerical-conservative party, his only base of native support, organized intrigues and opposition against him for his moderation. Only the fear of Juárez and his men in the hills and the presence of French troops prevented new conservative insurrections. Napoleon began to meditate upon the withdrawal of an expeditionary force which had proved a longer and more costly and less effective venture than he had imagined. What was the good of troops in Mexico if they could not pacify the country, command the hills, work the mines, and pay the huge costs of the expedition and anticipated profits? He had counted on a Confederate victory and a divided and weak United States; but the North won the war, and in 1865, still in battle array, demanded the withdrawal of his troops. The war clouds of 1870 were already looming on the European horizon. Almost without warning, he notified Maximilian that he was leaving him to his fate,

135

unless the Emperor of Mexico wanted to go back along with the French bayonets that were sustaining him.

Prodded by Carlota's notions of imperial honor and the reluctance of his brother, the Austro-Hungarian Emperor, to let him return, Maximilian decided to remain: thereby his fate was sealed. In vain Carlota went to Europe to plead with Napoleon to leave his troops, to the Pope to back up the moderate prince against the demands of the immoderate clergy. Then a merciful madness descended upon her, preventing her from realizing the tragedy of the end of her splendid imperial dreams. Her empire was to fall, Napoleon was to fall, in the fullness of time even the Austro-Hungarian Empire was to crash to the ground, but Carlota lingered on far into the next century in a world of dreams that no clericals and liberals and calculating clergy, nor any wars or revolutions could shatter.

Maximilian and the clerical-conservatives, abandoned by Napoleon, threw themselves into each other's arms; but in vain. His advisers had told the Emperor that his enemies were mere bandits, but near the end he was to write:

The republican forces which were incorrectly represented as disorganized, demoralized and solely animated by the desire of plunder, are proving by their acts that they constitute a homogeneous army . . . sustained by the grandiose idea of defending national independence which they believe in danger through the founding of the empire.

His generals had persuaded him after a momentary victory that his opponents were dispersed, and induced him to sign a decree that any remnants who did not lay down their arms were to be shot on sight without trial (decree of October 3rd, 1865). It only served to seal his own death warrant. Step by step as the French troops withdrew, the Republican Army of Juárez reoccupied the main centers of the country. At last, the Emperor was caught at Querétaro: with him were almost all the conservative generals who had battled Juárez before and during the French invasion for over a decade. By a queer coincidence this vanguard of reaction was made up of men all of whose names began with "M": Miramón, Márquez, Méndez, Mejía and Maximilian. Márquez was defeated in a sally to relieve the siege of Puebla. Méndez was captured in battle and summarily shot. Maximilian, Miramón and Mejía were courtmartialled and executed by a firing squad on June 19th, 1867. The Emperor permitted Miramón, the former anti-president, to stand in the center, and with that generous act of chivalry, the Maximilian adventure was ended.[6]

The costly miscarriage of his Mexican venture paved the way for the downfall of Napoleon III, as the unexpected stubbornness of the Spaniards had marked the beginning of the end for Napoleon I. The Mexican struggle for freedom cost Mexico over seventy thousand lives, and its misery and bankruptcy were many times compounded. But its sovereignty was saved; the clergy and reaction were too discredited ever again to attempt a monarchistic frontal attack; the liberal constitution and Reform Laws were at last identified in the popular mind with the cause of national independence and progress; and under the leadership of Juárez and his liberal and popular supporters, the foundations of modern Mexico had been laid.

[6] Shown in plate 224 where the three figures facing the firing squad, reading from left to right, are Mejía, Miramón and Maximilian.

X. REIGN OF DON PORFIRIO

The nation wanted rest. It had known nothing but struggles since the birth of its independence. It needed tranquillity to restore the blood it had lost on a thousand battlefields. Its revolutionary leaders had acquired demortized church lands, had upset the old monopoly of generals, clerics and landowning families, had acquired a scope for the exercise of their abilities, had cleared the way for industrialism and capitalism. They were even a little frightened by the extent to which the masses had been aroused to active participation and to eager expectation of a change in their lot. The new class was too lacking in self-confidence, too weak to rule alone. Its modest ambitions were satisfied, its little supply of revolutionary energy exhausted. It wanted above all things a chance to digest what it had won, it wanted rest, tranquillity, peace. The day of the hero of struggle was at an end. The longed-for "hero of peace" appeared in the shape of the liberal general, Porfirio Díaz.

True, there was an obstacle in the general's way, not easily surmounted. Benito Juárez was still there, looming large, victor of the War of the *Reforma*, victor of the war against Maximilian, father of the Constitution: his figure filled the entire horizon. But time and the unheroic days of peace were on the side of the ambitious young general who coveted his place. Juárez faced the staggering and ungrateful tasks of reconstruction with open eyes, free from illusion.

When a society like ours, he declared, *has had the misfortune to pass through years of internal upheavals, it is seamed through with vices whose profound roots cannot be extirpated in a single day nor by any single measure.*

He reduced the swollen army to 16,000 men: army officers responded by fresh attempts at rebellion. He amnestied his bitterest opponents, commuted into mere fines the confiscation of their estates. His inevitable reward for failing to undermine the economic base of counter-revolution was fresh conspiracy. He reestablished freedom for the conservative press; he was answered by a veritable torrent of abuse and unjustified criticism.

In 1871 he ran for reelection, calling upon the nation to let him complete the reconstruction. He was opposed by two men from his own camp: Sebastian Lerdo de Tejada,[1] civilian, radical liberal like himself, brother of the famous author of the Ley Lerdo which demortized the lands of the Church; and General Porfirio Díaz, hero of the War of the *Reforma* and the struggle against the French, and celebrated for having ended his campaign with a surplus of 87,000 pesos which he had turned over to the public treasury!

A close contest, in which as usual almost nobody voted, gave no one a clear majority; a Juarista Congress decided the election in the President's favor. Díaz greeted the decision with a new military pronouncement, the "Plan of Noria," but like the conservative revolts, it was easily put down by the regular army under Sostenes Rocha. The uprisings were tapering off, and Benito Juárez was beginning to overcome the obstacles to his long dreamed-of and so often postponed liberal reconstruction of Mexico. But now a new power intervened, against which the stubbornness and intrepidity of Juárez availed nothing. The new power was the hand of death. Juárez's enemies lowered their arms in tribute to the fallen hero. Porfirio Díaz came weeping to lay a wreath on the tomb of his leader whose closing days he had embittered. Unchallenged, Lerdo de Tejada assumed the presidency.

The new president attempted to continue the policies of Benito Juárez. He incorporated the Reform Laws directly into the Constitution, and generals Alatorre and Sostenes Rocha easily suppressed the Catholic revolt that followed. He inaugurated the first railroad, begun years ago under Juárez. He initiated the first steps for the division of the Indian village lands; awarded the first concessions to foreign capital. Dimly the outlines of "modern Mexico" were beginning to emerge. But in 1876 Lerdo proclaimed his own reelection and once more the defeated opponent Díaz raised the standard of revolt. A military pronouncement against a civilian in office, but with two unique features: (1) the "plan" did not propose a new constitution but accused the president of violating the old one; (2) it was directed against dictatorship and reelection, pledging itself to a war-weary people that it would guarantee genuine elections and thus be "the last revolution."

[1] Plate 225, the slightly twisted face to the left of the revolutionary newspapers. The man with the sword above him is Porfirio Díaz, and just below the sword-hand is the chief military support of Juárez's last years, General Sostenes Rocha.

In that respect at least, it turned out to be what its leader had promised, the last "old-style" revolt. It initiated a period of over a third of a century of peace, of unchallenged dictatorship, of slow and steady drift toward reaction, of prosperity (for the ruling class and foreign capital) and of rapid industrialization. It brought about Mexico's Augustan Age.

ESTABLISHING THE DICTATORSHIP

Don Porfirio began his long reign as uncrowned monarch of the Mexican Republic with great skill and caution. Having won power on the issue of "no reelection," he wisely abandoned the presidency at the end of his first term after engineering the election of his puppet, a disreputable, pleasure- and loot-loving rascal, General Manuel González. The bargain was a simple one: González was given a free hand to loot the treasury and the nation for four years, to enrich his friends, to accumulate a fortune, to build himself a pleasure-palace at Chapingo,[2] to fill the presidential mansion with his mistresses and boon companions, in short, to make himself so pleasantly, disreputably unpopular that he could not possibly continue himself in office and, at the end of his term, the "nation" would clamor for the return of the upright Porfirio Díaz.

The plan worked admirably. The Constitution was amended to permit Díaz's return, then to permit his reelection indefinitely. And he settled down in 1884 to more than a quarter of a century of consecutive office. In fact, his reign began with his successful revolt in 1876 and lasted over thirty-six years till old age and the gathering forces of an entirely new era put an end to his rule.

ELEMENTS OF PORFIRIAN POLICY

After every revolutionary struggle, history poses the problem of alternative programs of reconstruction: Bolshevik or Menshevik, Jacobin or Girondin. The War of the *Reforma* was a peculiar form of bourgeois revolution. It was a bourgeois revolution without a developed bourgeoisie, without powerful plebeian driving forces in the capital city, without Jacobins or *sans-culottes* to carry it to a successful conclusion. The program of Juárez was full of contradictory elements: against the Church lands and against the village common lands; against the feudal landlords

[2] Today the Agricultural School which houses the Rivera murals (Plates 162 to 187).

140

but creating out of the Church and village estates a new landowning class; against the French invaders but offering perilous concessions in exchange for Yankee help; against the forces of reaction but unable or unwilling to destroy their economic base. Díaz took up the program of Juárez, but he systematically developed its conservative and eliminated its radical implications. The bipolar bourgeois revolution, as has so often happened elsewhere, was "depolarized" by the exclusion of one of its poles, and thereby ceased to be revolutionary.

THE "HERO OF PEACE"

Díaz made no attempt to repeal the anti-clerical laws: he merely let them fall into disuse. The convents reopened. The public processions reappeared. The Church began to reacquire some of its former lands and add new ones. It reasserted its control over education. It violated every Reform Law in the Constitution. The "Hero of Peace" merely smiled beatifically, and looked the other way. The Church in turn blessed the "liberal" who had done what, through Santa Anna, Paredes and Bustamente, through Márquez and Miramón and Maximilian, it itself had been unable to accomplish. No more uprisings now, no more clerical intervention in politics, except to bless the perpetual self-succession in office of the Church's new idol.

He soon became the idol of the ruling class too, of its old families and newly rich ones alike. He established peace, the kind of peace for which Warsaw became famous under the Czars. The aroused peons crept back into their huts. The lords of the land, old and new, became absolute dictators in their own feudal domains. They absorbed the village lands, and the landless Indians became peons, tied by perpetual debt to the estates of their masters. While in the rest of the world agricultural prices were falling, in Mexico, backward, soil-impoverished, they rose. Despite its small agricultural yield, the price of an acre of land rose steadily, reached fabulous prices which put American corn and wheat land to shame, for its sale price was a reflex of the rich yield of unabated exploitation of its human appurtenances. A few powerful families acquired rights of life and death, even to the exercise of the "right of the first night," over the families of millions of disinherited villagers. The *hacendado* and his family went abroad, to New York, to Paris, to Madrid, to live on the income of unmitigated exploitation. Mexico City became a pleasure city, a "City of Palaces" that eclipsed even the plans of Maximilian. On the *haciendas,* some of them bigger in extent than many a small nation, the administrator occupied the feudal palace, a veritable fortress or military citadel, and ground out a steady stream of income. The workers received cloth, beans, corn, a hut of straw, alcohol, and "ghostly instruction." These were sold to him at fantastic prices, and a bottle of alcohol and a few yards of cloth were enough to start a debt which his children's children would inherit. Prices rose steadily, but wages continued to be the traditional ones of ten, twenty, fifty centavos a day, paid not in cash but in food, clothing, rent. One life was never enough to pay the debt accumulating from its economic outset, and one's children were born into a heritage of indebted slavery. Debt peonage was forbidden by the Constitution, but even in the United States where the Constitution is a fetish there arose the saying, "What's the Constitution between friends?" And the landowners were firm friends of Porfirio Díaz.

THE LAW OF "IDLE LANDS"

In 1875 under Lerdo and in 1883 under Díaz were passed laws for the measuring of "idle lands." Any one denouncing the existence of unclaimed land and surveying its limits was granted a third of its extension as premium. Special companies, mostly Spanish or American-owned, were formed to find and survey such lands. Woe unto the village or the peasant whose title rested only on the memory of man back to time immemorial! By the end of the century twenty-eight persons or companies had surveyed themselves 38,249, 375 hectares. (One hectare equals nearly two and one-half acres.) The California Land Co., Ltd., acquired 2,488,315 hectares; the *Compañia Mexicana de Terrenos y Colonización* 5,387,158 hectares, and so with the others. By the time Díaz fell, 178,742,000 acres had been given away and the revenue for the state amounted to a mere seven million pesos paid in its own bonds.

The *latifundio* had attained heights undreamed of in colonial and pre-*Reforma* days. Genuine land monarchs domestic and foreign had appeared. The entire state of Morelos, which was soon to produce Zapata and the Zapatistas, was the property of thirty-two landowners. In Chihuahua, where Pancho Villa was already in the hills, General Luis Terrazas owned an estate of six million hectares, as large as a Central American land. The "modest" estate of William Randolph Hearst, fiery

Mexican-eater, occupied over a half million hectares or 1,252,797 acres. In the State of Hidalgo the railroad travelled all day over 135 consecutive kilometers of land without ever leaving the estate of José Escandón. And the rest of the country was the same. Eight hundred-odd families occupied two-thirds of the land, and several million peons and their families did not own the few square feet on which stood their miserable huts, or a tiny patch on which to grow their own corn and beans. All the "best families" in Mexico still sigh for the "good old days of don Porfirio."

"PORFIRIAN PROSPERITY"

The foundations of Porfirian prosperity were laid by Juárez: the release of the Church wealth into the main stream of national economy, the first foreign concessions, the first railroad. With Díaz mechanical progress became a passion, an overpowering obsession. Civilization to him meant telephone and telegraph wires, railroad lines and textile factories, ports and tunnels and bridges and palaces, a balanced budget and the ability to borrow money abroad at a low rate of interest. In return for these accomplishments, and they were genuine accomplishments, he was willing to give fabulous concessions, hand away the nation's soil and subsoil and economic independence.

THE STORY OF PETROLEUM

His oil concessions are typical and fraught with fatal consequences. In colonial times, the wealth of the sub-soil had been an exclusive possession of the Crown: the right to exploit it was granted by temporary concession with payment of royalties. With Independence, the right passed into the hands of the nation. But in the reign of Díaz, in 1884, a law was passed which declared:

Exclusive property of the owner of the soil are . . . the salts which exist on the surface, the waters, superficial or subterranean, the petroleum and the gaseous, thermal or medicinal springs.

In 1887 petroleum concessionaires were exempt from taxes. In 1901 sweeping concessions were granted to drill for oil in remaining govern-

143

ment lands, without export tax, with the right to buy at nominal sums any land on which oil was discovered, and to prevent the opening of new wells by others within three kilometers in any direction of a well already opened. Within a few years, the whole oil-bearing sub-soil of Mexico lost its nationality.

MEXICO'S "GREATEST CITIZEN"

No president of Mexico has obtained such fame and praise in foreign parts as don Porfirio. Had he not brought peace, and law and order to turbulent Mexico? Had not his brilliant Minister of the Treasury José Ives Limantour [3] balanced the budget and accumulated a little surplus? Had not he brought "civilization" to the land, and wealth to its foreign "civilizers"? Had he not beautified Mexico City? brought the imperial splendor of courtly life to its "best" families? enabled their occasionally talented sons to study abroad and cultivate the arts and social graces at home? Had he not kept the peons in check? labor cheap and plentiful? property safe and profitable? Mexico a Mecca for foreign investors?

His dictatorship became a model for a whole school of Latin-American dictators. That it was "benevolent" became axiomatic; its despotism a triviality to be overlooked or a social or "racial" necessity to be justified by apologetics. When in 1910 he approached the eightieth year of his life and Mexico the one-hundredth of its struggle for independence, governments showered decorations and honors upon him from all over the world. His patriotic breast became inadequate, on days of state, for the display of all his decorations.[4]

A SCIENTIFIC DICTATORSHIP

His statesmanship was exemplary for the kind of government he had developed. He knew how to create loyalties by creating personal obligations. Desiring nothing but power himself (after thirty-five years of autocratic rule he left the presidency with only $750,000 in his possession), he complacently allowed others to enrich themselves under the aegis of his benevolence. He permitted the Church to grow richer than

[3] Plate 225, the man in the silk hat next to Porfirio Díaz. On Díaz's left is his wife doña Carmen Romero Rubio de Díaz, to her left, don Próspero, Archbishop of Mexico, and below him her father, Romero Rubio one of the most powerful and wealthy figures of the Díaz regime.
[4] He is shown in full regalia in plate 225.

144

ever, and ever more interested in the permanence of his rule. Powerful landowning families became more powerful thanks to him, and eager to sustain his power. The brains of the country he enlisted in enterprises that glorified him and enriched them: he made them cabinet ministers, diplomats, concessionaires. Positivism, Pragmatism and Progress saturated the intellectual atmosphere, rejecting romantic ideals, justifying the "practice that worked," singing paeans to the author of visible progress.

Descending from his august presence was a network of created interests that reached to the remotest corners of the Republic and to banking houses in distant metropoli. His friends were appointed as senators, deputies, governors and occupants of other official posts. And they appointed their friends, and their friends' friends. The personal nature of the structure was emphasized by its dependence on him; its feudal nature by the fact that every lower unit depended on the person immediately above it, each village group owing loyalty to its local *cacique*, each military unit to its immediate chieftain. At the top, immediately surrounding the dictator were his friends, the self-styled *Científicos*, the intellectual aristocracy of his regime. "Scientist" was, thanks to them, to become in the end a term of popular execration! Recognized chief of these scientific exploiters of the land was the Secretary of Hacienda, Limantour.[5]

And so everybody—at least everybody that was "anybody"—was satisfied. Only the impoverished masses were unhappy, and their unhappiness was inarticulate. The *cura* ruled their consciences; their landlords their lives. If they could not keep the peon in order, there were the *rurales* and the military levy. The independent press had long ago been silenced and destroyed. An outlawed editor who had tried to carry on in Texas was simply assassinated by Mexican police agents. When some young sailors mutinied at the very beginning of don Porfirio's reign he wired the Governor of Vera Cruz: *Aprehendidos in fraganti; mátalos en caliente.* ("Caught with the goods; kill them in hot blood.") Blood so "hot" that the Governor didn't even take time to find out which of his prisoners were innocent. Intellectuals that could not be

[5] Below Díaz and Limantour in plate 225 are a number of prominent figures of the Porfirian regime, Ignacio Mariscal, Carlos Pacheco, Guillermo Prieto, Gabino Barreda, and Justo Sierra. The last three (bottom row) were leading educators and men of letters.

bought, intimidated or ridiculed into silence were arrested and killed "while trying to escape" (the famous *ley fuga*), drowned in the "tanks" or subterranean dungeon cells of the Island fortress of San Juan de Ulúa which were submerged at high tide, or sent to the frightful penal jungle of Quintana Roo where cruelty and fever silenced them forever.

All vocal opposition disappeared. The dictatorship of the "Prince of Peace," like that rugged frame which had lasted as long as the Republic, seemed destined to last forever. But there was one enemy that even the scientific dictatorship could not suppress: that enemy was time.

Don Porfirio was eighty, two of his cabinet members past eighty, the youngest fifty-five. The Senate was "an asylum for gouty decrepits, and the House of Representatives . . . was composed of a host of veterans, relieved by a group of patriarchs." Of twenty state governors, two were past eighty, six past seventy and seventeen past sixty. One of the government-subservient newspapers called the bureaucracy the "Pyramids of Egypt, joined to the Pyramids of Teotihuacan." It was a dictatorship of old men. Young talents, educated abroad in lands of ballots and constitutions, students who found no career on graduation because "politics" was a senescent closed corporation and because foreign capital brought its own engineers and technicians—the young intellectuals were becoming impatient, politically restive, potentially revolutionary. His cabinet and immediate circle was cracking too. He had always encouraged antagonisms between them to weaken potential rivals, but now they began to count his years, and try a tentative crown upon their heads, and form rival cliques, and scheme against each other.

And foreign capital was doing some calculating too. How long would he last? Would his successor favor British or American investors? In 1901 he had angered American elements by giving Pearson and Son sweeping drilling rights for oil. It made Mr. Pearson baronet, baron, then Viscount Cowdray. But when in 1907 a million barrels of oil were brought in and in 1911 nearly twelve million, the ground became slippery under don Porfirio's feet. Certain American interests began casting around for a suitable successor. Some American newspapers discovered that he had been a "self-perpetuating and autocratic tyrant."

But time was working against the aged dictator in another sense. His concessions, his sale of the nation's wealth, his railroads built at fantastic construction rates, and generously treated mines and factories, were creating forces that were incompatible with his feudal dictatorship. Native industrialists, however weak, were developing interests and ideologies of their own. They needed a more mobile and more "educated" working class, a better paid one, of course at the expense of foreign capital, to form a domestic market for their goods. They required a protective tariff against foreign competition. Modern industry began the separation of the peon from the soil, was marshalling him into the cities, proletarianizing him, developing in him the rudiments of solidarity, and bewildering him with scraps of information about anarchism, socialism, syndicalism.

In 1906 the first strike broke out on a Yankee mining concession in the frontier town of Cananea. The administration received the strikers with bullets, and when they fought back, the mine boss, with the approval of the government, brought armed "reinforcements" from Texas till Díaz's *rurales* could come to finish the job of "restoring order." In 1907 the government killed scores of workers in the first textile strike at Río Blanco.[6] The dikes of the old order were beginning to crack, and behind them were accumulating the angry waters of a new revolutionary tide.

[6] The woman shown in the upper part of plate 225 is Lucrecia Toriz, one of the leaders of the strike at Río Blanco. She is still alive today.

XI. REVOLUTION OF 1910

In 1901 the opening convention of the Liberal Party formed to combat the growing power of the priesthood was electrified by the speech of a young intellectual, Ricardo Flores Magón, whose burning words indicted the Dictator himself for a series of crimes against the Mexican people. Preliminary lightning flash across a still cloudless sky.

The Liberal Party spread. Its meetings were raided, its leaders jailed and exiled, but its smuggled propaganda continued to appear. In 1906 it challenged the perpetual reelection of Díaz: its exiled leaders crossed the border and raised the standard of revolt. In 1908 they tried again. The sky was darkening, the lightning flashes becoming more vivid and continuous. Only the Dictator and his senile court, and the admiring civilized world that was quoting Mexican 4½% bonds at par, failed to hear the rumblings of the approaching storm. Then the aged ruler himself unleashed the torrents that were to overwhelm his regime.

THE CREELMAN INTERVIEW

The year 1908. Don Porfirio called in an American newspaperman, Creelman of Pearson's magazine, and through him told his astonished people he would not run again.

Mexico is now ready for a democratic government; I am resolved to leave the presidency at the end of my present term. . . . I would welcome the emergence of an honorable opposition party. . . .

A first-class earthquake would have caused less excitement. Mexico was used to earthquakes; it was not used to the voluntary abdication of dictators.

Limantour had been disqualified by virtue of the French nativity of his father. The *Científicos* groomed the unpopular Vice-President Corral for the presidential succession. His majesty's shadow-opposition thought itself referred to in the remarks about an "honorable opposition party" and rallied around General Bernard Reyes, Díaz's chief military man, opponent of the *Científicos* who for nearly a decade had been building up a military, a Masonic, and a student-club network of *Reyista* supporters. Then don Porfirio calmly announced that he could not resist the "demand of the Nation" that he run once more, and rejecting Reyes, picked the unpopular Corral as Vice-President and heir-apparent. Everybody expected General Reyes to revolt. Men of prominence began negotiations with him. Younger elements espoused his cause. Older ones began calculating the chances and estimating the appropriate moment to jump. And down below the surface continued to accumulate the gathering forces of social revolution.

The *Magonistas* of the Liberal Party were in jail or exile again, and the only other visible opposition figure was the somewhat laughable one of the rich landowner, Francisco I. Madero.[1] Of one of the wealthiest families of the North, most of his relatives were pillars of the regime. He himself was a mild-mannered idealist who had acquired some fame as a *loco* (in our political terminology a "crackpot") because of his spiritism, his theosophy, his homeopathy, his consultation of table-rappers and ouija-boards, and his generous experiment in philanthropy with the large peon population of his great estates. In 1908, at the time of the Creelman interview, he published a little tract entitled *The Presidential Succession in 1910*. It was an adulation of the Dictator, tempered with mild criticism and an insistence that the time was ripe for genuine suffrage and the democratic selection of a successor. The book was a sensation. It became a best-seller! And it gave birth to a new democratic, anti-reelectionist party. Then, in 1909, when the nation was buzzing with General Reyes's preparations for revolt, the latter suddenly surrendered to the Dictator and accepted a "diplomatic" exile. The *Reyistas*, left hanging in the air, foreswore politics. But their organized following was gathered in by the *loco* idealist Madero. A best-seller was making him presidential timber!

Don Porfirio was amused. He even had a friendly chat with his opponent. Madero's party had *Científicos* like Manuel Calero on its executive board, and disgruntled *Reyistas* like the Vázquez Gómez brothers. Don Porfirio had seen it all before: just one more legal shadow-opposition. But the President did not realize how far the maneuvers of the last few years had disintegrated the political superstructure of his rule. And he did not comprehend, any more than Madero, the subterranean social forces that were undermining its very founda-

[1] The bearded figure with the presidential band on his shirt front in plate 225.

tions. Nor did he reckon with the social power in a corrupt and decadent milieu that can be acquired by a fanatical devotion to an honest ideal, be the ideal ever so thin and shallow. The little figure of Madero soon assumed the gigantic proportions of an apostle.

The nation was crying for a change. Change of administration, thought the political opposition. Change of generation, said the student youth. Change of attitude towards labor, demanded the embryonic labor movement. A change in our whole miserable way of living, cried the peon, the Yaqui, the Maya. A change in the electoral machinery and its functioning, was the limit of the vision of the standard-bearer. But all the aspirations and longings for change continued to coalesce around his quixotic person.

The old Dictator laughed no longer. Madero's papers were raided, his presses smashed, his meetings broken up, his friends jailed, here and there assassinated. Then he himself was thrown into jail, but his influence continued to grow stronger. Of course Díaz was "reelected": his army, his governors, his bureaucracy, his courts and congress, determined who was to vote and how many and which votes were to be counted. It should have been all over, Madero not being a military man: but Madero proceeded to petition the incoming Congress to declare that it and the President had been elected by fraud, and to invalidate the elections. When that was rejected, having exhausted all "legal" means, he fled across the border, and raised the standard of revolt.

FRANCISCO I. MADERO: THE POLITICAL REVOLUTION

The revolt moved slowly at first, for it was not a defection of the military. The seasoned *Reyistas* like Vázquez Gómez and Carranza declared against it and abandoned Madero. But the revolution began to create its own armed detachments. It created its own leadership: made them out of shoe-store owners like Pascual Orozco, outlawed peons like Pancho Villa, peasants like Emiliano Zapata, young intellectuals like Pino Suárez. All but the most determined came over from the *Magonista* party. Then the *Reyistas* changed their mind and joined the growing rebellion, supplying experienced and reputable, if vacillating, leadership. Soon "neutrals" were joining. Then bandwagoners. Then second-line

150

Porfiristas. It began to acquire the land-slide character of a winning cause. Suddenly, Porfirio Díaz and Francisco I. Madero negotiated a peace-treaty, stopping the revolution before it had really gotten started on the job of plowing up the social foundations of the country. Díaz abdicated and sailed for Paris. But his Secretary of Foreign Relations, De la Barra, assumed the provisional presidency, and the Porfirian Congress and bureaucratic apparatus remained intact, pending the holding of elections. The narrow aims and limited social vision of Madero had become an unconscious brake upon the Revolution.

MISTAKES OF MADERO

At that moment Madero had virtually the whole people behind him. Backed by the victorious forces of an aroused peasantry, looked upon by all disinterested people as a great national hero, he might easily have begun the breaking up of the great estates, reduced the Church to its pre-Porfirian dimensions, stimulated labor and peasant organization, de-stroyed the economic and social base of the otherwise inevitable counter-revolution, and laid the foundations of the freest, most democratic economic and political structure in the pre-1917 world. But his vision did not extend to such horizons.

He made every mistake a revolutionary leader can make—except one: he did not become unfaithful to his own principles. However, those principles—democratic suffrage and non-reelection—were hopelessly in-adequate to the needs of a revolutionary transformation. They were not even realizable in Mexico without such a prior transformation. With the mentality of a large, albeit benevolent, landowner, he could not conceive of breaking up the great estates by revolutionary action. All his peon followers could get out of him was a promise to have the courts investigate and restore land unjustly taken under the Díaz law for surveying idle lands. At best, that would return the peasants to the abominable pre-Porfirian misery.

At the end of the first Revolution, said a soldier to John Reed, *that great man, Father Madero, invited his soldiers to the Capital. He gave us clothes, and food, and bull-fights. We returned to our homes and found the avaricious again in power.*

Madero soon alienated his peasant base and was left alone among the wolves of the Capital.

The ABC of revolutionary strategy is to smash the bureaucratic-military apparatus of the old regime. But Madero left the army intact. He left the civil bureaucracy intact. He alienated even moderate "public opinion" by accepting De la Barra and the Porfirian Congress as the provisional government, by keeping generals like Huerta in active service, by making *Científicos* like Calero members of his cabinet. He opposed the carrying out of the laws of the *Reforma*, continuing the Porfirian policy towards the clergy. He laid himself open to the charge of continuing the Díaz system of nepotism, by surrounding himself with members of his own family in office: Ernesto Madero, ex-*Científico* as Secretary of the Treasury; Rafael Hernández, a relative, in *Gobernación*; two Maderos were Deputies, Gustavo and Alfonso; and Raúl Madero was made Governor of Morelos. Then he set the stamp of bourgeois calculation upon the leadership of the Revolution by trying to recompense it for its financial sacrifices out of the public treasury. Revolutions throughout history have ever been a labor of voluntary sacrifice unrecompensed save by the sometime triumph of their cause and the inner satisfaction that comes from living up to the dictates of one's own intellect and feelings. When the Secretary of the Treasury gave Gustavo Madero 642,000 pesos, no doubt less than he had spent on the struggle, and Gustavo refused to give an accounting to the public, the President left himself open to the darkest suspicions and the vilest slanders. No doubt his motives were of the best, but a revolutionary leader must be fool-proof and demagogue-proof. The innovation of open monetary recompense for all the cash "invested" in the Revolution was little short of disastrous.

As the popularity of Madero waned, his opponents became bolder. From the left, Zapata refused to lay down his arms because the Revolution had not given land to the peasants. In his own camp the ex-*Reyistas* rebelled in the name of Vázquez Gómez and under the military leadership of Pascual Orozco. On the right General Reyes reappeared to head a revolt, and after him Felix Díaz, nephew of don Porfirio. Each of these revolts was suppressed, but their leaders, where captured, were merely imprisoned, and General Reyes and Felix Díaz continued to plot from prison in Mexico City.

Then, sixteen months after the inauguration of Madero, came the inevitable. A small section of the metropolitan garrison and the aristocratic military cadets revolted, liberated General Reyes and Felix Díaz from jail, attacked the National Palace, and failing to take it, seized an urban fortress, the *Ciudadela*. The revolt would have been easy to suppress, for the garrison of the National Palace had repulsed the attackers, killing General Reyes. But treachery, the old enemy of governments and, above all, of "apostles" in Mexico, had been rendered easy, even certain, by Madero's own political illiteracy as a revolutionist. General Huerta, Porfirian heritage, ambitious, unscrupulous, cruel, generally drunk, was permitted to become commander-in-chief of the loyal forces defending the person of the President and besieging the *Ciudadela!* [2]

GENERAL HUERTA: THE COUNTER-REVOLUTION

For ten tragic days a grim farce was enacted. General Victoriano Huerta directed a mock siege against the *Ciudadela*, sent loyal troops in close formation at a dog trot against withering machine gun fire, sprayed the surrounding neighborhoods with deliberately misdirected shells, allowed food and munitions to be smuggled to the beleaguered forces, and bargained with Felix Díaz for the rescue of his lost cause in return for the provisional presidency of the Republic. Huerta held these trump cards in his hands: the command of the loyal forces, the person of the President, the power to blow the citadel to pieces, and the support of a master intriguer, the leading spirit of the diplomatic corps, Henry Lane Wilson, Ambassador of the United States. In fact, the American embassy was the center of the whole intrigue and Wilson the chief go-between in the negotiation of the Díaz-Huerta agreement. Once consummated, Madero and Pino Suárez, his Vice-President, were arrested by their loyal defenders, forced to abdicate under a promise of safe-conduct out of the country, and then murdered in cold blood. The Apostle of Democracy was thereby transformed into the Martyr of the Revolution. And Huerta forced a cowardly and terrified Congress to accept the abdication and elevate him to the provisional presidency. The counter-revolution had triumphed.

[2] General Huerta is the figure with sword drawn, to the right of Porfirio Díaz, in plate 225; the general to his right and behind him is Mondragón, leader of the cadet uprising.

153

THE INTERVENTION OF HENRY LANE WILSON

The active share of Henry Lane Wilson in this bloody intrigue has puzzled many historians. His resignation was soon accepted by the American government, and Woodrow Wilson categorically repudiated his recognition of Huerta. The United States showed unrelenting hostility to the murderer of Madero throughout his regime, exercised an economic boycott against him, permitted munitions to reach his enemies, landed troops in Tampico in a mistaken notion that intervention would hasten his overthrow, and accorded recognition to his chief antagonist, Venustiano Carranza. What were the secret springs of the opposing actions of the two Wilsons, the Ambassador and the President?

American financial interests had watched with complacence the fall of Díaz. They had little to complain of except that in his closing years Limantour was veering to English interests as a modest offset to the Yankee preponderance which Díaz himself had created. Their chief grievance was the Pearson Oil concession and the Pearson-Government partnership in the construction of the Tehuantepec Railway. Madero was permitted to organize his revolution and his gun-running on American soil. He was given friendly support, although his inability to reestablish order was viewed with alarm and was the subject of many prejudicial and prejudiced reports by Ambassador Wilson to his Government. But English interests were outspoken against him, and anxiously cast about for a rival and successor who would reconfirm and restore their Díaz concessions.

Great Britain and France were indecently prompt in recognizing General Huerta. When American banks placed a boycott on him, the Bank of London gave his Government a loan. Woodrow Wilson publicly declared that he would never recognize a Government "which is stained by blood" and "not supported by the consent of the governed." Huerta soon added more blood stains by the assassination of Belisario Domínguez who had dared to criticize him in the Senate. When Congress voted to investigate the disappearance of the Senator, he dissolved it, and clapped 102 of its members into jail. "I am shocked at the lawless methods employed by General Huerta," declared Woodrow Wilson in a speech at Mobile; and the British Government chose that exact moment to have Sir Lionel Carden present his credentials to the Mexican President! The line-up was perfectly clear, except for the equivocal position of Henry Lane Wilson.

The tangled web of intrigue in which British and American interests played and plotted with the fate of the Mexican people will never be fully unravelled till the archives of oil and mining companies of both hemispheres, and the secret records of State Departments are opened to the light of day. But this particular mystery is in a fair way to being solved if we but bear in mind that Henry Lane Wilson was sent to Mexico by President Taft, and that Lord Cowdray, the British oil magnate of Pearson and Son had Henry W. Taft, brother of the President, and George W. Wickersham, Taft's Attorney General, as members of the Board of Directors of the company over which he presided! [3]

Beginning with Huerta, every candidate for the presidency for the ensuing decade was forced to choose between opposing internal class forces, and opposing groups of foreign capital. He had to favor either the landowners and the Catholic Church, or the peasants, workers and revolutionary petty bourgeoisie. And he had to seek support either from British or American capital. Huerta, despite Henry Lane Wilson's apparent Americanism, was supported by the interested elements of British capital, and by the clergy and landowners.

The Catholic hierarchy greeted his ascent to power with *Te Deums* in the great Cathedral of the Capital. Four days after the murder of Madero, *El País*, Catholic daily, reported "a solemn religious function to give thanks to the august Patroness for having conceded the salvation of the Republic." But the climax came when *El País* carried a cable from the Pope congratulating Huerta "for having restored peace" to Mexico! However, the congratulations were more than premature: Huerta was never to know a day of peace throughout his brief and troubled regime.

THE REVOLUTION CONTINUES

The real tragedy of the Mexican Revolution lay in its ideological and political unripeness. It possessed neither leaders, nor program, nor party, adequate to an hour of revolutionary decision. It was blind, elemental, anonymous, full of heroism and readiness for sacrifice, but devoid

[3] The upper background of plate 225, showing oil sheds, tanks and wells, is Rivera's reference to the foreign forces intervening in the succession of revolts from 1910 to the present.

155

of understanding of its own forces and needs. It possessed no Lenin or Marat, no Bolshevik Party or Jacobin clubs. Its driving force was an outraged peasantry, with no leadership, theory, program or party of its own, no classwide or nationwide consciousness, only local grievances, local enemies, local and sporadic organs of struggle, and a narrow village horizon of understanding. Peasant revolutionary movements have invariably had necessity of alliance with and leadership from some urban revolutionary class. But the proletariat in Mexico was not yet out of its swaddling clothes; the petty bourgeoisie, anemic, unreliable, self-seeking, fearful of the peasantry and lacking confidence in itself; the great bourgeoisie almost non-existent except in the shape of foreign capital and its hangers-on. The lack of class consolidation, clear grasp of the situation, definite program and sound organization, left the revolutionary movement (or rather, the Revolution in motion) a prey to confusion, opportunism, careerism and betrayal. It fell victim, first to vague idealism, inspiring but impotent, then to unscrupulous demagogy and unprincipled thirst for power. Figure after figure was temporarily invested with revolutionary greatness by forces which each beneficiary understood only well enough to utilize them as means to a brief and factitious career of power and glory. Then the waves of the Revolution closed over him again, tossing up another swimmer on their crest. *Claudicación*—betrayal of revolutionary promises made on the way up—became the counter-pole of *Revolución*. Betrayal was elevated into a system, the invariable rule for figure after figure and government after government as each was elevated to the summits of power. But the revolutionary energy, the *élan*, the reckless courage and determination of the masses to achieve their vague aims, seemed to be inexhaustible.

Madero's incompetence and social conservatism cheated them of their hopes: they gathered around Zapata, Pascual Orozco and others in efforts to overthrow him and carry the revolution farther. But Orozco betrayed, and Madero, having alienated the revolutionists, was vanquished by the Reaction. Thus the apostle was redeemed by his martyrdom and acquired in the popular imagination all the virtues opposed to the vices of those who had overthrown him. He became a banner which could rally the masses around anyone who promised to avenge his death and continue the Revolution. Out of the confusion of men and movements finally emerged the figure of Venustiano Carranza. For want of adequate leaders the revolution was inventing them.

VENUSTIANO CARRANZA: THE "CONSTITUTIONAL REVOLUTION"

Carranza, like Madero, was a great landowner. He had formed part of the Porfirian regime, as Senator, as Governor of Coahuila, as a leader in the *Reyista* legal opposition. Stranded by the shameful surrender of Reyes, he went reluctantly into the Madero camp. There is reason to believe that he was himself plotting a revolt against Madero when the news reached him of Huerta's *coup d'état*. He immediately declared himself in rebellion against Huerta, and by virtue of his dignity, his years in office and his possession of an already prepared governmental and military machine, he was soon able to assume the title of "First Chief of the Constitutionalist Army Charged with Executive Power." No authorized body gave it to him, and he was to have to fight for it later with a dozen contenders, but it gave him a head start.

Stubborn, pedantic, narrow-visioned, fond of flattery, eager for power, temperamentally conservative, mistrustful of the Villas, Urbinas, and Zapatas with whom he had to deal, Carranza had no social program beyond the empty formula of a "return" to the Constitution which had never been carried out. The agrarian movement he mistrusted and in his heart opposed. The labor movement, which supplied "Red Battalions" for his forces, he trusted even less, and when he felt strong enough he outlawed the unions and shut their headquarters. But without peasants and workers and radical gestures, no army, no victories, no ascent to power was possible. So, frigidly, with ill grace and misgiving, he permitted radical theoreticians, civilian politicians, accomplished demagogues and guerrilla peasant leaders to gather behind his solemn political vacuity and speak in his name. He became a very fiction of the movement that was lifting him to power.[4]

The military men who organized his victories (he won none himself), he mistrusted too; their names might easily dim his feeble luster. Therefore he spent much of his time hamstringing Villa till he turned against him. As for Obregón, brilliant organizer of Carranza's military

[4] Carranza is the figure with white beard and moustaches to the right of the arch in plate 225. In his hand is a reference to the Constitution of 1917.

157

victories, he was less impulsive than Villa and no less stubborn and ambitious than Carranza. He contented himself with redoing what the "First Chief" undid, building up his own prestige within the Constitutionalist machine, organizing his own future while developing the forces which were to elevate Carranza into the presidency. He was young, and till recently, unknown, and could bide his time. Thus the "Constitutionalists" schemed and fought and intrigued and mistrusted each other and played with radical phrases and programs until the anomalous situation reached its climax in the Constitution of 1917.

THE CONSTITUTION OF 1917

The new Constitution was a modification of that of 1857 by the incorporation of a more advanced social program. Its agrarian section, Article 27, cancelled the oil concessions which had handed away the natural wealth of the land, reasserted the doctrine of national ownership of the subsoil resources, and made mandatory the distribution of some portion of the great estates to landless villages—with compensation for the landowners unless theft were proved. The labor section, Article 123, provided for a minimum wage, right of workers and employers to organize, double time for overtime, social insurance, profit sharing. It voiced a categorical recognition of private property, but, on paper at least, it was the most advanced constitution in the world till the Russian Revolution in November of the same year in which it was promulgated. Carranza was proud to be the "Father" of a Constitution, just as the great Juárez had been; but he shuddered at the nature of his offspring.

Yet he dared not throw doubt on its paternity. Zapata and his followers had been battling since 1911, first against Díaz, then against Madero, then Huerta, and now against him. The armed peasantry that had long ago swamped the old professional army were expectant, exigent. Revolutionary phrases were so many cards to be played in a game for which the high stakes were a more or less brief enjoyment of power. The reactionary Huerta, when he felt himself slipping rapidly in the closing months of 1914, had sought to save himself with a radical agrarian law. The clever Cabrera, most brilliant civilian in Carranza's camp, had retaliated by promulgating the "Law of the Sixth of January," 1915, in Carranza's name. Slowly, inevitably, as the struggles continued, resting always on the armed people, the blind elemental aspirations of the masses

158

were forcing their imprint upon the originally programless Revolution, and to some pitifully small extent even upon its practice.

EMILIANO ZAPATA: THE AGRARIAN REVOLUTION

Emiliano Zapata became a folk hero even before he was dead. He is the protagonist of more popular ballads than any other figure in the Revolution—and, with the exception of Villa, than all of them put together. He was the greatest figure that the agrarian revolution produced.[5]

Among the people, he was soon a legend. Among the well-to-do he was a legend too. How the good house-owners and merchants and men of wealth and maiden-ladies of well-aged chastity trembled when his "bandit hordes" advanced on Mexico City, driving out even the forces of the great chieftain, General Obregón! Now surely the scourge of God was upon them and the end of the world was nigh! But the humble, gentle-voiced soldiers of the army of the apocalyptic terror came to their doorways, huge *sombreros* held in their hands, and with phrases of quaint formal politeness asked for a *taco* or a drink of water! Were these the terrible hordes of Attila that the Metropolitan press had been maligning for years with such hair-raising stories of violated nuns, outraged virgins, quartered babies, frenzied loot and destruction? Not one of the successive armies of occupation had taken as little.

They were not after women other than the army of *soldaderas* who followed their detachments, satisfied their desires, nursed their *chamacos* and cooked their food. They were not after jewels, nor bonds, nor family heirlooms, nor after gold except for the military requisitions by which all factions financed their campaigns. They wanted land. And when they got to Mexico City, they did not know how to ask for it, hat in hand, nor how to exact it, rifle at shoulder. Puzzled and bewildered, lost on the stage of national politics, they withdrew to their native state of Morelos. Twice more they occupied the Capital, but they did not know how to get the one thing they were after, nor did they care to take anything else.

They wanted land; they wanted it with all the single-mindedness of purpose arising from their needs, embodied in their "Plan" and incarnated in their leader. That was it: *single-mindedness of purpose*. That

[5] Zapata is shown in plates 204, 205, 208, 222, 225, 226 and elsewhere in Rivera's paintings.

159

was the distinguishing feature that made Zapata the greatest driving force, the best revolutionist, the most important figure the Revolution of 1910 produced. All the aspirants for power published manifestoes called "Plans": he alone had a plan in the social sense of the term. Madero's Plan of San Luís had been a mere negation: to overthrow Díaz, to abolish reelections and manipulated suffrage, to undo a few of Díaz's worst injustices. Carranza's "Plan of Guadalupe" aimed to overthrow Huerta, to restore the Constitution, and primarily, though not stated, to raise Venustiano Carranza, Governor of Cuahuila, to the presidency of the nation.

But Emiliano Zapata's plan, the "Plan of Ayala," provided for the direct revolutionary seizure of all the robbed estates, for the slicing off of one-third of each great *hacienda* to endow every village with land, and for the confiscation without indemnity of the entire estate of every landowner who fought against the Revolution. Let the peasants take the estates first, said the Plan, and then if the landowner thinks he has been unjustly treated, let him prove it without use of his present enormous preponderance of power, in courts to be instituted by the Revolution. There were weaknesses in the Plan of Ayala, but it was the only significant social program the struggle produced. It forced fragments of itself on Huerta, on Carranza's "Law of the Sixth of January," on the Constitution of 1917: ever greater fragments, though no program or government has yet caught up with it.

The Plan of Ayala was drafted on November 28th, by Emiliano Zapata and his school-teacher lieutenant Otilio Montaño,[6] and never thereafter abandoned by its propounders. It was altered from time to time, but only to incorporate new experience with men and events, to be made still clearer and more definite. Its preamble was the portion that suffered the greatest alteration: first it was a denunciation of Díaz for despoiling the people of their lands; then a denunciation of Madero for failing to carry out the program for which they had taken up arms; then a denunciation of the murderous and reactionary Huerta; then of Carranza. The changing preamble reflected the unchanging course of the single-minded and untiring fighter.

No betrayal could disillusion Emiliano Zapata, no fine words deceive

[6] Montaño is shown next to Zapata, holding in his hand the Plan of Ayala, in plate 225. He and Zapata were models for the buried bodies, plate 178.

160

him, no bribe buy him off, no "decisive" battle put him out of the struggle. He was often defeated, but for him there were no decisive battles short of final victory. No one could dislodge him and his band from the precipitous slopes of the uptilted state of Morelos. Each new government in turn proclaimed: "The Revolution has triumphed. Let us have peace." But always he returned the hopeful, stubborn answer: "Let us have land. Then there will be peace and we will know that the Revolution has triumphed."

It was a strange army, these *Zapatistas*. It increased and diminished with the planting and the harvest. It shrank with defeats and swelled with victories, almost disappeared with each promise-fed illusion, and re-formed mightier than ever with each disillusion of fulfillment. When federal troops surrounded one of its peasant-clad detachments, it simply disappeared, buried its rifles and blended into the surrounding peasantry as it tilled the soil. The danger past, the *Zapatistas* dug up their rifles, counted their cartridges and reassembled.

There was at all times a heavy price on Emiliano Zapata's head, but not one of his followers could be bought to betray him. At last he died, a "ballad-hero's" death, by ambush and treachery. It was not a *Zapatista* but the guile of the *Carrancistas* and his own devotion to the revolution that betrayed him. Nine years Zapata had been in the field. Carranza troops under Pablo González had invaded his native Morelos and were trying to "restore order," capture him dead or alive, return the land to the *hacendados*. A quarrel was staged between Colonel Guajardo and his superior, General González, where it could be overheard by a Zapatista prisoner. Then Guajardo let himself be persuaded to go over to the Zapatistas and the cause of land for the peons. Zapata, like all peasants, was *desconfiado:* he mistrusted army officers and the slick politicians who came from the Capital of the country. So Guajardo arranged proof: he attacked and took the town of Jonacatapec! Its defenders had been provided with blank cartridges, and it is even said that Guajardo lent realism to the game by executing some of his prisoners! Now Zapata was convinced and marched with a staff of thirty men to meet Guajardo in a trap surrounded by 600 soldiers. He was riddled with machine-gun bullets while advancing into the Judas embrace of Colonel Guajardo. The Carranza government, "emanated from the Revolution," author of the Constitution of 1917, rewarded Pablo González and Guajardo with

161

prizes of fifty thousand pesos each, and promoted the assassin to a general-ship! The press applauded almost universally, and the radical Carrancistas under Obregón continued to form the "left" pillar of his government!

Zapata dead, his forces were soon demoralized without their leader. Montaño, rural school teacher, intellectual adviser of Zapata and co-author of the Plan of Ayala, had been killed earlier. Other intellectuals were being taken into the Obregón camp via the newly formed *Agrarista* Party. Zapata was dead, but *Zapatismo*, the ghost of the man, his spirit incorporated in the Plan of Ayala and enshrined in the hearts of the peasants—that would not down. It had forced every opponent to adopt some sort of agrarian program, to embody some portion of the Plan of Ayala in its decrees and promises. And it was to force each subsequent government, that of Obregón, of Calles, of Cárdenas, to comply in some measure with its dictates. Woe unto the president of Mexico who would frankly disavow it: even today the spirit of Emiliano Zapata is powerful enough to "disrecognize" him and overthrow him.

RICARDO FLORES MAGÓN: THE PROLETARIAN REVOLUTION

Ricardo Flores Magón was the leading figure of the proletarian forces in the Revolution of 1910 as Zapata was of the peasant forces. Of middle-class family, his revolutionary career dated from his student days. In 1892, at the age of twenty, he first saw from the inside the "humiliating walls" of a Porfirian jail. In 1901 he, his brother Enrique, Díaz Soto y Gama, subsequently a *Zapatista*, Librado Rivera, Juan Sarabia, and other young democratic anti-clericals formed the Liberal Party, a radical party of middle-class intellectuals, which under Ricardo's leadership became more and more anti-Díaz and more and more peasant and proletarian in program and class outlook. The subsequent history of Magón is a tale of raids, arrests, flights, exile, uprisings and jail sentences, mostly jail sentences. It is safe to say that he spent more time in jail, both in Mexico and the United States, than all the other leaders of the Revolution put together.

After spending most of the years 1901, 1902, and 1903 in Mexican jails, he fled into exile and from El Paso, Texas, continued the publica-tion of his paper, *Regeneración*. It was so effective that Díaz sent police agents to El Paso to assassinate him. A timely contribution from one

Francisco I. Madero, rich landowner stirred by his paper and not yet dreaming of a party of his own, enabled the little band of exiles to leave for St. Louis, at a safer distance from the border. There in 1905 they published the program from which all future movements in Mexico were to draw something of their inspiration: non-reelection of Díaz; enforcement of the anti-clerical provisions of the Constitution; an eight-hour day and minimum wage law; abolition of debt peonage; seizure of idle lands by the State and their distribution to those in need of land and ready to work them. There in brief were the germs of the anti-reelectionism of Madero, the land program of Zapata, the constitutionalism of Carranza, Articles 27 and 123 of the Constitution of 1917, and the agrarian and labor legislation of all subsequent governments from Obregón to Cárdenas. They do not yet go beyond the frame-work of the bourgeois-democratic revolution, but they reveal Ricardo Flores Magón as the real theoretical father of the 1910 Revolution.

In 1906 and 1908 the *Magonistas* crossed the frontier, and each time held out for several months in armed revolts against Porfirio Díaz. Thus they were precursors in the field of insurrection as well. But from then on the American government took a hand. It was quite complacent with the program and gun-running of Madero, permitted Villa and Carranza to receive munitions, gave open support to Obregón and his successors, but it was not minded to tolerate a revolutionary movement on its borders which based itelf on the workers and peasants. All the *Magonistas* but Ricardo were jailed in El Paso. He escaped to Los Angeles, where the Mexican Ambassador tried to buy him off, Mexican police agents attempted to kidnap him with the knowledge of the authorities, and when he and his defenders successfully resisted, he was jailed by the American government.

In jail he completed his evolution in the direction of the view that the proletariat was the basic revolutionary class of our epoch. He became a "Libertarian Communist," that is to say an Anarcho-Communist. This was a reflex of the backwardness of the immature Mexican working class, of its Spanish heritage, of the influence of the American I.W.W. which was then capturing the imagination of the Mexican workers, and of the moth-eaten opportunism and conservatism of the American Federation of Labor and the American Socialist Party. His letters from prison contain trenchant criticism of those two organizations as well as of the

Yankee spirit, which seemed to his ardent temperament to be "incapable of enthusiasm and indignation."

In 1910, coming out of jail after a second term of two years, Magón directed another revolutionary effort which, despite him, was absorbed by the all-engulfing movement of Madero. Thereupon he began a critical analysis of the shallow political aims and lack of social vision of Madero, which criticism, like Zapata's preamble to the Plan of Ayala, was to be directed in turn against each of Madero's successors. The following year saw *Magonistas*, American "Wobblies" (I.W.W. members) and filibustering adventurers unite in a raid into Lower California. For a time they were victorious, but Anarchism, with its abstract formalistic dogma of decentralization, played into the hands of American filibuster separatism and as the danger of another Texas case became manifest, the movement was discredited. The adventure ended in failure and the arrest of Ricardo Flores Magón and Dick Ferris, "President of the Socialist Republic of Lower California," for violation of the neutrality laws of the United States. From a California jail Magón issued a new program for taking the land, the machines, the means of transportation and the houses, by direct action of the workers and peasants in arms. The program earned him yet another indictment and a sentence of two years on MacNeil Island for him, his brother, Librado Rivera and Anselmo Figueroa. Out in 1914, he was back in jail by 1916 for a proclamation calling on the Carranza soldiers to turn their guns on their officers and use their arms to realize the revoluntiary aspirations of the masses from whence they had sprung. The same year saw General (later "Comrade") Plutarco Elías Calles smash a mine strike at Cananea by armed force and order the execution of its *magonista* leader, Gutiérrez de Lara, by a firing squad.[7]

Scarcely out of jail once more, Ricardo Flores Magón and Librado Rivera were indicted again under the "espionage" act for publishing an internationalist manifesto while America was at war. This time Magón was given twenty-one years, Rivera fifteen. In March of 1918 the walls of the jail closed upon him, never to open again except to carry out his dead body. He was still a young man, yet the years behind prison bars

[7] In the upper center of plate 225 are portrayed Ricardo Flores Magón (soft hat and glasses), his brother Enrique, next to him, wearing a derby. Below Ricardo are Librado Rivera, Juan Sarabia, and Anselmo Figueroa.

had broken his health if not his indomitable spirit. His sight was failing, his heart going back on him, but the revolutionary flame burned clear and steady as ever within him. In December, 1920, the *Obregonista* Mexican Congress voted him and Rivera a life pension in acknowledgment of their services to the Revolution, but Magón responded for the two of them that "money torn from the people by you would burn our hands."

In 1922, the war long over, he petitioned in vain for temporary release to consult a heart specialist; the Government refused his request. His last letter, charged with presentiment of death, reviewed the revolts of 1906 and 1908 as the "first flutterings of the eye-lids of an awakening giant," deplored the divisions in the ranks of the young labor movement in Mexico and urged a united front of *Crom*, Anarchist, Syndicalist and Communist movements for their common aims.

If my sufferings and my chains serve to accomplish the unification of the proletarian organization, he wrote, *I bless my sufferings and I love my chains.*

On November 21st, 1922, the American Government delivered him to Mexico, a corpse. There is a monument to Obregón in Mexico; Carranza, whom Obregón overthrew has received official recognition, Madero has innumerable memorial streets and buildings named in his honor. Even Zapata, who fought all these with an ample part of Magón's program, has been tardily admitted to the revolutionary family. But Ricardo Flores Magón is not part of the official martyrology. Thirty years after his first revolt, no government monument, no anniversary ceremonies commemorate his life and death and leadership in the cause of freedom. Is it because of his anarchism? (Mexican governments were never afraid of "isms.") Or is it because of his emphasis on the independent action of the masses and independent role of the proletariat, and because his life ebbed away in the jails of the "Good Neighbor" across the Rio Grande? When the revolutionism of Carranza, Obregón and Calles have been reduced to the stature of occasional good wishes, exploded myths and gestures of convenience, when Madero is seen in his true light as a courageous apostle of doctrinaire electoral democracy incapable of comprehending the social forces that lifted him for a few months to the crest of a revolutionary wave, Ricardo Flores Magón and Emiliano Zapata, men who fought all the other "heroes of the Revolution" in turn, will come to be recognized as its real makers and leaders and the living source of inspiration for the worker and peasant movements of Mexico.

PANCHO VILLA: THE INSTINCTIVE REVOLUTION

Neither the greatest, nor the most consistent, nor the most revolutionary, nor ever quite strong enough to reach for the presidency, Pancho Villa is nevertheless the most typical figure of the Revolution of 1910. He is the symbol of all its confusion and social backwardness, its recklessness and cruelty, its dash and heroism. Like Zapata, he captured the folk imagination and while yet alive became a ballad hero, and like Zapata he died a ballad hero's death in ambush. He is a figure comparable to England's Robin Hood and Russia's Stenka Razin.

Son of poor and ignorant peons, Doroteo Arango (for so he was christened) murdered some local despot, and at the age of sixteen fled to the hills, an outlaw. There he assumed the name of a famous bandit of tradition, gathered other brave and desperate characters around him, and became Pancho Villa, the scourge of the landowners, the hero of the poor, the living realization of their dreams of freedom and vengeance upon their oppressors.[8]

When the Governor of Chihuahua and the President of Mexico put a price upon his head, he enlarged the circle of his enemies to include them and all their police and armies. When he heard that Madero was fighting his enemy, the President, he gladly made a pact of alliance with him. His little band swelled into an army of many thousands of men, and without ever ceasing to be *mi jefe*, he also became *mi general*. But when Madero consolidated his power, Pancho Villa found yet another *jefe* above him commanding the army of the North, the former Porfirian officer, General Huerta. He was not used to executing the commands of others; before long, General Huerta ordered him shot for insubordination. It was Madero who saved his life by imprisoning him in Mexico City, and, before a year was out, by letting him escape to the United States. Thereby Madero, the incomprehensible Apostle of Democracy, won his undying, almost doglike devotion. While in jail, slowly and painfully he

[8] Pancho Villa is the genial figure in the big sombrero near the right curve of the arch in plate 225, midway between Montaño and Carranza.

166

learned to read, to spell out and half comprehend some of the big, hard words that propagandists were subsequently to spread in his name.

When Huerta assassinated Madero, Villa was swift to cross the border into his native state and take up arms against "the traitor." His gallant leadership crushed the federal army and insured the victory of the Constitutionalist cause in the North. Pancho had never read the Constitution. But he hated big landowners, overseers, the clergy, *gachupines* (only later was he to add *gringos* to the list) and his enemies, and above all that *viejo cabrón traidor*, Victoriano Huerta.

No one who offended him was too insignificant to escape his wrath, none too great to feel his defiance. When Carranza and Obregón angered him, he added them to the list. When the United States gave aid to Carranza, he took on the United States as well. Such was his noble progress from fighting a local despot to fighting governors and presidents and entire countries. It is doubtful if he would have stopped short of defying the entire world.

Out of bandit tactics and genuine innate talents of a high order, Pancho Villa developed a technique admirable for guerrilla warfare: the night attack, the wild cavalry charge, the swoop down from the hills, the mastery of the swift, the sudden and the unexpected. Leaving their *soldaderas* and *chamacos* behind as encumbrances, his *Dorados* (Golden Lads) would appear out of the darkness in wild night cavalry charges, whooping at the top of their lungs and spitting flames into unguarded camps many leagues from the place where they were supposed to be resting. Pancho Villa acquired fame as invincible. With the aid of a master of strategy, General Felipe Angeles, Villa became the greatest military man in Mexico—until Álvaro Obregón, general improvised too by the years of struggle, raised the Revolution's fighting tactics to a new level, based on lines of communication, continuous supply of ammunition, carefully chosen terrains for giving battle, retreats for strategical purposes, mobility of supplies and reserves. Then Pancho Villa was hopelessly outclassed, and his disappearance from the stage of history was inevitable.

For Francisco Villa, despite his acquisition in the course of the years of an entourage of military experts, politicians and intellectuals, never rose above the levels of instinct in military affairs, in social questions, or in politics. Throughout his life he had not the slightest conception of the bigness of the world, or the complexity of its social organization. He

167

listened with bewildered intensity and fitful humor to the intellectual camp-followers that gathered around his victorious person, issued naive and absurd decrees on money and trade and exchange, and tried in vain to terrorize invisible laws and forces into compliance with the aid of the firing squad, but all the while he continued to be the same shrewd, arbitrary, impulsive, instinct-guided peon who at sixteen defied a local despot, took to the hills and assumed the name of a semi-legendary bandit hero.

As bandit he had done well by himself, taken what he pleased: money, horses, rifles, provisions, women. As revolutionary general, he continued to do the same: everything, even the women, on a more magnificent scale. As bandit he had spared the poor as a matter of common sense and out of sympathy; he had been occasionally generous to poorfolk who crossed his path, and became an heroic legend because he incarnated the inchoate dreams of freedom and vengeance of those who could not escape their oppressive lot. His life as a revolutionary leader merely extended the size and import of the legend. Therefore, so long as he was victorious, his power of attracting adherents among the peons was limitless. The revolutionary "theory" he incarnates finds its best summary in one of the songs they sang:

> *No quiero más que tener*
> *lo que me quitó el patrón:*
> *un rancho y una mujer,*
> *un coyote cimarrón,*
> *una mesa en que comer*
> *y una tierra en que poner*
> *un grano y una canción,*
> *comadre, y a ser feliz*
> *con tu amor y mis chamacos,*
> *unos besos, y unos tacos,*
> *y unas cargas de maíz.*

> I only want to have
> what the boss took from me:
> a ranch and a woman
> and a wild *coyote*,
> a table on which to eat

and some land in which to put
a seed and a song,
and, *comadre*, to be happy
with your love and my kids,
some kisses and some *tacos*,
and some loads of corn.[9]

The masses rallied around Pancho Villa because those were their wrongs and the modest limits of their desires, as they were in essence the wrongs and desires that had made him bandit and revolutionary leader. But a revolution which does not go beyond such theoretical understanding, program and leadership, is bound though victorious, to end in self-defeat or betrayal. Several times Pancho Villa took the capital, but he was beyond his depths there. As organization outgeneralled him on the field of battle, so it outgeneralled him on the field of politics, social legislation and diplomacy. The same genius which Obregón was beginning to show in organizing the military forces of the Revolution, he was also applying to the organization of its labor and peasant forces, and was subsequently to employ in the field of government. Then the Villas were to become an anachronism altogether.

There was nothing left to do but to make his peace with forces that had gotten beyond his comprehension, and bide his time, perhaps, for a more favorable situation. He accepted an offer of land for him and his Golden Lads at Canutillo, some few thousand pesos in cash to buy supplies and seeds, the retention of rifles, and, no doubt, of buried treasure. Then, when Pancho Villa the bandit and general had become Francisco Villa the peaceful citizen and cultivator of the soil, he was shot down like a dog from treacherous ambush lest in the approaching De la Huerta rebellion against Obregón, he and his men might take up arms again. The Villas and Zapatas and Flores Magóns were no more. The day of the romantic revolution was over: the day of the "Organized Revolution" had begun.

[9] *Coyote* here means dog; *comadre* addressed to the loved one has about the same flavor as under similar circumstances would be conveyed by the use of the word "sister"; *tacos* are the universal sandwiches consisting of a tortilla wrapped around anything edible.

XII. MEXICO TODAY

National and foreign opinion looks for the Obregón coup as an inevitable outcome in the evolution of the present anarchistic situation in Mexico. This can be predicted with almost mathematical precision from the precedents of Mexican history.

So wrote Francisco Bulnes at the beginning of 1916. At that moment General Obregón was busy organizing Carranza's government for him: developing the beginnings of a modern army; defeating Villa and Zapata; building up a government-controlled and government-subsidized peasant movement; penetrating into the incoherent anarcho-syndicalist labor movement with the aid of a painter of dubious principles, one Dr. Atl; preparing for the great constitutional convention to be held the following year at Querétaro; negotiating for recognition, loans and munitions from the United States; winning and organizing support everywhere for the "First Chief," Carranza, through the channel of support for the First Chief's right-hand man, General and War-Minister Álvaro Obregón.

Bulnes's prediction from the precedents of Mexican history was a sound one, but General Obregón was in no hurry with his coup. He was young; he was careful and thorough; he had no intention of displacing the venerable figure in whose name he was working; but he was determined to succeed Carranza at the end of the latter's term. When the First Chief alienated the peasants by his too obvious impatience with the agrarian program that Obregón and his "radicals" had put into the new constitution; when he outlawed the labor movement which, under Dr. Atl, had organized "Red Battalions" on Carranza's behalf; when he angered the United States by platonic flirtations with Germany; when he alienated all who surrounded him except little men and unconditional flatterers—General Obregón tactfully repaired part of the damage, suggested patience, and let the hopes of the resentful and the discontented center around his own person.

When Carranza, near the end of his term, prepared to ditch his heir apparent in favor of a more tractable and less independent figure through whom the First Chief might continue to rule, General Obregón easily turned his electoral campaign into the "Revindicating Revolution." It began in Obregón's home state, Sonora, under the lead of two *Sonorenses*, Adolfo De la Huerta, the governor of the state, and its former governor, Plutarco Elías Calles, Carranza's Minister of Industry, Commerce and Labor. The "Plan" of the revolution, that of Agua Prieta, was as vague and conservative as any in Mexico's history: protection for all citizens and foreigners; development of industry and commerce; the resignation of Carranza in favor of De la Huerta as provisional president; elections under the latter's supervision; "effective suffrage, no reelection." Obregón had done his preliminary work so well that he had no need of radical phrases: his concern was to win the more conservative elements and especially American support.

Within a month after the outbreak of hostilities Carranza was in flight for Vera Cruz. On the way, he was assassinated by an officer wishing to curry favor with the new regime. That was on May 18th, 1920, and from that day till the moment of this writing, nearly two decades later, there were to be no more successful revolutions. Rebellions there were aplenty, but on a constantly diminishing scale. Álvaro Obregón, most civilian of military men and most military of civilians, most conservative of radicals and most radical-sounding conservative, a military genius, a born leader of men, a statesman of the first rank and a consummate organizer, was to work out a pattern for relative stability in this world of flux and change and to become master of the contradictory devices required to keep afloat on the stormy sea of Mexican political life. His successors, Calles and Cárdenas and the intervening puppet appointees of Calles, had only to follow the pattern he laid out. They developed and perfected and refined it, but it is the Obregón system of statecraft that rules Mexico today.

THE OBREGÓN PATTERN

For internal support, every candidate for the Mexican presidency since 1910 has had to choose between popular peasant-worker support, and that of the landowners and their ideological apparatus, the Catholic clergy. The peasants are the most numerous class in Mexico, but large sections of them still follow the leadership of the landowners and the Church. The working class elements are so immature and lacking in independent organization and consciousness that they do not form an important separate force. Thus the two camps, the popular and the land-owner-clerical, are nearly equal in balance and strength. What the land-owners lack in numbers they make up with their economic power, which enables them to put large numbers of armed and mounted men in the field. This deadlock of class forces makes the government military-bureaucratic apparatus relatively independent of class control and capable of developing and fostering vested interests of its own. The opposing pulls of the radical peasants and workers on the one hand, and the backward landowner-church peasant combination on the other, are so nearly equal that the government is always in unstable equilibrium and easily upset by some shift of support or the pressure of some outside force. Such an outside force, pressing constantly upon it, is that of foreign capital.

Here too the presidential aspirant has been obliged to choose between European (principally British) and American capital. Díaz favored the latter, but in his closing years sought relative independence by increasingly calling in European interests. Madero received support in the United States, and, upon reaching power, cancelled some of the Díaz English concessions. Huerta based himself on the Church and the land-owners for internal support, and upon the backing of British interests. This, as we have seen, explains Wilson's unconcealed hostility to his government.

The World War prepared the basis for a more stable regime by ending the mutual counter-pulls of British and American interests. There was a definite growth in the influence of the United States in Mexico and a definite recession of the power of England. At this juncture Obregón struck out boldly on the basis of what seemed to him the strongest combination of forces: the peasant-worker bloc as the internal, and American capital as the external support of his regime. A circus performer riding bareback on two horses at once has an easy time in comparison; for Obregón's two high-spirited horses were not trained to run together!

He would have to make solid concessions to American capital without alienating the nationalist-minded, anti-imperialist masses; make concessions to the masses without alienating suspicious, conservative American capital. He would have to contrive to blow hot and cold, if not in a single breath, at least in successive ones. Only a man of audacious vision would have attempted it: only a major statesman could have gotten away with it.

Obregón soon discovered a rough mathematical formula for his pattern: the masses could generally be kept contented with a maximum of radical phrases and gestures and a minimum of actual deeds; on the other hand the hard-boiled financiers were not too exigent as to phraseology but fearfully exacting as to actions.

How to convince American interests made jittery by Russian Bolshevism that his revolutionary phrases should not be taken too literally, that he must have free play for demagogy if he was to remain in power at all? How to convince the masses that his government was really revolutionary; that if it tried to go farther or faster there would be American intervention? How to measure out the crumblike concessions that would keep the regime from getting unpopular, and yet surround each tiny crumb with a shining ruby mist of socialistic phraseology so that few would perceive how little was the crumb after all? How to keep the partially awakened masses, stirred by a decade of civil strife, under sure and subtle control? These were no minor problems of statecraft. They were brilliantly and consciously solved by Obregón, and his methods of solution were consciously adopted and extended by the two succeeding bosses of Mexico, Calles and Cárdenas. They are working better than ever today.

Therein lies the explanation of the constant tacking and veering of the Mexican ship of state: therein the missing background to reconcile the apparently contradictory policies and principles that have left observers so bewildered and helpless to make up their minds as to the nature of the Mexican regime. This explains why on one day Obregón nullifies the oil sections of Article Twenty-Seven of the Constitution, granting every demand to the American oil companies, and the next day makes one of the most radical pronouncements as to governmental theory ever heard outside of the Soviet Union; why with one hand (figuratively of course, for he lost his left arm in a battle against Villa at Celaya) he gives land in homeopathic doses to the peasants, and with the other gives away the land as a whole to oil and mining companies; why one decree deports the papal delegate as a "pernicious foreigner" and the next expels a foreign-born leader of the Mexican Communist Party on a similar charge; why the government assures the victory of

173

a strike in which neither American interests nor those of the native governing group are involved, and smashes the next strike which happens to be directed against American interests; why the very administration which institutes "Socialist" education can also devise secret plans for military cooperation with its imperialist overlord, the United States, in the next war.

THE HOUSE OF MORGAN STEPS IN

The Obregón revolt occurred in April, 1920; yet the leading article in the May number of *The Americas*, published by the National City Bank of New York, declared:

Now that events in Mexico are moving towards final settlement, there is every reason to believe that the plans repeatedly made and postponed may be put into execution, and trade relations established between the business men of this country and the merchants of Mexico that will be permanent and profitable to both groups. . . . In spite of troubles that may come during the next few months and outward appearances that make it appear that Mexico is merely keeping up its favorite pastime of revolution and civil war, there is sound reason for believing that constructive influences are at work and that a happier and more prosperous epoch is nearly at hand.

The National City Bank is not given to empty optimistic prediction in such matters. . . .

Yet there were a number of minor obstacles in the way of the new course and Obregón spent much of his four years removing them. Chief of these were the pressure of accumulated and more than justified anti-United States sentiment in Mexico on the one hand, and the pinheadedness of the American state department and diplomatic apparatus on the other. Ambassadors like Lane Wilson and Fletcher and Sheffield and pedantic and unrealistic Secretaries of State like Hughes and Kellogg were frightened into epileptic fits by the radical phrases so lightly uttered and more lightly taken in Mexican political circles. Hughes would not hear of face-saving and radical phrase-saving in Mexico. He wanted Obregón openly to sign away Mexico's sovereignty and publicly to abjure radicalism as a condition of recognition; whereas the latter was proffering a tacit engagement to nullify the land and oil provisions of the Constitu-

174

tion simultaneously with or immediately after recognition. More than that, he was offering an administration that could deliver what it promised, thanks to the retention of popular support.

At last the American bankers, disgusted with the needless delay and pedantic quarrels about abstract formulae, simply thrust the diplomatic messenger and office boys aside and Thomas W. Lamont, Morgan partner, stepped into the situation in person. The effect was magical.

THE REAL ISSUES

Obregón and Lamont were men who could understand each other. So, at a later stage in the same development, were Calles and Morrow. The Bankers' Committee which Lamont represented knew exactly what it was after and had the good sense to know that they must leave the Mexican government in a position to deliver it without being overthrown by popular indignation. They wanted Mexico to settle the claims of American enterprises damaged during the years of revolution. They wanted the railways returned to private control on the basis of a guaranteed dividend yield. They wanted the existing government to recognize the loans made by Díaz, even those contracted after revolution had broken out against him. They wanted recognition of the loans made to Huerta. They wanted all loans consolidated, funded, guaranteed by some sure source of government income, and provisions made for the resumption of interest payments. They wanted the cancellation of the oil provisions of Article Twenty-Seven of the Constitution.

But Lamont could see in an instant what phrase-frightened diplomats living in a rarefied atmosphere of abstractions and phrase-fetishism of their own making seemed incapable of seeing in a decade: that it was useless to get a government of Mexico to yield openly and publicly on this issue, since any government frankly proposing to abolish Articles Twenty-Seven and One Hundred and Twenty-Three of the Constitution would not last long enough to make the first deliveries of the promised goods. The same hard-boiled economic realism that permitted financiers to back Mussolini in Italy, radical phrases and all, and subsequently Hitler in Germany, was applied by the clear-headed Lamont and his successor Morrow to Mexico. But Morrow's follow-up has been overpublicized and Lamont's pathfinding role scarcely noticed by American commentators.

The Bankers' Committee was formed in 1919, while Obregón was preparing his *coup d'état*, while Ambassador Fletcher was compiling an inflammatory list of 217 Americans killed between 1911 and 1919, while Albert B. Fall, oil senator and chairman of a Senate sub-committee on Foreign Affairs was still recommending the use of military force to compel Mexico to change her Constitution or publicly exempt American interests from its operation.

In the late summer of 1921 Thomas W. Lamont, Chairman of the Bankers' Committee, went in person to Mexico on a trip "combining business and pleasure." (They have a tendency to overlap in a man like Lamont and in a land like Mexico.) There was a pleasant exchange of courtesies with President Obregón and his Secretary of the Treasury, Adolfo de la Huerta. Within a month thereafter, Mexico had assumed the Díaz and Huerta debts; had agreed to the installation of a new "American-model" banking system; had entered into a debt-funding, annual-payment-with-increasing-annuities arrangement similar to the Dawes-Young Plan; to the putting of the railroads on a paying basis by government subsidy, purchase of new rolling stock, slashing of wages and smashing of the railway unions; to the return of the railroads to private control under the management of a bondholders' committee headed by J. P. Morgan and Company; and to the settling of the oil dispute with a committee of oil executives.

The attitude of the present Mexican government, said Lamont in a public statement on leaving the Mexican capital, *is satisfactory to American interests, indicating an intention to protect and encourage American interests in Mexico.*

THE OIL CONFLICT

A few days later directors of the Standard and various other oil companies went to Mexico. Less flexible than Lamont about certain details and handling a much more delicate subject, they nevertheless found a satisfactory formula: the "non-retroactivity of Article Twenty-Seven."

Virtually all of Mexico's petroleum wealth had been given away by Díaz prior to 1910. The revolution, in its anti-imperialist aspect, had been fought to cancel these concessions. Hence Article Twenty-Seven reads:

176

All contracts and concessions made by former governments from and after the year 1876 which shall have resulted in the monopoly of lands, waters and natural resources of the Nation . . . are declared subject to revision. . . .

The intent was clear. The demands of the oil men modest. All they asked for was the "non-retroactivity" of Article Twenty-Seven, that concessions made prior to 1917 *should not be subject to revision!* A few days after the agreement was arrived at, the Mexican Supreme Court declared that Article Twenty-Seven could not be applied to rights acquired prior to May 1, 1917.

There was some further squabbling by hold-out oil men and the still uncomfortable State Department. But on August 31st, 1923, the Government of the United States and the Government of Mexico exchanged mutual declarations of recognition on the terms originally arranged by Lamont and Obregón. Thereby the anti-imperialist or nationalist revolution was liquidated and American interests became more completely dominant than they had ever been under Díaz.

Endowed by nature with the richest subsoil for its area of any country in the world, Mexico's chief rival is the ex-Mexican portion of the United States. Now the oil and mineral companies of the northern land dominated both sides of the line. Mexico's oil, minerals, railroads, banking, an indebtedness several times the size of Mexico's highest annual budget to date, and ninety percent of her import-export trade passed into the hands of United States capital: all the rest was a mere shadow and all subsequent assertions of sovereignty mere shadow-boxing. Mexico's fate was sealed as a semi-colonial land so long as the Obregón pattern should endure.

The agreement came none too soon. Less than a month after recognition was accorded, Secretary of the Treasury Adolfo de la Huerta handed in his resignation to the President. His purpose was to head an armed rebellion to block Obregón's plan to name Calles as his successor. De la Huerta himself aspired to the post. Behind him was a majority of the Chamber of Deputies, the dominant *Cooperatista* [1] Party, a number of state governors and most of the leading generals in the army. For a while

[1] The Cooperation Party: party names from now on become more and more radical. Calles was "elected" by the *Agrarista* and *Laborista* Parties, Cárdenas by the National Revolutionary Party which has absorbed the others.

Obregón's plight looked desperate. But the Government of the United States acted with amazing energy to sustain the administration with which it had just made an agreement. It rushed to Obregón arms, ammunition, airplanes. He had no funds, so it opened a $10,000,000 credit to pay its own munitions-makers. Such action is unprecedented in the history of Mexican-American relations.

At the same time, the workers and peasants of Mexico rallied to Obregón's support in great numbers, more than offsetting the military defections. Between them, American capital and the Mexican masses turned the tide. The Obregón pattern was working. Both pillars were holding firm. The epoch of successful revolutions was over: the epoch of unsuccessful rebellions had set in.

THE SECOND PILLAR: POPULAR SUPPORT

American governmental support was secured by direct negotiation with the House of Morgan, first with Lamont, then with Morrow. Popular support was secured by direct control of the masses. For this purpose government-instituted and subsidized labor and peasant movements were set up, captained by carefully selected agents of the administration. These agents disposed of funds, patronage, and occasional support in struggles with rivals, or with opponents of the government, or with economic interests which the government did not wish to protect.

Carranza's labor agent was Gerardo Murillo, the artist whose *nom de plume* or rather *de pinceau* is Dr. Atl. The little bearded second-rate painter suddenly appeared in the labor movement in 1915 armed with vast quantities of Carranza's own printing-press pesos, given him by Obregón to relieve the distress of the workers during the stormy war-torn days of a year of political chaos and economic prostration. Thereby Dr. Atl acquired sufficient influence to organize the famous "Red Battalions" for Carranza. Obregón further gave the nascent labor movement a palatial headquarters: the *Casa de Azulejos*, formerly the Jockey Club and today the continentally famous restaurant, Sanborn's. But when Carranza had consolidated his power he outlawed the labor movement, prohibited and smashed its strikes, jailed its leaders and dispossessed it from its elegant home. Thereby Dr. Atl was discredited and went back to painting volcanoes. He was lost from the surface of political life until he bobbed up again last year as an agent of the German embassy in Mexico

178

and a paid propagandist for fascism and anti-semitism. But Obregón, even while working through Dr. Atl in 1915, was already grooming a much more important labor lieutenant for his purposes.

LUIS N. MORONES

Luis N. Morones is the *caudillo* in the labor movement. The type is as old as Mexico, but the field of operations is a new one requiring new formulae and new methods. Gross, fleshy, thick-lipped, heavy-jowled, soft and pudgy-handed, redolent of perfume, fond of silk underwear and diamonds, he looks more like the newspaper cartoon conception of a capitalist than he does like a labor leader. His sybaritic softness of exterior gives no inkling of the ruthless hardness and lust for power that enabled him to bestride the confused, chaotic, mistrustful and immature labor movement of the twenties and bend it to his will.[2]

Obregón first met his future labor lieutenant during an electrical strike in 1915. The meeting took place in the course of one of General Obregón's intermittent occupations of Mexico City before Carranza's power was definitely consolidated. The general settled the strike by "seizing" the properties of the British-owned telegraph and telephone company and "giving" them to the strikers to run under the management of a company foreman. The foreman was Morones. Like so many of the Mexican government's melodramatic "seizures" of plants and properties, the arrangement was only temporary. But the association between Morones and Obregón there initiated was a prolonged one. With the disappearance of the diminutive Dr. Atl from the labor scene, Morones, the ex-electrical worker, became the main transmission gear from the government to the organized workers.

In 1918 the *Obregonista* Governor of Coahuila, Gustavo Espinosa Mireles, issued a call to the various local labor movements, unions and workers' propaganda groups, to unite in a single nation-wide labor movement. The call is typical and revealing:

The Government of the State of Coahuila, watchful not to remain behind in the evolutionary march of time . . . desires that the worker himself

[2] Morones is portrayed plate 226 (the fleshy face with straw hat over the eyes, just behind Obregón) and symbolically in plate 246 (the pig beating the cymbals behind a figure representing Calles).

meeting fraternally and freely should study and determine the points on which his well-being can be based . . . thinks that the opportune moment has come to invite all workers of the Republic to realize their unification and provide a solution of their needs. . . .

This was accompanied by an offer to pay all expenses of the transportation, lodging, lost wages and other needs of the delegates, and provide free meeting halls and other expenses attendant on the holding of a national convention. Out of this government-fostered and government-financed meeting was born the *Confederación Regional Obrera Mexicana* (*Crom*), with Luis N. Morones as its inevitable leader. The next year a similar conception and gestation process gave birth to the *Partido Laborista Mexicana* (Mexican Labor Party), again with Morones as its leader. True, not all labor elements accepted the new government gift horse; but state subsidies, government favors, and their obverse—government repression—soon made the *Crom* and the *Partido Laborista* dominant, and they continued so till 1935.

The next year, 1920, both movements supported Obregón against Carranza's handpicked candidate for the presidency, and backed the Sonora group (Obregón, De la Huerta, Calles) in their subsequent uprising. Morones was rewarded by appointment as the director of the government munitions factory (a strange revolutionary labor leader that can be put in charge of munitions!); his fellow laborite, General Celestino Gasca was made Governor of the Federal District with all the patronage involved, and a number of other labor leaders were given fat government jobs.

Armed with government funds and political patronage, Morones gathered around him a little group of labor leaders of his own selection. He even included capable opponents and critics when they proved amenable to softening by the persuasive methods the administration had put into his hands. This little band of chieftains, never elected by any labor body, was known as the *Grupo Acción*. Limited at its height to twenty-five men of whom less than half were important, it nevertheless controlled an ever widening circle of active agents in the labor movement, including the *Casa del Obrero Mundial* (House of the World Worker), also a non-representative body, the *Crom*, the *Partido Laborista*, the principal unions and state federations of labor.

A much less publicized organism than the *Grupo Acción* was the mysterious *Palanca*—the "lever" or "crowbar"—Morones's specially selected strong-arm squad. A Mexican *caudillo* cannot maintain power merely by bribery of his enemies: he inevitably makes more of them than he can buy, and among them will always arise unpurchasable competitors who can be satisfied by nothing short of his displacement. Nor could Morones always count upon the government to put his enemies out of the way: sometimes they were even fostered by opponents in the cabinet or by the administration as a whole to prevent its agent from becoming too powerful. Hence the *Palanca*.

If one is active in Mexican political life he must expect to shoot and be shot at. Morones was shot at more than once, even wounded on occasion; but he was too good an organizer to do his own shooting. It got done just the same, as men like Senator Field Jurado could testify were it not for the proverbial reticence of the dead.

Those opponents of Morones who were opponents on principle of the entire system of government-controlled unionism, the government itself took care of. Those who were not amenable to purchase, were handled by two other characteristic methods of "persuasion." "For foreigners," a high government official once told the writer, "we have the thirty-three; for natives the thirty-thirty."

The "thirty-three" in question refers to Article Thirty-Three of the Constitution of 1917 which permits the president "to expel from the republic forthwith, and without judicial process, any foreigner whose presence he may deem inexpedient." Under it Obregón and Calles deported dozens of Argentinians, Cubans, Spaniards, Americans and workers from various European countries: Communists, Anarchists, Syndicalists, and even the bombastic poet Santos Chocano, of no particular ideology whatsoever.[3]

[3] It is hard to believe that the well-informed Ernest Gruening did not know this when he wrote:

Whereas in the United States a foreign labor agitator is deported for activities deemed against "our form of government," in Mexico it is the foreign capital agitator, the superintendent who violates constitutional provisions and refuses to comply with the labor laws, who may have Article Thirty-Three applied to him—a policy both nationalistic and popular. (Mexico and Its Heritage, p. 358.)

Vastly more use has been made of Article Thirty-Three against foreign-born labor leaders, including the Spanish-speaking Latin-Americans and natives of Spain, than against foreign-born capitalists or their superintendents.

As to the instrument reserved for the native-born, the "thirty-thirty," it refers to the calibre of the rifle used in all Mexican revolutionary campaigns; the best, the most incorruptible and clear-eyed of the native leaders of the Mexican workers and peasants have been eliminated and their mouths have been stilled by its action. As victims of the Obregón and Calles regimes I cite at random: Mauro Tobón, tireless and selfless Communist textile worker and leader in the industrial center of Orizaba; Gutiérrez de Lara,[4] follower of Flores Magón and organizer of a copper mine strike against American interests at Cananea; José Guadalupe Rodríguez[5] and Primo Tapia,[6] two of the bravest and best beloved of Communist peasant leaders. These are the greatest of the victims of these "*laborista*" regimes, but the list could be extended to cover many pages and include local leaders in every village and industrial center of the country.

PEASANT ORGANIZATION

The same procedure as was used to "organize" and harness the labor movement was applied more slowly and delicately to the peasantry. Once Zapata had been eliminated by the Carranza government aided by the "thirty-thirty," Obregón skillfully gathered around him intellectuals who had served with Zapata and agrarian elements who had opposed him, and out of them built up the leadership of the *Partido Nacional Agrarista*. Then the governors of Vera Cruz and Tamaulipas, Tejeda and Portes Gil, called into being statewide peasant organizations and attempted to extend their scope into a national peasants' league. But Communist influence was stronger here and the jealousy of other state governors more of an obstacle. Only after much maneuvering and many assassinations did Portes Gil finally develop a national peasant organization safely under governmental subsidy, leadership and control.

The distribution of land in small parcels was a potent means of winning control and support among the peasantry. The government worked through innumerable village leaders or *caciques*, local politicians whose recommendations on land distribution gave them prestige and power.

[4] Portrayed by Rivera on the National Palace Wall, Plate 225, the figure with rifle, to the left of Villa.

[5] Plate 226, figure with rifle just above the word "Libertad."

[6] Plate 226, next figure to the right and slightly below that of Guadalupe Rodríguez.

Where the landowners were strong and bitter in their opposition to the government, it permitted the peasants to bear arms for their own and its defense. Where the peasants were strong and militant, the government disarmed them by force and garrisoned the region with troops under notoriously reactionary generals. In such places assassination of *agraristas* and military raids on whole villages were common. Such assassinations by landowners and military are still common today.

In Vera Cruz the peasants were radical, well organized, conscious of their goal, and under Communist leadership. The land they sought to seize was rich and fertile. To Vera Cruz, therefore, President Obregón sent one of his most reactionary military men, General Guadalupe Sánchez, with twenty thousand troops, and instructions to disarm the *agraristas*. General Sánchez was the first to raise the standard of revolt against Obregón in the De la Huerta rebellion! Statesmanship as the President was working it out was a game of delicate calculation, and in Vera Cruz he came perilously near to overreaching himself.

In Yucatán he did overreach himself. Here too the peasants were well organized in *Ligas de Resistencia* under the leadership of Felipe Carrillo Puerto. The Yucatán peasants were peons; they were united by Mayan blood and tradition, by the ruthless exploitation of the great henequen producers, by uniform labor on a large scale with a single universal cash crop, henequen or sisal. Under Governor Salvador Alvarado, ex-apothecary with vague socialistic leanings, Felipe Carrillo Puerto had been encouraged to form the *Ligas de Resistencia*. Then Carrillo had come into contact with foreign socialists and communists, had been stirred by the Russian Revolution (as had Zapata who shortly before his death declared his belief in the soviet system as the salvation of Mexico), and had helped form the Communist Party of Mexico.

Theoretical confusion is a fertile mother of opportunism: Obregón had little trouble weaning the politically illiterate Felipe Carrillo away from the Communist movement by a promise of the governorship and a free hand in his native state of Yucatán in return for support against Carranza. Then, to curb Carrillo, he sent another of his most reactionary generals, Ricárdez Broca, to Yucatán with instructions to disarm and curb the *Ligas*. He too joined the De la Huerta rebellion, and having performed well and thoroughly his task of disarming the peasantry, was able to capture and execute their leader, Felipe Carrillo.

183

With his death, chargeable directly to the subtleties of Obregón's states-manship, the great peasant movement of Yucatán fell to pieces and to this day has not fully recovered.[7]

THE DE LA HUERTA REBELLION

The De la Huerta rebellion represented an extremely close shave for General Obregón. The revolting generals already mentioned were joined by such military men of established reputation as Generals Estrada, Diéguez, Figueroa, and Salvador Alvarado, the one-time "so-cialistic" governor of Yucatán. They took with them about half of the army, most of the military equipment, and the main fortified *plazas* of the country. Then General Maycotte came rushing in to the capital from Oaxaca, embraced President Obregón, protested his loyalty, and went out to meet the "enemy" with most of the funds, munitions and garrison of Mexico City. No sooner outside the city than he "pro-nounced" for the rebellion!

General Obregón's situation now seemed hopeless. Band-wagon jumpers began to jump forthwith. Those too closely identified with the regime to switch, prepared to go into hiring or flee the country. General Calles, whose succession to the presidency was at issue, took a military train to the North, intending to escape to the United States.[8]

But General Obregón recruited the metropolitan police, union mem-bers, peasant bodies, added loyal troops, received fresh munitions and supplies from the United States, agreed to accept the conditional sup-

[7] Plate 222. Felipe Carrillo Puerto is the central figure (in the soft hat) between Emiliano Zapata and José Guadalupe Rodríguez, just above the banner bearing the words *Tierra y Libertad* at the top of the picture. Next to the three agrarian martyr leaders stands a worker in overalls. He is pointing the way for the Mexican peasants, over the heads of Obregón and Calles, to the figure of Karl Marx on the left wall. It is interesting to note that Rivera painted this at the top of the central arch of the stairway of the National Palace at a time when Calles occupied the palace as President of Mexico. Echoing the line of the worker's hand is that of Morelos, the leader with the most advanced social program in the struggle for independence, and the pointing sword of the leader of the first great Indian revolt.

[8] The story of the projected flight of General Calles has never been made public before. The writer is in a position to know the facts since he was invited to make one of the specially selected list of passengers. He was told that Maycotte had just switched (the news was not yet public), that Obregón was through, that this would be the last train to make the border, and that De la Huerta would be in the capital within a few days and all *Laborista* and Communist and union leaders would face a firing squad. Besides Calles the train contained Morones, Gasca, Haberman and other *Laboristas*.

port offered by Communist-led peasants and furnish arms for such contingents while permitting them to operate independently under their own command, seized all busses and taxis in the Capital to form a motorized army, and struck with incredible swiftness, skill and vigor at the Vera Cruz rebel line. While his "omnibus cavalry" attacked from in front, the Vera Cruz peasants demoralized the rebellious regiments by an unexpected attack on their rear and by cutting their line of communications. The first decisive battle was brilliantly won. As for General Calles, he let on to have gone North to raise troops, and returned to support Obregón and accept the presidency from his victorious hand.

ACHIEVEMENTS OF THE OBREGÓN REGIME

This victory completed the relative stabilization of the Mexican political structure. During his four years in office Obregón had made a settlement satisfactory to the United States on oil, debts and railways, had won recognition, balanced the budget, restored a sound currency and banking system, and enriched a number of his friends who were laying the foundations for the development of a new native bourgeoisie. At the same time he had appointed a Minister of Education, José Vasconcelos, with a well-nigh fetishistic belief in schools and literacy, and appropriated more for schools than for the army, something unprecedented in the turbulent history of Mexico. (The press, short of memory, has erroneously reported that the Cárdenas education budget comes nearest to equalling the military appropriation of any regime since 1910. During two years, Obregón's education budget actually exceeded that of the army.)

Gingerly he had begun the reduction of the number of generals and the size of the army. He was enormously aided in this by the De la Huerta rebellion: the number of generals in active service was rapidly reduced by the firing squad and by flights to foreign parts. But, despite his cautious disarmament of the more militant peasantry, he left his successor with the problem of their having been rearmed on a bigger scale than ever, to cope with the uprising of the very generals he had sent to curb them.

He had further developed a stable and docile labor movement under government control, and made important strides in the same direction

185

with the peasantry. The direct seizures of land had been largely checked; the agrarian laws had been whittled down to distribution by slow-moving government action of small and inadequate tracts to strategically selected groups of peasants, with provision for compensation of the landowners in the shape of government bonds, acceptable in payment of taxes. Obregón was handing over to the next president a going concern and a pattern of statesmanship clearly defined and initially successful. All that Calles had to do was to continue the use of its methods and develop it further in the direction in which the country was already moving. And in any emergency he could still count upon the guidance and support of Mexico's greatest military man and most skillful statesman, the inventor of the devices of stability.

A "LABOR" GOVERNMENT

Politically Calles had proclaimed himself a *Laborista*, and with his accession to the presidency the fortunes of Morones and his little group reached their zenith. By 1927 they possessed one cabinet member (Morones himself in the ministry of Industry, Commerce and Labor), eleven senators, forty deputies, two governors, innumerable state legislators and political appointees, and the governor of the Federal District, rich in patronage since it included Mexico City.

As Secretary of Industry, Commerce and Labor, the head of the *Crom* fulminated against the "wastefulness of strikes," urged the "collaboration of labor and capital to foment national economy," broke a number of strikes, principally those of non-*Crom* unions or those directed against American interests, declared the railway shopmen's strike of 1927 illegal after a Mexican court had pronounced it legal, renewed the promises to the oil companies of the "non-retroactivity of Article Twenty-Seven," and publicly proclaimed to Mexican labor: "It is time to declare a truce in the class war." On the First of May, 1927, the Minister's International Labor Day speech to his demonstrating cohorts culminated with a description of President and "Comrade" Calles as "the greatest continuer which the world has known of the work of the men who died in Haymarket, Chicago, forty-one years ago."

While all this was going on, incapable and self-blinded observers of both Catholic and liberal and socialist tendencies were working themselves and their readers into fevers over the "Socialism" of Mexico. The

Catholic commentators found it an unmixed evil; the liberals and so-cialists an unadulterated good. Actually the working class was gaining very little, and "socialism" was but a phrase to be played with. A certain positive residue or sediment of all the turgid demagogy is of course inevitable, but even today in 1937 the Federal District with its large bureaucratic and middle class population consumes more meat than all the rest of the country put together, a staggering index to the poverty and malnutrition of the great mass of the Mexican people. The minimum wage laws required by the constitution, are still being "regulated and investigated" and the writer has personally entered rural areas where not one laborer receives even the legal minimum. In much of the country the traditional wage of less than fifty centavos a day (fourteen cents in our money) still prevails. Even in the capital, the workers receive the legal minimum, which there ranges from one and one-half to two pesos (forty-two to fifty-six cents), only in those industries where their organized force is sufficient to enforce it. Among the greatest positive gains, however, should be noted the fact that in those industrial areas and occupations in which labor is strong, they do pretty generally get three months' notice or three months' wages as required by law, if fired unjustifiably. What this does in the way of inspiring confidence and self-respect in workers, the American laborer can only begin to imagine.

If the gains of the working class were small and slow, those of the self-appointed labor leaders were rapid and considerable. Brother Mo-rones by this time had become the owner of several commercial enter-prises, including a hotel and a textile factory, a number of realty de-velopments, and a mansion or group of mansions in the suburb of Tlalpam, fitted out with the luxury of a millionaire's country club, with tennis court, *frontón* court, bowling alleys, swimming pool, and a retinue of servants, all to entertain Morones's actress and labor-leader friends. Minister Morones's public ostentation of his diamonds became at last a public scandal (political opponents with access to the press saw to that), such a scandal that a publication of the *Crom* was forced to "ex-plain" them in an article called, *Los Brillantes de Morones*, where they were justified as a "reserve fund" for the labor movement! Since then the *Crom* has passed through some dark hours, and Morones is in exile today, but it is not on record that he has disposed of any of his proper-ties, and if he makes a somewhat less ostentatious display of his diamonds today it is because such display is less safe in the United States than in Mexico.

MORROW IN MEXICO

In 1927 Dwight W. Morrow resigned his Morgan partnership (but not of course his properties, interests and personal connections) and went to Mexico as Ambassador, to conclude what Lamont, as "private citizen," had so ably begun. Mexican securities on the New York Exchange experienced a rapid boom upon the announcement of his appointment. The United States had travelled far from its populist and trust-busting days, when a Morgan partner could go as Ambassador to Mexico, a Guggenheim in the same capacity to Cuba, and Andrew W. Mellon assume direct charge of the American Treasury. And Mexico had travelled even farther, for it could receive a Morgan partner as "viceroy" without a hostile popular demonstration. To make sure of popular feeling, however, Mr. Morrow hit upon the clever stunt of the "goodwill flight" of his future son-in-law, Charles A. Lindbergh.

Morrow extended a warm and friendly hand to the "Socialist" President of Mexico, and used the time-honored and efficacious method, learned in his years in the House of Morgan, of putting his new-found friend on the preferred list for a number of fine investments. Calles was an apt pupil and issued forth from the brief period of association a millionaire, in fact, the richest man in Mexico! Morrow put his financial experience and wisdom at the disposal of the President and his intimate associates. He helped them to form a number of companies, in some of which Morrow is reported to have been a silent partner, which trustified most of the still unorganized industries of Mexico. The Calles group of companies has grown steadily since, so that today one cannot take a lump of sugar or a Mexican-made cracker, buy a new tire, have a road paved, build a cement or concrete house, strike a paper match, use a corrugated box or a section of plate glass in Mexico, without paying tribute to the Calles group who form the substantial nucleus of a rapidly growing native capitalist class.

The group includes the banker Rodríguez, whom he subsequently made President of Mexico, Aarón Saenz and Alberto Pani who formed parts of both the Obregón and Calles cabinets, De la Chica, manager of the big and flourishing Monterrey steel enterprises, Pascual Ortiz Rubio,

188

also a Calles-made President,[9] and a number of others. Through inter-locking directorates they control something like a score of enterprises. So far they have no conflict with foreign interests because they have made no serious attempt to invade the fields of oil and minerals, but monopolize the construction industries (steel, concrete, cement, rubber, glass, building construction and road-making) and have branched out into various consumption industries such as milk, crackers, *garbanzos* (chick-peas) and realty and resort and hotel developments. When in 1935 Cárdenas, the fourth Calles-made President, broke with the *Jefe Máximo* (as Calles had come to be called), he deported both the *jefe* and his chief political lieutenants such as Morones and León and re-moved many of his friends from military and political posts, but he either did not care or did not dare to disturb *callismo*, the native capi-talist group and financial-industrial system built up under Morrow's brief tutelage by the apt pupil "Comrade" Calles and his intimate associates.

"THE MEN OF THE REVOLUTION"

These, the real *Callistas*, are known as "Men of the Revolution." From the Revolution they issued and through it acquired generalships, gov-ernorships, cabinet posts, presidencies, prestige, power and wealth. As generals in the field they confiscated "enemy" properties, made forced levies on stocks of gold and currency, "purchased" supplies with the paper pesos they printed over their signatures, acquired estates by "agrarian expropriation" and seized and carried off and sold everything movable in the regions through which they passed in their campaigns.[10] Obregón began life as a mechanic and petty rancher: he ended it as a big landowner and the chief *garbanzo* grower of Mexico. Calles began as an undiplomaed rural school teacher: today he owns the rich *haciendas* of Trinidad, Soledad de la Mota, Santa Bárbara and El Tambor. These men represent a new capitalist-minded land-owning class; but under Morrow's tutelage they became more than that: bankers, builders, road-makers, realty men and modern industrialists. This development seems likely to mark a new epoch in the history of Mexico. And in it lies

[9] Plate 236. The central figure dictating to a stenographer is Rodríguez, the one in profile to his right, Ortiz Rubio.

[10] "General Pork Barrel" in Plate 248 is meant to symbolize these "Men of the Revolution." He is shown dancing with a peasant girl representing Mexico, and at the same time robbing fruits from the crate on her back.

the secret of the growing conservatism of the Calles group. Having acquired land, they began to call for even the slow, makeshift, inadequate land distribution to come to an end. Having acquired industrial properties, they began to fear the Frankenstein labor movement they themselves had called into being. Strikes were all well and good as an aid to American interests in their competition with other foreign capitals, as a crusher of small enterprises in favor of growing native monopolies, as a weapon against "reactionaries," i.e. government opponents. But suppose the labor movement should become less discriminating? get out of hand? Suppose the *Callistas* should cease to be in control of the government? The "Men of the Revolution" began to wish that the demagogy they themselves had started would cease.

THE JEFE MÁXIMO

"I have proved," said President Obregón when handing over his office to Calles, "that the presidential palace is not necessarily the antechamber to the cemetery." Towards the close of President Calles's administration, they had the Constitution amended so that "no reelection" was modified to read "no reelection until an intervening term has elapsed." That made Obregón eligible for a constitutional return to the presidency. Was this the beginning of a new Díaz self-perpetuating regime, people asked, or were Obregón and Calles planning to alternate indefinitely in office? The usual uprising was easily suppressed but General Obregón never reentered the national palace as president. On the eve of his inauguration in the course of a great banquet celebration, a young cartoonist, José Toral, fanatical Catholic, approached him to "draw his caricature" and then put a bullet through his brain.[11] From then on, Plutarco Elías Calles became the undisputed "Strong Man" of Mexico.

The next four presidents of Mexico were Calles appointees. First he had Congress select Portes Gil for a term of a year as provisional

[11] The assassin Toral is portrayed in the upper left of plate 226, receiving a pistol from Madre Conchita, the Mother Superior of an illegally maintained Mexican convent. Behind Obregón is the shadowed face of Morones, perhaps in reference to the fact that Toral in his confession said that present with Madre Conchita was a stout fleshy man whom Morones's enemies professed to identify as him. At the time he was quarreling bitterly with Obregón and his non-*Callista* followers, but I cannot find the slightest evidence that Morones was actually implicated in this crime.

190

president pending a new election. Then he arranged for the "election" of Ortiz Rubio. At the end of two and a half years in office the latter got into a quarrel with one of Calles's favorites, the Governor of Morelos, whereupon the *Jefe Máximo* called in the reporters and informed them that the President was resigning because of "ill health"—leaving it to the press to inform the President! The rest of his legal term was filled out by the Calles banker, Abelardo L. Rodríguez, and he was succeeded in office on December 1, 1934, by Lázaro Cárdenas, the last Calles appointee and present President—and ruler—of Mexico.

When that election took place, Calles had dominated Mexico continuously for more than a decade. He was, erroneously I believe, regarded as Mexico's greatest military man after Obregón: as a general he had never won an important battle. But a strong man he was, beyond a shadow of a doubt. His strength lay in his wealth, in the vested interests he had built up about his person, in his ruthlessness, his organizing ability, his hard-boiled realism and financial genius. Above all, it lay in the fact that with Obregón dead he was the last of the great *caudillos* produced by the stormy and epic years of revolution. The rest had died violent deaths: Zapata and Villa and Carranza in treacherous ambush, Obregón by an assassin's bullet, innumerable lesser generals in unsuccessful rebellions. Those who had not died had knuckled under, become part of the Calles machine, or gone into voluntary or involuntary exile. On his shoulders was the mantle of the Revolution; he was the inheritor and hitherto the faithful continuator of the Obregón pattern of rule. He had even improved upon the pattern, invented the ultimate refinement in demagogic devices: a smashing blow at the defeated but ever provocative Church every time he was engaged in any particularly nefarious acquisition or delivery to American interests of Mexico's wealth. It created much noise and smoke: thunder of excommunications and smoke of hell-fire: it led to feeble and sporadic rebellions of backward peasants under the leadership of militant clerics: it was the cheapest way to cover up a dubious action, reconsolidate popular support and retain the mantle of revolutionary.

The rule of Calles seemed destined to last indefinitely. Without ceasing to be a reality, he was already becoming a legend. In his palace in Cuernavaca he held court and from there directed the affairs of the nation. To him came presidents and generals, deputies and governors, industrialists and bankers and foreign agents and diplomats. The particular man in the presidential palace had become a mere elongation of his shadow. Calles had made him, had named his cabinet and dictated his policies and prescribed his share of the spoils of power, and if he should but quarrel with the least of the "Strong Man's" friends or thwart the most insignificant of his wishes, Calles had shown that he could unmake him again. The "Political Party," now that he had reduced all so-called parties to one, was another elongated shadow of the *Jefe*. He had created it: all his appointees and government employees had to belong to it and contribute from their earnings to its maintenance. Through it he named governors, senators, deputies; personally made out in advance the lists of those who were going to be elected. After his fall, men were to compare this to Porfirianism: but while he was in power it was the living incarnation of the Revolution and democratic institutions. Now that Cárdenas has continued the same practices, the "renovated" *Partido Nacional Revolucionario*, the same apparatus with a new *jefe* is still the incarnation of "revolutionary" procedure. In Mexico press and politicians are ever blind to the defects of the presence in power and voluble to the point of nausea about the crimes of his immediate predecessor, while the one that that predecessor denounced and overthrew is already on the road to "rehabilitation."

The "Strong Man" had become more than a dictator: he had become the savior of his people and the ideals of the Revolution. In every emergency they turned to him for counsel, for orders, for direct assumption of leadership. In 1929 during the rebellion of Topete, Manzo and Escobar, Calles returned from his "retirement" to become Minister of War. In 1931 Ortiz Rubio's cabinet resigned and once more the Strong Man took the war ministry. When the peso dropped and silver hit the toboggan, he became head of the Bank of Mexico. Something was always calling Calles out of retirement! The country could never get along without him.

Then the Strong Man made a slight error: he chose the wrong man to occupy the presidential palace. He rightly felt that it was time to install a younger man in the presidency, and he selected one of his faithful and undistinguished subordinates. Lázaro Cárdenas was the first president of a new generation. He was only fifteen when Madero initiated the Revolution of 1910. At eighteen he left his job as printer and village jailkeeper to "take the field" against Madero's assassin, Victoriano Huerta. He saw service under General Obregón, fought against Villa and Zapata, joined the revolt against Carranza, and carried out with efficiency and probity a number of military and political tasks during the Obregón and Calles regimes. At the end of 1933, when he received the unanimous nomination of the Calles-bossed convention of the *Partido Nacional Revolucionario*, he was only thirty-eight years of age. As all other parties such as the *Laborista* and the *Agrarista* had long been merged into the National Revolutionary and the only truly independent organization was the weak and semi-illegal Communist Party, his nomination (barring a successful rebellion) was tantamount to election.

Lázaro Cárdenas had always been a faithful and unexceptionable subordinate, yet there was something in his presidential campaign that should have made the Old Man suspicious. With his election assured and automatic he made an electoral tour unprecedented in the history of Mexico: he covered 27,000 kilometers in plane, train, ship and on horseback, reaching innumerable remote villages that had never seen a presidential or even a gubernatorial nominee. It was all very well to put up a pretense of a contest, but the candidate was overdoing it: he acted as if he were determined to see every peasant in the Republic!

"What do you want?" he asked everywhere.

"Some land. A dam. A school. A street."

The President-to-be made a note of it. "I will attend to it personally."

Calles became a little uneasy. He surrounded the newest creature of his will with a strong cabinet of picked agents. He even put his son Rodolfo there as Minister of Communications. But the cabinet rarely saw the President. After his election as before it, Cárdenas kept trotting around the country: arranging for local leaders in the villages to make simple requests; promising to fulfill them, keeping his promises, going back in person to inaugurate the little strip of road, the one-room schoolhouse, the well or tiny dam asked for and promised; building up the local leaders who had made the request; building up a rural political machine and building up the shadow-presidency into substance. Meanwhile the presidential palace remained vacant: affairs of state continued to be transacted as before by the Strong Man from his palace in Cuernavaca.

The uneasiness of Calles continued to grow. He wheeled one of his biggest guns into action: he gave orders to his governors to sharpen to the utmost the war with the Church. His governors closed churches and inaugurated "Socialist Education." Armed bands of "Red Shirts" appeared in the Capital itself under the direction of Garrido Canabal, former *Callista* Governor of Tabasco, noted anti-clerical, now Minister of Agriculture. Soon there would be a new revolt of *Cristeros*, clerical-led peasants fighting for Mexico to be governed by "Christ, the King." Then Cárdenas would have to call the Strong Man into the War Department as Portes Gil, Ortiz Rubio and Rodríguez had done before him, and all would be well. But the President seemed not to notice what was being brewed: *mestizo* with Tarascan blood in his veins, he possessed the stoical uncommunicativeness of the Tarascans: silently and undeviatingly he continued his expeditions around the countryside.

For six months the mute struggle, the maneuvering for position, continued: then Calles gave the President the opening he had been waiting for. The *Jefe Máximo* who had been bossing the country in the name of the Revolution, who had been wielding the power based on the pattern invented by Obregón, abandoned one of its two pillars. In a statement to the press he denounced the "marathon of strikes" that was sweeping the country, demanded greater economic peace and progress, declared that the land distribution had gone far enough, that the communal lands were unproductive and economically inefficient, that it was time to consider ways and means of stimulating agricultural production and stabilizing the countryside. Thus he laid aside for a moment the mantle of Revolution, and Cárdenas, waiting his chance, seized it. It was the lever needed to rise from the presidency to actual power.

Within a few days Cárdenas rallied great sections of the labor and peasant movements around him, smashed Morones and the *Crom*, formed a new labor movement with a new labor lieutenant at its head out of the pieces of the old, and then with swiftness and energy that impressed the bandwagon boys, he removed *Callista* governors, senators, deputies, generals and cabinet ministers in so clean a sweep that experienced politicians who had been expectantly waiting for the lightning to strike him ran for cover cheering and shouting: "Viva Cárdenas! Viva la Revolución!" Calles hesitated in bewilderment before the unexpected melting away of his forces, and while he hesitated, was lost. When, too late, he began to speculate on the possibilities of a rebellion

Cárdenas acted again with an energy worthy of Mexico's Strong Man, and without troubling about Constitutionalism or legal warrant, simply picked up the fallen dictator with a few of his closet friends such as Morones and León, put them on an airplane under police escort, and deposited them in the United States. He had already reached an understanding with the American Government, and no demurrer was made about their being dumped over the border. The Strong Man of Mexico was finished: a new Strong Man had taken his place.

XIII. LAND OF THE SIX YEAR PLAN

The entire year 1936 General Cárdenas employed in consolidating his power. The circumstances of his break with his former Boss gave him the complete support of the Left. There were still many problems on that score, but his most immediate concern was the Right: the Church and the landowners. By the peculiar logic of politics there was danger of the clergy's rallying to the support of their arch-enemy of yesterday, General Calles, before the latter's hold on the government apparatus and his revolutionary prestige could be completely liquidated. In that case he would have a combination of forces capable of making an effective bid for power. If the reader wonders how the Church might support the arch Jacobin and arch anti-clerical of the past decade, he may be helped to grasp the logic of politics involved by contemplating the evolution of such a figure as Alfred E. Smith from the shining hero of the liberals into the darling of the Liberty League and the Union League Club.

Cárdenas set about at once quietly patching up the deliberately aggravated conflict with the Church: he permitted the harshest laws to lapse, let the closed churches reopen, arranged for the courts to "revise" the legal seizures of Church property by the government. The clergy had long been trying to evade these property laws by "selling" their holdings to trusted parishioners and lay leaders of the Church apparatus. Now the courts repeatedly found that these "innocent third parties" as "purchasers in good faith" should not have been disturbed in their possession of the properties in question, and that restitution should be made. The Church-State tension grew noticeably weaker.

But his problems with the peasantry were by no means completely solved either. In breaking with Calles he was glad of all the band-wagon jumpers he could get. Among them were Portes Gil, chairman of the National Revolutionary Party, and official patron of the National Peasants League. He was a potential rival for the post of *Jefe Máximo:* Cárdenas could not altogether trust him, nor could he rest secure until he had grouped the organized peasants around his own person. Another

Callista whose support he was able to keep was General Cedillo. An old revolutionary leader, a military man, the governor and absolute boss for the better part of a decade of the rich state of San Luis Potosí, and the possessor of a vast and well equipped private armed force, he was a power to be reckoned with. In latter years, following the trajectory of the other "Men of the Revolution," Cedillo had become rich, a big landowner, conservative, and increasingly popular with the Catholic clerical party. Cárdenas put him in his cabinet in the influential post of Minister of Agriculture. This was effective in retaining Cedillo's support, but made it necessary that the President should keep his Minister of Agriculture from attending to the duties of his office which would bring him into contact with the peasantry outside his domain of San Luis Potosí: it was more than ever imperative that General Cárdenas should continue his trips around the countryside and personally attend to land distribution, irrigation, school installations, and road openings. The presidential palace still continues to be vacant most of the time.

THE DISTRIBUTION OF THE LAND

To consolidate his peasant base and emphasize his differences with Calles, General Cárdenas greatly speeded up the program of land distribution. In the first twenty months of his administration he awarded nearly four and one-half million hectares of land to about three thousand villages. Thereby he distributed over half as much land as all of his predecessors together. However, one must not get the impression that the Mexican agrarian problem is now in a fair way to being solved. Here are a few of the reasons:

1. Only the larger villages are eligible. About two-thirds of the recorded rural settlements in Mexico are not entitled to receive any land under the law.

2. The majority of those eligible are too terrorized to apply for land. Cárdenas may now be expected to slow up, not only on the basis of the precedents of Mexican history and the superior sweeping powers of new brooms, but because the Agrarian Department is actually running out of applications for land, with the bulk of the eligible villages not yet benefited.

3. The law does not propose to do away with the *latifundio*. The

197

great estates, where touched, have been trimmed, not carved up, and generally only of their poorest lands.

4. Precisely those states where land concentration is greatest are the ones with the smallest rural settlements ineligible under the law.

5. The land is not being confiscated except where previous robbery of village lands can be *legally* proved. Out of the first 1,649 distributions only sixty-six were such "restitutions" of stolen lands. Since then (January 1st, 1927) "restitutions" have practically ceased.

6. The economic and hence political power of the *hacendados* is not being seriously impaired. They are compensated for the land taken by payment in agrarian bonds, which bonds are acceptable in payment of taxes. Where improved lands are taken, some improvements are paid for in cash.

7. The amounts distributed even to the eligible villages are in general inadequate for the maintenance of life. The average per family is between eight and nine hectares, but this average is arrived at by including forty-hectare tracts in Chihuahua where the land is arid and sterile, and three-hectare tracts in the State of Mexico and grants of one and one-half hectares in the Federal District. Even the latter are no farmer's paradise. Yet so jealously does the law protect the *hacendado* that in the populous State of Mexico there is no longer any eligible land to be taken from the large estates despite the smallness of the grants and despite the fact that the legal needs of the eligible villages are far from satisfied. The reported yield per hectare for the year 1934-5 in the distributed lands was worth about 100 pesos ($28.00)! This includes crops consumed as well as those sold. The yield for non-distributed land in Mexico is not much higher, but it is compensated by the size of the estates.

8. The years of relative stability mean a rapidly growing population for which no provision is made. Only about one-third of all villages, concentrated in the main in less than half of the states, will be benefited at all, even after the law has been fully carried out. This creates a dangerous situation whereby in the next social upheaval (I do not refer to mere rebellions preliminary to presidential elections), the benefited villages and states may be used against those where the land concentration, land-hunger and rural exploitation are at their worst. The majority of the rural population, and the worst off, have as a whole not

been affected, nor will they be affected in any favorable way by the workings of the present law.

THE LABOR MOVEMENT UNDER CÁRDENAS

Since the *Crom* was an instrument of Calles it could not survive his fall. Today, like the CGT, it is reduced to a mere shadow. Like every institution that wishes to survive in Mexican public life, the *Crom* continues to offer itself to Cárdenas as more loyal than the new organization which he created at the time of his defiance of Calles. It plays a definitely reactionary role. The new government-favored labor movement, constructed largely from the fragments of the old *Crom* plus independent unions, is the *Confederación de Trabajadores Mexicanos* (CTM), with Vicente Lombardo Toledano, intellectual and ex-*Cromista*, at its head. It is better organized than was the old *Crom* in its best days, for the working class has grown in numbers and consciousness since then. Having been born in the Cárdenas-Calles left-right fight, it is definitely to the left of the *Crom*, even as that organization was in its earlier years.

Where Morones was gross, blatantly corrupt, cynical and corpulent, Lombardo Toledano is thin, ascetic, poetic and patrician. He has none of Morones's greed for wealth nor love of display: desire for leadership and power are his only incentives. He is undoubtedly less demoralizing in his influence upon the growing labor movement than was Morones, yet his political rôle is essentially the same. He bears the same relation to Cárdenas as Morones did to Calles. When Cárdenas broke the railroad strike of 1936, to Lombardo Toledano fell the task of curbing the wave of indignation and protest and directing it into harmless channels. It seems a matter of ritual that every message he directs to the labor movement should end with a pledge of support to "the progressive policies of President Cárdenas."

The new labor leader is a man of acute intelligence and would like to "indulge" his high ideals. But he is forced to work with much of the old, corrupt Morones machinery. The writer has seen a list of his chief lieutenants, inherited from the past, with a price next to the name of each of them. The list is provided by the Chamber of Commerce of Mexico to trustworthy members to let them know how much it costs to settle a labor dispute: the price varies with the delegate who does the negotiating. Lombardo is undoubtedly aware of this and it is distasteful to him. He himself is not for sale, but it is part of the game as he plays it; he needs to work with these men if he is to fulfill his function.[1]

A STRIKING PARALLEL

A year after Calles became the "first Labor President of Mexico," he was called upon to face two important strikes. The first was a strike of the street-car workers against the British-owned Light and Power company. He gave the company an ultimatum: three days to give in or he would "take over" the properties involved. The corporation surrendered before the time-limit was reached.

The second was a railway strike: the men were resisting a wage cut, a reduction to the rank of civil-service employees ineligible to strike, and the liquidation of their union. He presented an ultimatum, not to the company this time but to the men. The company involved was the bondholders' committee headed by J. P. Morgan. True, the railwaymen were so well organized that Calles finally had to make important concessions, but the difference in the two "solutions" was obvious.

In 1936, the second year of Cárdenas's presidency, he too faced two strikes: again the Power and Light Company, involved in a general electrical strike, and again the railwaymen.

The electrical strike the government pronounced "legal." In Mexico, when a strike is "legal," the strike is as good as won. The workers nail up the union flag on the doorway and the police and army are charged with seeing to it that it is not removed. Picketing is unnecessary. Needless to say, the electrical workers won their demands.

In the case of the railwaymen, the government declared the strike "non-existent," which is the opposite of "legal." The men were given one day to get back to work under penalty of losing their jobs, with the same police and army protecting the workers who would replace them. The strike was lost, though part of the demands were subsequently granted by arbitration. After all, the railwaymen are the best organized and most independent aggregation in Mexico, and Cárdenas, like Calles, had to yield to them though he yielded less. More than ten years elapsed

[1] "The Labor Leader," plate 249, is a caricature of Lombardo Toledano, and "The Big Boss and his Labor Lieutenant," plate 246, represents Calles and Morones.

between the two parallel incidents and their internally "contradictory" solutions. Clearly, though Cárdenas has broken with the openly conservative millionaire Calles of recent years, he has not broken with the Obregón pattern of statecraft. Calles tried to break with the pattern in 1935: that was the cause of his fall. Cárdenas continues the pattern: that is the secret of his power.

CÁRDENAS AND THE LEFT

One decisive advantage that General Cárdenas has over his predecessors is the absence of any critical opposition from the Left. In the past, the Communist Party had given support to Obregón-Calles at difficult moments like the De la Huerta rebellion, but the support was critical, based upon the independent arming of the proletariat and peasantry, aiming at the defeat of the rebellion, but also, if possible, at the overthrow of Calles and Obregón. It was like the support that Lenin gave Kerensky in the face of the revolt of Kornilov.

But the break between Cárdenas and Calles coincided with the heyday of the People's Front policy in the Communist International. The Communist Party, as in the past, rallied to the support of the government against forces attacking it from the Right, but this time the support was unconditional, enthusiastic, essentially uncritical, not conceived in terms of the independence of the labor movement and the proletariat. It was in nowise comparable to Lenin's "support" of Kerensky, rather like the Social Democracy's support of Bruening, Von Papen and Hindenburg. They no longer run candidates for office but content themselves with supporting Cárdenas's left arm against his right and supporting the "Left Wing" of the National Revolutionary Party. They cover up as does everybody else the fact that there is no such party, that there are no real elections, that Cárdenas bosses party, Senate and Chamber.

When Cárdenas delivered his annual message for 1936, *el Machete*, Communist organ, called for a demonstration in front of Congress to "support Cárdenas." The demonstration was then described as "the festival of the oppressed. The popular multitude on the march is the blood of a people that lives and expresses itself with Liberty. Long live Cárdenas! Long live the deputies and senators of the left!" They preferred to ignore the fact that Cárdenas had just ordered the so-called "Left

Wings" of Congress dissolved on the ground that all Congressmen support him and therefore there can be no Left and Right. *El Machete* thunders, as does the President, against "the reaction" and "*callismo*," but never against the native capitalist class, the heart of *callismo*. In fact it has ceased to talk in terms of class at all.

On the First of May it called upon the peasants to "strengthen the struggle for the land *within the framework of the law*." Calles and Obregón always had to reckon with Communist agitation *against* the agrarian law and for the peasants to take the great estates by their own action. Obviously this new respect for the agrarian law simplifies matters for Cárdenas. As for the army, the Communist Party now indites such slogans as this: "The Mexican People's Front salutes the glorious national army in connection with the 126th anniversary of our independence." Again Cárdenas's tasks are enormously simplified: his budget for 1937 includes the largest military appropriation in the history of Mexico, while his Under-Secretary for War is one of the most reactionary landowner-generals that Mexican militarism has produced.

THE SIX-YEAR PLAN

Much has been written of Mexico's Six-Year Plan. Apologists for Cárdenas have presented it as a sort of Soviet Five-Year Plan with another year of planfulness added. And they have treated it as a revolutionary invention of Cárdenas after he broke with Calles. Actually it is nothing of the sort.

Mexico's Six-Year Plan is the high-sounding name given by the Calles-controlled convention of the National Revolutionary Party to the presidential platform adopted by it in 1933. Its six years come from the fact that that is the length of the presidential term: its title "plan" is a reflex of the general demagogic tributes to economic planning fashionable in America and Europe during the depression. Despite its length and Russian-sounding name it is really inspired in and comparable to the analogous "New Deal" platform of Roosevelt, promulgated in his campaign the year before.

A genuine planned economy must begin with the abolition of private ownership, at least in basic industry and finance. The so-called Six-Year Plan begins with a declaration of the principle of private property. It promises, as have previous presidential programs, to improve the lot of the workers, encourage industry, complete the land distribution within the law, establish public works, promote education and improve Mexico's relation with foreign countries. One looks in vain through all its pages and promises for any sign of planned economy or socialism.

"SOCIALIST EDUCATION"

The writer has heard scores of flying-tour visitors to Mexico swear that with their own eyes and ears they saw and heard Marxian Socialism being taught to the entire rising generation of Mexican school children. Catholic reactionary and People's Front Communist observers are agreed on this.

"Why are you keeping your children out of school?" the writer asked of a poor couple, a *portero* and his wife, who are participating in the waning Catholic boycott of the Mexican school system.

"I don't know," said the husband, "the *padre* told us they are teaching evil."

"I don't see why we shouldn't send our boy to school," said the wife. "With the girl's it's different. After all, the boy is a man-child, and sooner or later he'll have to know how women are formed. . . ." To them "Socialist Education" meant sex education. To ninety-nine out of every hundred schools in the republic it doesn't even mean that.

What the government really means by "Socialist Education" is:

(1) Education by the State; (2) ultimately universal and compulsory education—today there are not enough schools for that; (3) use of State-outlined courses and texts in private schools; (4) non-sectarian, non-religious instruction; (5) the rigid enforcement of the constitutional prohibition on the intervention of ministers and priests in primary, secondary or normal school instruction. Here is the government's own statement, through the mouth of its Under-Secretary for Foreign Affairs, Licenciado Ramón Beteta:

To the foreigner, this name, Socialist Education, will connote an idea which is not one our legislators had in mind when amending the Constitution. . . . Thinking only of the literal meaning of the word (the last thing one should ever think of in interpreting Mexican political phraseology—B.D.W.) one could well imagine that this new school is attempting to teach communism, the destruction of the family and the

203

establishment in Mexico of a classless society in which the right of pri-vate property would not be recognized. The plan of the so-called so-cialistic school in Mexico is by no means so ambitious.

On the contrary, the government recognizes the existence of a con-stitution which provides a federal, representative, democratic and re-publican form of government, and which expressly acknowledges the right of private property as a social function. It would not be possible therefore, for that government to teach officially a doctrine contrary to its very existence. . . .

"AT LAST WE ARE REVOLUTIONISTS"

After Cárdenas broke with Calles on the issue of radicalism, the phraseology of the refurbished government's pronouncements for pop-ular consumption became more astonishing, and less a key to reality, than ever. This demagogy reached what is possibly its climax in the summer of 1936. At that time, leaders of the self-styled "Left Wings" of Senate and Chamber of Deputies made speeches repudiating their whole past as a "deception" and "mystification" of the Mexican masses.

Cándido Aguilar, old and experienced politician who had managed to hold on with various ups and downs since the days of Carranza, declared:

We have deceived the Mexican people, the workers of our country, making them promises which we cannot fulfill. We who call ourselves Left are not Left. Among us there is no Leftism, but what might be called "conveniencismo" (politics of convenience). We have never developed a frank policy in favor of the cause of the proletariat. We have limited ourselves to receiving orders from political leaders and from high officials. How can we be Lefts if we have remained silent before a decision of the Commission of Conciliation and Arbitration which injures the interests of the railwaymen? (Referring to the railway strike broken by the gov-ernment earlier in the year.)

Soto y Reyes said truly: the P.N.R. (National Revolutionary Party) has committed great faults. We have not been sincere nor honorable; we have only defrauded the hopes of the working people, while we worried about our political interests. I think my words will not please; and hereby I invite you to work loyally for the cause of the proletariat.

As for the Soto y Reyes referred to in this remarkable parliamentary address, he was the chairman of the "left wing" of the Chamber, and he had started the flood of confessional oratory by maintaining that the whole Revolution had been nothing but falsehood and deception till Cárdenas broke with Calles. He had not intended to refer to the breaking of the railroad strike, which was Cárdenas's doing, for he dated the era of revolutionary purity from Cárdenas's attack on the *Callistas* a year before.

We ought to be sincere with the workers . . . , continued Soto y Reyes. *And let no one tell us that we of the Left Wings want to implant exotic regimes . . . that we are communists, for it is not communism to try to relieve the miseries of the people. What we are doing, gentlemen deputies and senators, could be called humanism, which could be practiced by a Catholic and a reactionary if he were sincere. . . .*

Only today can we say for the first time that we have a proletaristic government, for we believe that the worker who does not have the weapon of money ought to have the weapon of the law. . . .

We do not try to destroy organized capital; it is infantile to say that we want to organize the dictatorship of the proletariat. . . . How can we be called extremists when we ask for the forty-eight hour week and see that there are countries which decree one of forty hours?

The last question we must admit is unanswerable. As for the outburst of oratory, it was a preliminary move in the fight for the elimination of Portes Gil from the chairmanship of the National Revolutionary Party. No sooner was he out than President Cárdenas ordered the dissolution of the "Left Wings" of both houses as no longer useful nor desirable. They dissolved without a murmur, forgetting all their special Leftness, and declaring that there was unanimity in both houses anyhow, since every one aimed only to support the President and carry out his wishes.

MEXICO'S "MARXISM"

On November 20th, 1936, there was an unusually impressive celebration of the outbreak of the Madero Revolution of 1910. The Senate and the Chamber of Deputies delegated official spokesmen to express their views on the occasion. From the words of Nicéforo Guerrero, spokesman for the Senate, we cull the following:

> *What is the Socialism of our Revolution? We must say it frankly, the Socialism of our Revolution cannot be anything but Marxian Socialism. . . .*
>
> *For many, to speak of Marxism is to invoke the disappearance of private property . . . but that is the phantasma of the uninformed. . . . Neither the Revolution nor the Government is trying to implant Communism in Mexico. The Revolution includes in its program restraint, not abolition, of private property. . . ."*

Such is the Marxism and such the Marxian Socialism of Mexico. With this airy shadow of a specter, clerical propagandists would terrify the United States and make it believe that "Red Bolshevism is rampant in Mexico." And with these same phrases in lieu of substance the Communism of the People's Front variety would content the Mexican masses and work up international revolutionary enthusiasm for "Socialist" Mexico.

CÁRDENAS MEXICO

If one seeks for a description in sociological terms of Cárdenas Mexico, one finds the following:

(1) A personal dictatorship of President Cárdenas which enables him to name all governors, senators, deputies, the executive committee of the sole existing party, the *Partido Nacional Revolucionario*, and will presumably enable him to name, perhaps even control, his successor.

(2) This government is run primarily in the interests of native capital, as the junior partner of American capital.

(3) The dictatorship is thinly overlaid with the phrases and trappings of democracy and constitutionalism. There is a Congress but its members are in practice selected by the president or by the National Committee of the *Partido Nacional Revolucionario*. This year, as usual, it voted away its legislative powers to Cárdenas after spending the period of its sessions making resounding revolutionary speeches and protesting its loyalty to the President. At the end of the year it voted him "extraordinary," i.e. dictatorial, powers in the following fields: commerce, cooperatives, mines, oil, electricity, weights and measures, irri-

206

gation, land distribution, patents and trade marks, monopolies, income, credit, currency, banking, public debt, social insurance, labor legislation, pensions, public accounting, treasury and taxes. What else is there left to legislate on?

(4) Even the labor movement openly acknowledges his rule. Throughout the past year they have repeatedly asked him to step in and settle not merely disputes with the employers but even factional disputes within the organized labor movement. The *Crom* and the CTM have accepted his decisions in their disputes with each other without question and have vied with each other in the indecent competition as to who is the more loyal in carrying out those decisions and which movement is the more loyal to him in general.

(5) The dictatorship maintains itself without great difficulty through the army, backed by popular and American governmental support. In recent rebellions the United States has supplied munitions to the Government and embargoed them to the rebels, and has set up generous emergency credits for their purchase. Popular support is secured through radical phrase demagogy, which perforce deposits a growing sediment of actual though meager concessions and reforms: government-controlled but ever more inclusive organization, intermittent and limited distribution of lands, support of labor struggles when the rising governmental native capitalist and American interests are not involved. Supplementary measures for control are government subsidies and appointments which strengthen the hand of the government agents in the labor and peasant movements, and corruption or elimination (assassination and deportation) of "incurable" opposition elements. Thanks to the present attitude of the Communist Party, Cárdenas has not needed to have recourse to those severer measures.

ANOTHER LANGUAGE

Cárdenas leaves most of the demagogy to his assistants and supporters, though on occasion he has made the mountains of Mexico ring with his radical phraseology. When he speaks to American interests, he talks another language. On December 22nd, 1936, in his first public interview with the American press since the consolidation of his regime, President Cárdenas told the A.P. reporter what he had previously said in private to Ambassador Daniels:

Mexico would look with gratitude on elements with capital which might want to invest money in the country, giving them every class of guarantees within the law, and they ought not alarm themselves since our legislation is more protective of capital than that of the United States, where taxes are greater and wages higher.

This is the simple truth and no doubt a natural program for a semi-colonial, nascent capitalist government, but it is a far cry from the radical phrase-demagogy of "Socialism," "Marxism," "Revolution," with which his speeches for popular consumption within the country are wont to bristle. It is, too, a far cry from the fervid anti-imperialist sentiments that actuated the stormy days of the Revolution that began in 1910, and from the dreams of nationalization of the vast natural wealth of Mexico's subsoil.

WHITHER MEXICO?

The year 1937 dawns with Cárdenas as Mexico's Strong Man. He sits more firmly in the saddle than either of his two predecessors in that role. The Government of the United States is no less friendly to him than it was to them. His base of support inside the country is broader and stronger than theirs, for it includes a growing native capitalist class and capitalist landowning sector and ranges at present all the way from the moderate Catholics to the Communist Party. The force of the landowners is by no means broken but it can no longer count for the present on the support of any important foreign capital. Barring foreign support and inspiration, revolutionary attempts from the Right cannot for the moment be anything but feeble. Revolts as a constituent part of electoral procedure, to be sure, are likely to continue. Cárdenas may face such an uprising some time before the end of his term in 1940: the landowners and the Church perhaps backing elements in his own regime discontented by his choice of a successor. But since 1920 such revolts have been weaker and weaker and none of them have been successful. The indications are that Cárdenas will be able to name the next president, and presumably to control him.

Of course, international events have their repercussions in Mexico. Thus the fascist uprising in Spain aroused great sympathy among land-owners and clerical reactionaries in Mexico, stiffened their morale and enabled them, under the guise of attack on the Spanish Government, to carry on a terrific propaganda campaign against the regime of President Cárdenas, compelling him to line up with the Spanish Government to the limit that American desires would permit. A new world war, a victory of fascist or socialist forces in some important sector of the world, especially in the United States, would materially alter the situation in Mexico.

At present, Mexico continues to be ruled by the pattern invented by Obregón. Under it there has been greater stability than at any time since the Porfirian dictatorship. For sixteen years now it has prevented successful revolution. Faces change but the pattern remains. It was not Cárdenas that attempted to depart from it, but Calles, grown rich and openly conservative, who proposed a public shift from popular and American capitalist support to unconcealed reliance on native and Americal capital. He demanded the abandonment of the traditional demagogy and limited reformism of the government as, in the long run, dangerous.

Nor did Cárdenas make war upon the native industrialists, the so-called Calles group: rather has he entered into friendly alliance with it. He has not himself made conspicuous use of the presidency for his own enrichment. The only venture I have been able to learn of was a plunge in silver on the basis of a "tip" from the American Treasury Department and the National City Bank when Roosevelt was preparing to announce his silver purchase policy: a little deal, yet it was sufficient to make Cárdenas a millionaire. However, under the aegis of his presidency, personal friends and associates and relatives, notably his brother, have found ways and means of enriching themselves and prying their way into the privileged circle of the former Calles Group. The relations of the President with Saenz, Pani, De la Chica, Rodríguez, Ortiz Rubio and the rest are today most friendly. Native capital continues to be a growing factor in the regime.

Not only is it a growing factor in the regime, it is a growing factor in the land as a whole. The years of the world depression were for Mexico the proverbial ill wind that somewhere must blow good. After a year or two of deep stagnation and the disastrous effects of the drop in silver, Mexico actually entered into a period of unprecedented prosperity. No longer could capitalists and landowners withdraw their profits as formerly for investment in the United States. The American stock market, banking system, and industry were in no condition to absorb these winnings. Those who had been pumping profits out of Mexico for decades were now forced to reinvest them inside the country. Thereby they began an industrialization of the land such as has not been seen since the days of Díaz. New factories, roads, housing and hotel construction, realty developments, enlargement of existing industries and initiation of new ones, trustification of unmonopolized fields, expansion of the government budget and public works expenditures at a new high, surpluses in the treasury, growth of banking, beginnings of a commercial loan system at more reasonable interest rates, enlargement of the proletariat and expansion of the internal consumers' market: for the last few years the deepest depression in the history of world capitalism has coincided with a veritable boom in Mexico.

The boom was getting well under way when Cárdenas assumed the presidency; it greatly contributed to his popularity and the stability of his regime. But it also introduced new forces into Mexico which must ultimately change the present social pattern. Native capital and the working class are beginning to grow up together. The latter grows faster than the former, for foreign capital and native alike are begetters of a native proletariat.

The Revolution of 1910 is drawing to a close: not that its vaguely felt aims are fulfilled or the major causes of unrest removed, but because the situation is changing and the initial drive has spent its force. Its aims: the disruption of feudalism and the breakup of the great estates, the emancipation of Mexico from foreign domination, free play for the development of modern industry, parliamentary and electoral democracy and civil liberty, could not be carried to fulfillment because the bourgeoisie whose historical needs they represent was too weak and immature to carry them through. Moreover, the birth of the middle class in Mexico came at a time when on a world scale it was already senescent and reactionary. As in other lands, it brings with it into the world its "grave-digger," the proletariat, and leaves to the latter the fulfillment of its revolutionary aims.

Over the pattern of stability and compromise that Obregón, Calles and Cárdenas have established grow ever more visible the outlines of a gigantic question mark. How long can native capital and the native proletariat continue to grow up and yet live together in doubtful harmony? How long can the government speculate with the immaturity and lack of consciousness of this infant giant, the Mexican working class? When Obregón came into power it still wore the white "pyjamas" of the peasantry: today it wears the blue overalls of the factory workers. What does that symbolic change in its mode of living betoken for its way of thinking?

And the unsatisfied sectors of the peasantry, how long will they remain quiescent? The states where the land concentration is greatest and the land hunger and oppression most intense, the villages whose redemption is not even contemplated by the agrarian laws, the peasants whose essential needs are left unsatisfied when the distribution is over: when will their century-old accumulations of resentment break out anew?

Worker and peasant masses cannot continue year after year phrase-fed and promise-crammed while their elementary life needs remain unfulfilled, and not become more and more exigent of fulfillment. The next time the agrarian revolution breaks out, it may find a labor movement in the cities approaching maturity, ready to cut the leading strings that bind it to the government which is itself bound in turn by invisible but powerful threads to American capital. If Zapata had found such a labor movement when his forces occupied Mexico City, there would be a different story to tell. When the Mexican proletariat comes of age, the Obregón-Calles-Cárdenas pattern will no longer work. Then there will be a new situation in Mexico. . . .

I. THE LAND AND THE PEOPLE
(Oils, Watercolors, Sketches, etc.)

PLATE NO. 1   *Self Portrait*
Detail from fresco
Ministry of Education, Mexico

PLATE NO. 2 *Grasping Hands*
Wax painting, Nayarit 1931
Collection Edsel B. Ford, Detroit

PLATE NO. 3   *Hillside with Cactus*
Wax, Sonora 1931
Destroyed by Painter

PLATE NO. 4   *Purple Shadows*
Oil, Sonora 1931
Frieda Kahlo de Rivera

PLATE NO. 5 *Citlaltepetl*
Oil 1906
Private Collection

PLATE NO. 6   *The Village Water Supply*
Watercolor, State of Mexico 1934
Spanish Embassy, Mexico City

PLATE NO. 7   *The Carrier*
Tempera, Chiapa de Mota 1934
Walter Goldfrank, New York

PLATE NO. 8 *Street in Tehuantepec*
Watercolor 1935
Mrs. George Buller, Washington, D. C.

PLATE NO. 9 *House in Tehuantepec*
Oil 1930
Weyhe Gallery, New York

PLATE NO. 10   *Guanajuato Village*
Watercolor 1934
Private Collection

PLATE NO. 11   *Tavern in Acapulco*
Watercolor 1934
Private Collection

PLATE NO. 12   *The Ruined Estate*
Watercolor, Xilotepec 1934
Private Collection

PLATE NO. 13 *Bridge and Buzzards*
Watercolor, Tehuantepec 1935
Central Art Gallery, Mexico (Misrachi's)

PLATE NO. 14 *Cow and Trees*
Watercolor, Tehuantepec 1935
Central Art Gallery, Mexico

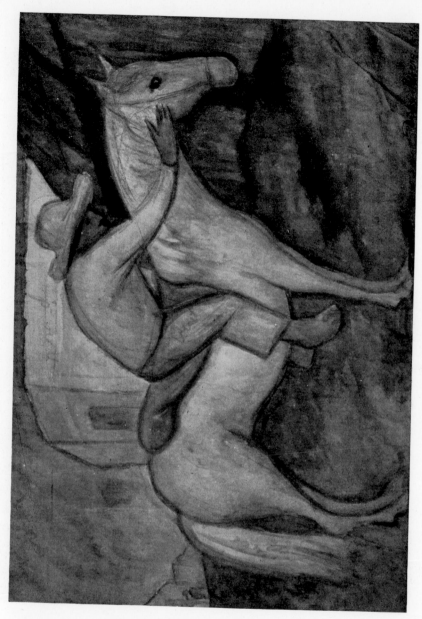

PLATE NO. 15 *The Yellow Horse*
Watercolor, Chalchicomula 1934
Rabbi Philip S. Bernstein, Rochester, N. Y.

PLATE NO. 16 *The White Burro*
Watercolor, Xilotepec 1934
Mrs. Schaeffer, New York

PLATE NO. 17 *The Tired Horse*
Watercolor, Xilotepec 1934
Mrs. Walter Hochschild, New York

PLATE NO. 18   *Avenue with Palms*
Watercolor, Tehuantepec 1935
Central Art Gallery, Mexico

PLATE NO. 19   *Man of Tehuantepec*
Watercolor 1928
Eustace Seligman, New York

PLATE NO. 20 *Man of Tehuantepec*
Watercolor 1935
City Art Museum, St. Louis

PLATE NO. 21 *Man of Tehuantepec*
Watercolor 1935
L. H. Morgan, London

PLATE NO. 22   *Head of a Young Yucatecan*
Oil, Yucatan 1921
Frieda Kahlo de Rivera

PLATE NO. 23 *Portrait of María Guillén*
Oil, Mexico City 1921
Frieda Kahlo de Rivera

PLATE NO. 24 *Portrait of Guadalupe Marín*
Wax, Mexico City 1926
Jackson Cole Phillips, New York

PLATE NO. 25   *Tehuantepec Girl*
Oil 1930
Private Collection, New York

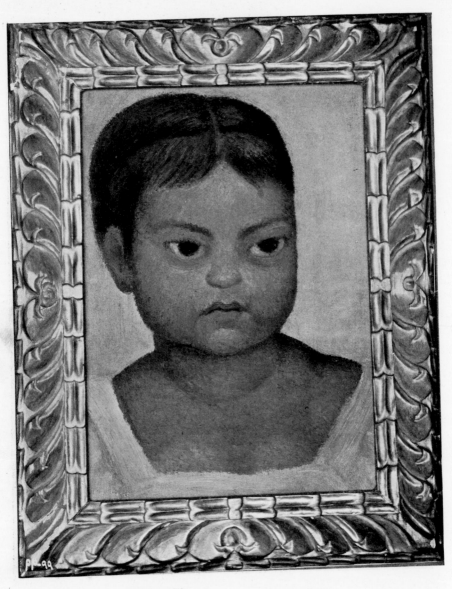

PLATE NO. 26   *Delfina Flores*
Encaustic 1927
Private Collection, San Francisco

PLATE NO. 27 *Torrid Siesta*
Watercolor on canvas 1936
Frieda Kahlo de Rivera

PLATE NO. 28 *Ignacio Sánchez*
Oil 1925
Private Collection, San Francisco

PLATE NO. 29   *Little Indian Girl*
Oil 1925
Private Collection, San Francisco

PLATE NO. 30   *Roberto Rosales*
Wax 1930
Edward M. M. Warburg, New York

PLATE NO. 31   *Delfina Flores*
Encaustic 1926
Mrs. Sigmund Stern, San Francisco

Retrato de la niña Delfina Flores a los 4 años
de edad. Mexico 9 de Abril de 1927. lo pintó Diego Rivera

PLATE NO. 32 *Delfina Flores*
Wax 1927
Ernestine Evans, New York

PLATE NO. 33   *Child with "Judas"*
Oil 1934
Private Collection

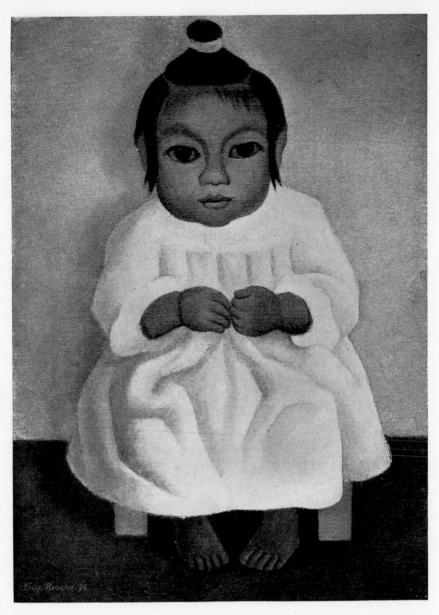

PLATE NO. 34 *El Copetón*
Oil 1930
Carl Van Vechten, New York

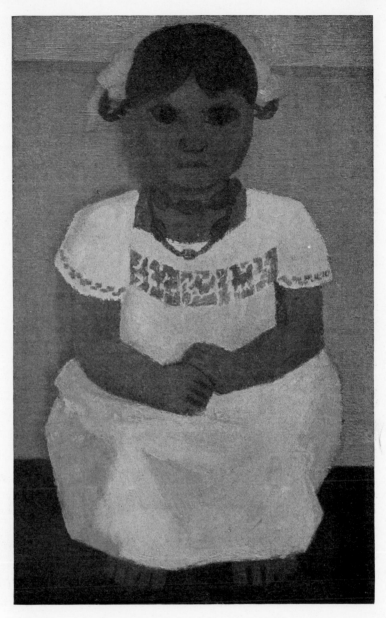

PLATE NO. 35   *Her Sunday Best*
Watercolor 1931
Private Collection, New York

PLATE NO. 36 *Juanita Flores*
Oil on tin 1931
Private Collection

PLATE NO. 37 *My Compadre's Children*
Oil on tin 1930
Private Collection

PLATE NO. 38   *Mother and Child*
Tempera 1934
Aline Brooks, New York

PLATE NO. 39 *Juana Rosas*
Oil 1934
Aveline Pugh, Racine

PLATE NO. 40   *Don Lupito*
Oil 1936
Painter's Personal Collection

PLATE NO. 41 *Girl on Petate*
Oil 1934
Central Art Gallery, Mexico

PLATE NO. 42 *Delfina and Dimas*
Tempera and oil 1935
Private Collection, New York

PLATE NO. 43 *Children at Lunch*
Tempera and oil 1935
Joseph P. Andrews, Newport, Ky.

PLATE NO. 44 *The Elegant Girls of Texcoco*
Watercolor 1935
Central Art Gallery, Mexico

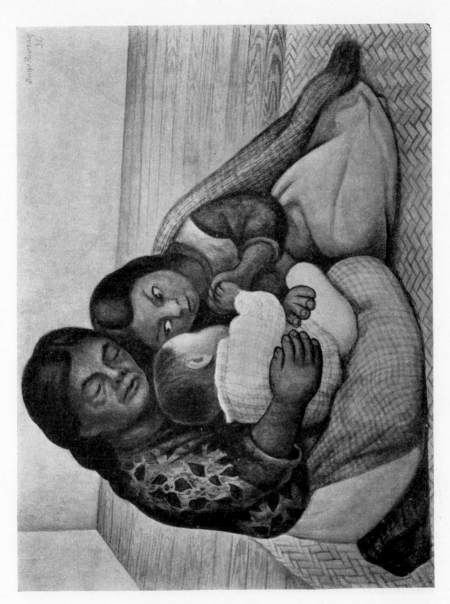

PLATE NO. 45 *My Compadre's Family*
Watercolor on canvas 1934
Owen Atkinson, San Francisco

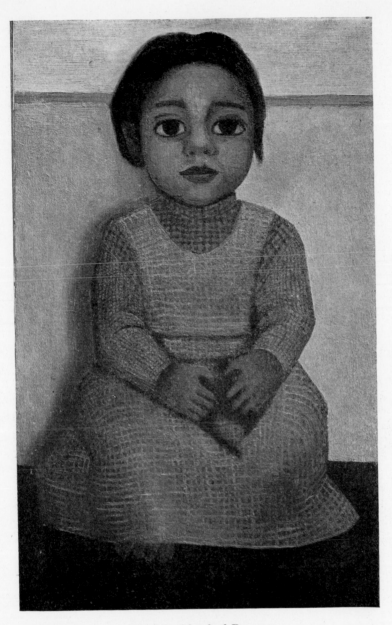

PLATE NO. 46   *Girl in Checked Dress*
Oil 1930
Private Collection, New York

PLATE NO. 47 *Juana Rosas*
Tempera 1935
Central Art Gallery, Mexico

PLATE NO. 48 *Jose Guadalupe Castro*
Oil 1936
Dena Barnett, Detroit

PLATE NO. 49   *Juana Rosas with "Judas"*
Watercolor on canvas 1934
Mary Thayer, Cincinnati

PLATE NO. 50 *Juana Rosas*
Oil 1935
Private Collection

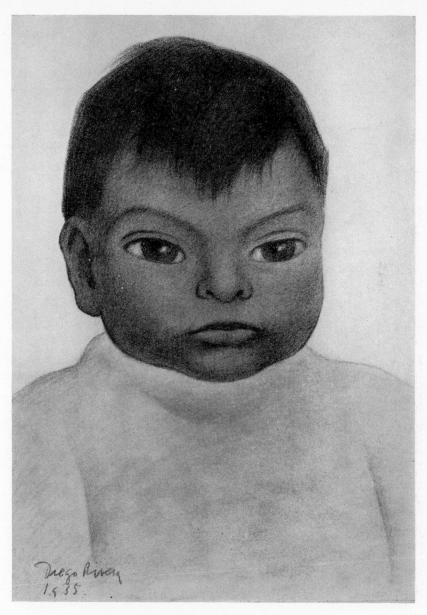

PLATE NO. 51 *Portrait of Dimas*
Sanguine and charcoal 1935
J. A. Slocum, New York

PLATE NO. 52 *Portrait of Jesús Sánchez*
Oil on tin 1930
Private Collection

PLATE NO. 53 *Sleep*
Watercolor on canvas 1936
Central Art Gallery, Mexico

PLATE NO. 54 *Bather*
Watercolor, Tehuantepec 1935
Rosa Covarrubias, Mexico

PLATE NO. 55 *Bathers*
Watercolor, Tehuantepec 1935
Mrs. G. S. Franklin, New York

PLATE NO. 56 *Washing Clothes*
Watercolor 1935
Stendahl Galleries, Los Angeles

PLATE NO. 57 *Women Bathing*
Oil 1925
Frances Toor, Mexico

PLATE NO. 58 *Sandunga*
Watercolor, Tehuantepec 1935
W. W. Lipper, Los Angeles

PLATE NO. 59 *Sandunga*
Watercolor, Tehuantepec 1935
King Vidor, Beverly Hills

PLATE NO. 60 *Tehuana*
Oil 1929
Solomon Hale, Mexico

PLATE NO. 61 *Fruit Vendor*
Oil, Tehuantepec 1928
Moisés Saenz, Mexico

PLATE NO. 62 *Morning Moon*
Oil, Tehuantepec 1928
Mrs. Charles Liebmann, New York

PLATE NO. 63 *Barter in the Market*
Watercolor, Tehuantepec 1935
Joseph P. Loeb, Los Angeles

PLATE NO. 64 *Market Scene*
Watercolor, Tehuantepec 1935
Mrs. Edgar Tobin, San Antonio

PLATE NO. 65 *Totopo Vendors*
Watercolor on canvas 1935
City Art Museum, St. Louis

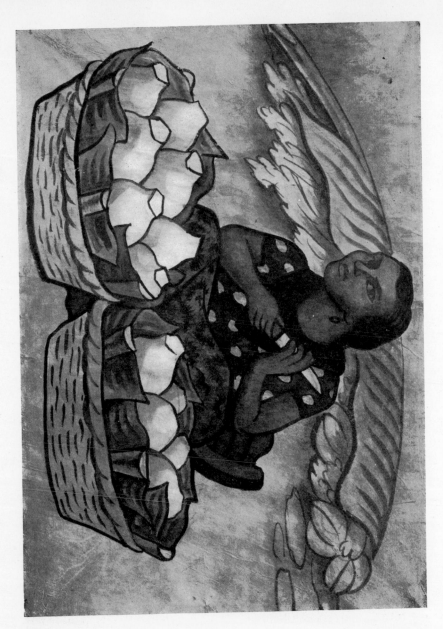

PLATE NO. 66   *Testing the Knife*
Watercolor 1935
Archibald Brown, New York

PLATE NO. 67　*Buying Melons*
Watercolor, Tehuantepec 1935
Frieda Kahlo de Rivera, Mexico City

PLATE NO. 68   *Potters Resting*
Watercolor, Tehuantepec 1935
Frieda Kahlo de Rivera

PLATE NO. 69 *Buying Flowers*
Watercolor, Tehuantepec 1935
Frieda Kahlo de Rivera

PLATE NO. 70 *Market Scene, Coyoacán*
Watercolor 1936
Misrachi Galleries, Mexico City

PLATE NO. 71 *Basket Sellers, Amecameca*
Watercolor 1934
Walter Goldfrank, New York

PLATE NO. 72 *Returning from the Market*
Watercolor, Chalchicomula 1934
Dr. Alfred Sollinger, Mexico City

PLATE NO. 73 *Woman with Bundle*
Watercolor 1934
Mrs. Schaeffer, New York

PLATE NO. 74 *Pig Vendor*
Tempera 1935
J. K. Dubasch, Bombay, India

PLATE NO. 75 *El Cristero*
Watercolor 1934
Private Collection

PLATE NO. 76   *Vegetable Seller, Tacubaya*
Watercolor on canvas 1935
Personal Collection of Painter

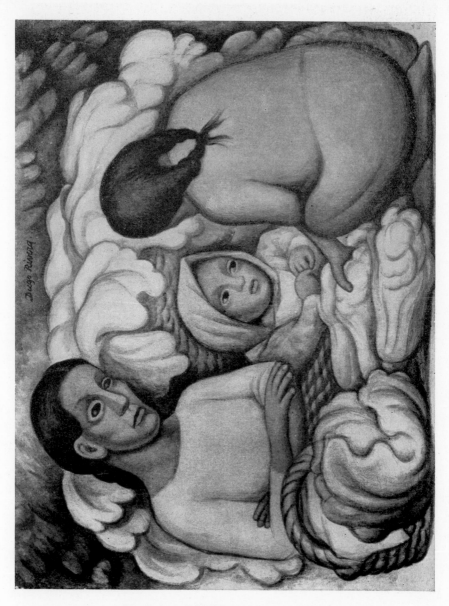

PLATE NO. 77 *Mother and Children*
Watercolor on canvas 1935
Solomon Hale, Mexico

PLATE NO. 78 *Market in Iguala*
Chinese Ink 1935
Central Art Gallery, Mexico

PLATE NO. 79 *Paper Flower Makers*
Chinese Ink, Iguala 1935
Central Art Gallery, Mexico

PLATE NO. 80 *Mother and Child*
Oil, Acapulco 1930
Weyhe Gallery, New York

PLATE NO. 81 *The Balcony*
Encaustic, Yucatan 1925
Robert Montenegro, Mexico

PLATE NO. 82 *Vegetable Carrier*
Chinese Ink, Xochimilco 1936
Central Art Gallery, Mexico

PLATE NO. 83   *Vegetable Carrier*
Chinese Ink, Xochimilco 1936
Central Art Gallery, Mexico

PLATE NO. 84   *Loading the Burro*
Chinese Ink, Xochimilco 1936
Personal Collection of Painter

PLATE NO. 85   *Making Rockets*
Watercolor 1928
Alfred Honigbaum, San Francisco

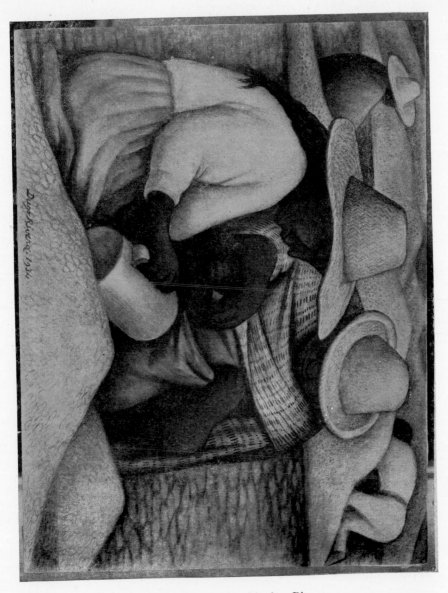

PLATE NO. 86 *Corn Vendors in the Market Place*
Watercolor on canvas 1935
Yascha Heifetz, New York

PLATE NO. 87   *Tortilla Maker*
Encaustic 1924
Emilio Portes Gil, Mexico

PLATE NO. 88 *Embroidering*
Oil, Tehuantepec 1928
Private Collection, New Orleans

PLATE NO. 89 *Spinning*
Watercolor 1936
Central Art Gallery, Mexico

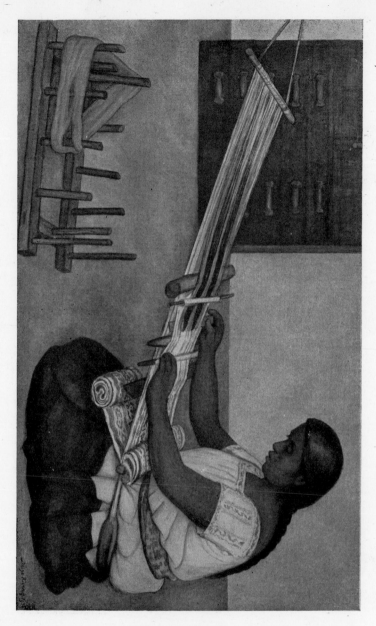

PLATE NO. 90   *Winding Thread*
Mrs. Alan M. Stroock, Ossining, N. Y.
Tempera and oil 1936

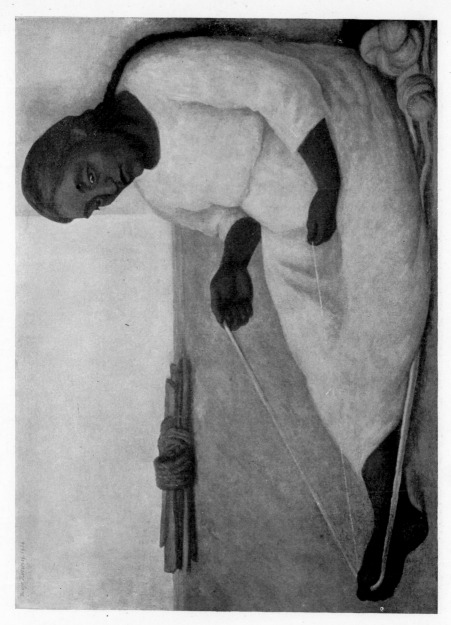

PLATE NO. 91 *Weaving*
Central Art Gallery, Mexico
Watercolor on canvas 1936

PLATE NO. 92 *Water Carrier*
Tempera 1935
Moisés Saenz, Mexico City

PLATE NO. 93   *Flower Carrier in Xochimilco*
Tempera and oil 1936
San Francisco Civic Center

PLATE NO. 94   *The Tough Overseer*
Watercolor, Hacienda de la Cañada 1934
S. B. Ward, Newton Center, Mass.

PLATE NO. 95 *Miners in Guerrero*
Chinese Ink 1936
Misrachi Galleries, Mexico City

PLATE NO. 96   *Beggars*
Watercolor 1934
Gregory Zilboorg, New York

PLATE NO. 97 *Garbage Carrier*
Tempera 1935
Cincinnati Public Library

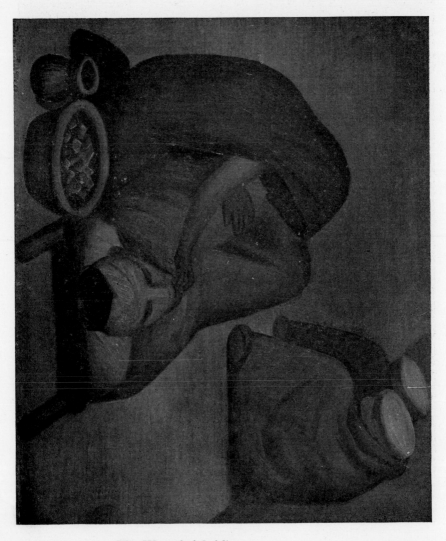

PLATE NO. 98   *The Wounded Soldier*
Oil on Tin 1931
Frances Flynn Paine, New York

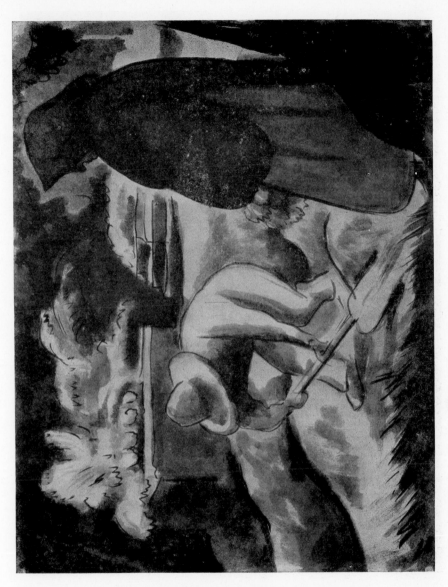

PLATE NO. 99   *Day of the Dead*
Chinese Ink, Amecameca 1935
Misrachi Galleries, Mexico City

PLATE NO. 100 *At the Father's Grave*
Chinese Ink, Amecameca 1935
Misrachi Galleries, Mexico City

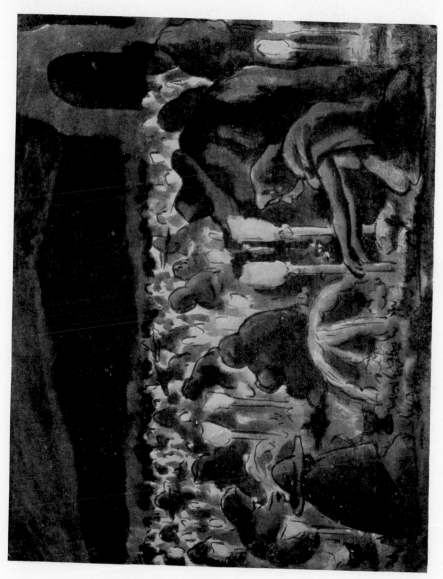

PLATE NO. 101 *Night of the Dead*
Chinese Ink, Mixquic 1935
Eustace Seligman, New York

PLATE NO. 102 *The Assassination of Altamirano*
Tempera, Mexico City 1936
Misrachi Galleries, Mexico City

II. THE COURT OF LABOR
Frescoes in the First Patio, Ground Floor
Ministry of Education, Mexico City

PLATE NO. 103 *Section of the Court of Labor*
North Side, Three Floors

PLATE NO. 104   *The Trapiche*
Rural Sugar Mill

PLATE NO. 105 *Entrance to the Mine*

PLATE NO. 106 *Searching the Miner*

PLATE NO. 107   *Waiting for the Harvest*

PLATE NO. 108 *Opening the Crucible*

PLATE NO. 109 *Pouring the Steel*

PLATE NO. 110 *The "Liberation" of the Peon*

PLATE NO. III *Schoolteacher on Communal Land*

III. THE ASCENDING LANDSCAPE
Elevator Entrance and Stairway Frescoes
Ministry of Education

PLATE NO. 112
Yucatecan Mother and Child

PLATE NO. 113
Tehuantepec Mother and Child

PLATE NO. 114 *The Tropics*

PLATE NO. 115   *The Hunter*
Detail from The Tropics

PLATE NO. 116 *Tropical Forest*

PLATE NO. 117   *The Plantation*

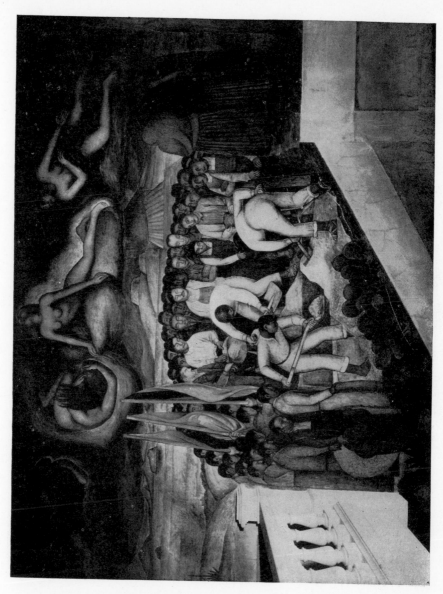

PLATE NO. 118 *Rain and Blood: Fertilizers of the Soil*

PLATE NO. 119   *Burial of Proletarian Victims*
Detail from Rain and Blood

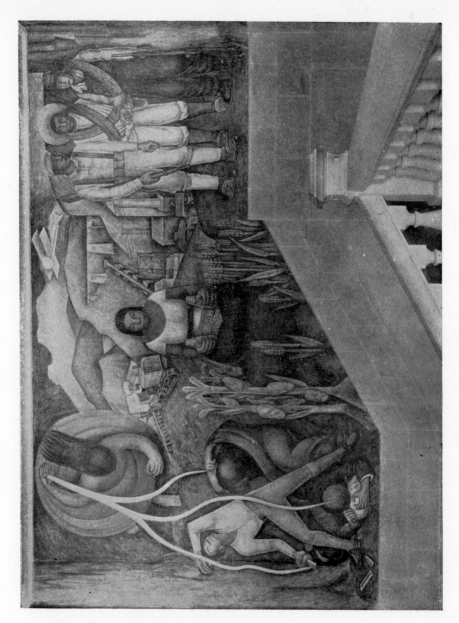

PLATE NO. 120 *The Industrialized Land*
Destruction of militarism, feudalism, clericalism;
science is brought to the land; and the earth gives
freely of its fruits

IV. COURT OF THE FIESTAS

Second Patio, Ground Floor
Ministry of Education

PLATE NO. 121 *Art Conservation in the Ministry of Education*
View of the Court of the Fiestas

PLATE NO. 122   *Festival of the Corn Harvest*

PLATE NO. 123 *Distribution of the Land*
First and Second Panels

PLATE NO. 124 *Distribution of the Land*
Second and Third Panels

PLATE NO. 125 *The Day of the Dead in the Country*

PLATE NO. 126 *The Day of the Dead in the City*

PLATE NO. 127   *The Judases*
The Bourgeois Politician, the General, the Priest

PLATE NO. 128　*First of May*
Unity of Workers and Peasants
Second and Third Panels

PLATE NO. 129   *First of May*
Detail from Workers' Demonstration
First Panel

PLATE NO. 130   *Flower Festival: Santa Anita*

PLATE NO. 131   *Dance of the Sun: Chalma*

PLATE NO. 132   *Tianguis (Market Fair)*
Second and Third Panels

PLATE NO. 133 *Tianguis (Market Fair)*
Second and Third Panels

PLATE NO. 134   *Yaqui Dance*
The Deer and the Hunter

PLATE NO. 135 *Tehuantepec Dance*
La Sandunga

V. REVOLUTIONARY BALLAD SERIES

Third Floor, Court of the Fiestas
Ministry of Education

PLATE NO. 136 *Ballad of Zapata*
"Over in Morelos there was a man..."

PLATE NO. 137   *Ballad of the Bourgeois Revolution*
Opening stanza

PLATE NO. 138 *Fixing the Plow*

PLATE NO. 139 *Distributing Fruit and Flowers*

PLATE NO. 140   *Disseminating Knowledge*

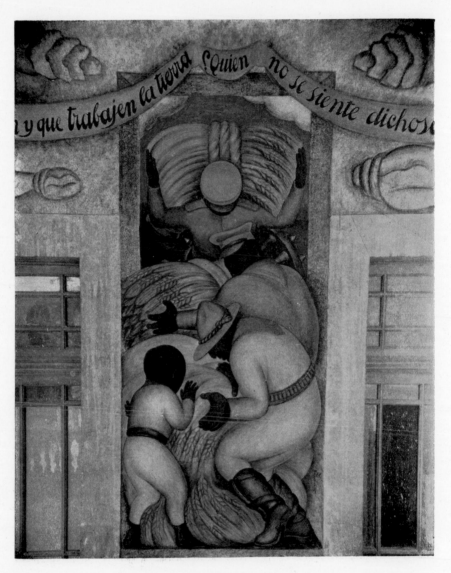

PLATE NO. 141 *The army which has served for war*
Can serve to till the soil....

PLATE NO. 142   *Who doesn't feel happy*
When it begins to rain?

PLATE NO. 143 *The Crowned Tractor*

PLATE NO. 144 *Gold is worthless*
If it cannot buy food...

PLATE NO. 145 *False Learning*

PLATE NO. 146   *Midnight approaches*
                 And the rich are still thinking
                 How their money
                 Can be made to increase

PLATE NO. 147   *Night of the Poor*

PLATE NO. 148 *Blessed Fruit of Knowledge*

PLATE NO. 149 *Night of the Rich*

PLATE NO. 150   *Wealth comes from the soil*

PLATE NO. 151   *Liquidation of the Feudal Order*

PLATE NO. 152   *Completion of the Bourgeois Agrarian Revolution*

PLATE NO. 153 *Insurrection*
Beginning of Ballad of Proletarian Revolution

PLATE NO. 154 *Barricade*

PLATE NO. 155 *Barricade*

PLATE NO. 156 *He who does not work*
Shall not eat. . . .

PLATE NO. 157   *The Workers Committee Takes over the Factory*

PLATE NO. 158 *The End of the Latifundio*

PLATE NO. 159   *United Front*

PLATE NO. 160   *Bread for All*

PLATE NO. 161   *Allegiance to the Soviet Power*

VI. NATIONAL AGRICULTURAL SCHOOL AT CHAPINGO

Stairway Frescoes

PLATE NO. 162   *Revolution Teaches the Sciences to Worker and Peasant*
(Here is taught the exploitation of the land, not of man)

PLATE NO. 163 *Distribution of the Land to the Peasants*

PLATE NO. 164 *The Engineer*
Detail from Distribution of the Land

PLATE NO. 165   *Good Government*

PLATE NO. 166 *Education and Construction*
Detail from Good Government

PLATE NO. 167 *Armed Agraristas*
Detail from Good Government

PLATE NO. 168   *Bad Government*

PLATE NO. 169 *Agents of Reaction*
Detail from Bad Government

PLATE NO. 170 *Organizers of Reaction*
Detail from Bad Government

PLATE NO. 171   *Reaction Rampant*
Detail from Bad Government

VII. NATIONAL AGRICULTURAL SCHOOL AT CHAPINGO

Chapel Frescoes

PLATE NO. 172   *The Corn Field Fertilized*
"The tree of liberty is kept green
with the blood of martyrs."

PLATE NO. 173 *The Agitator:*

PLATE NO. 174 *The Virgin Earth*

PLATE NO. 175 *The Virgin Earth: Detail*

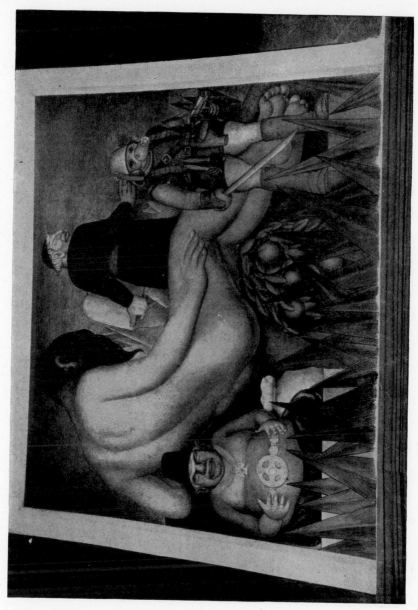

PLATE NO. 176 *Earth Enchained by Capital, the Army, the Church*

PLATE NO. 177
Social Disorder: Oppression of the Many by the Few

PLATE NO. 178 *Revolution: Germination*

PLATE NO. 179 *Revolution: Florescence*

PLATE NO. 180   *Revolution: Fructification*

PLATE NO. 181   *Subterranean Forces*

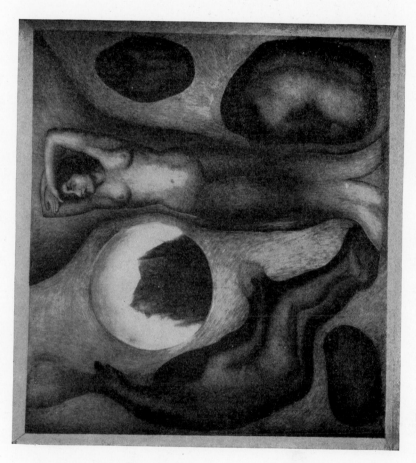

PLATE NO. 182 *Germination*

PLATE NO. 183   *Florescence*

PLATE NO. 184 *View of Chapel Vault*

PLATE NO. 185   *Detail from Vault*

PLATE NO. 186   *Detail from Vault*

PLATE NO. 187 *Rear Wall: Fruition: The Fecund Earth*

VIII. MINISTRY OF HEALTH
MEXICO CITY

Meeting Hall Frescoes
and Stained Glass Windows

PLATE NO. 188 *Corner of Meeting Hall*
Rear: Purity and Continence
Ceiling: Health and Life

PLATE NO. 189   *Strength*

PLATE NO. 190 *Knowledge*

PLATE NO. 191

The Four Elements: Earth

PLATE NO. 192

The Four Elements: Fire

PLATE NO. 193
The Four Elements: Water

PLATE NO. 194
The Four Elements: Air

IX. CUERNAVACA MURALS: PALACE OF CORTES

PLATE NO. 195 *The Attack on the Temple Square*

PLATE NO. 196 *Detail: The Knight of the Tiger*

PLATE NO. 197   *Detail: Battle between Aztec and Spanish Knight*

PLATE NO. 198 *Crossing the Canyon into Cuernavaca*
A Traitor Priest Shows the Secret Way

PLATE NO. 199 *The Taking of Cuernavaca*
Above: Pillage
Center: Gold Weighed Off before the Agent of the King
Foreground: Branding the Captured Slaves

PLATE NO. 200
Conquest under Cross and Sword

PLATE NO. 201 *Construction of the Palace of Cortés*
Cortés, as Marquess del Valle, Receiving Tribute

PLATE NO. 202 *Morelos Sugar Plantation*
The Conquest is Converted into
Permanent Feudal Exploitation

PLATE NO. 203   *Father Motilinia Teaching the Indians*

PLATE NO. 204 *Exploitation and Insurrection*
Right: The Church Receives its Tribute
Above: Building a Temple with Serf Labor
Above Portal: Human Sacrifice Continues—The Inquisition
Left: Zapata Leading the Agrarian Revolt

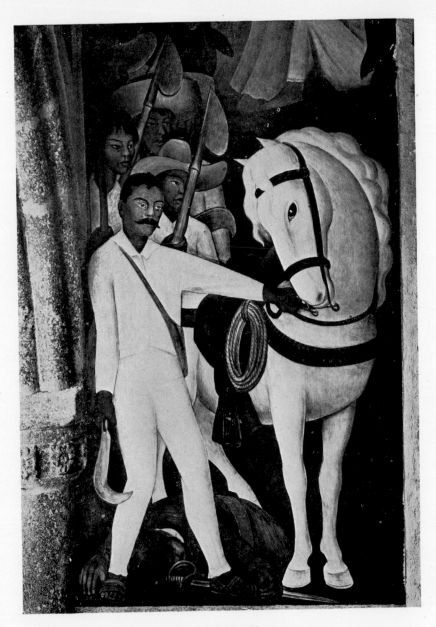

PLATE NO. 205   *Detail: Zapata and His Horse*

PLATE NO. 206   *Detail: The Church Receives Tribute*

PLATE NO. 207 *Portrait of Morelos*

PLATE NO. 208   *Portrait of Zapata*

PLATE NO. 209 *Cortés Disembarks at Vera Cruz*

PLATE NO. 210 *Cortés Receives the Ambassadors*

PLATE NO. 211

The Pact with the Tlaxacalans

PLATE NO. 212

*The Siege of
Tenochtitlán*

PLATE NO. 213

*Torture of Cuauhtemoc
and Tlacopan*

PLATE NO. 214 *Assassination of Cuauhtemoc*

PLATE NO. 215

Destruction of Indian Culture

PLATE NO. 216

Mining with Indian Slaves

PLATE NO. 217   *Las Casas Defending the Indians*

PLATE NO. 218 *Vasco de Quiroga Teaching the Indians New Trades*

PLATE NO. 219 *Death by Treachery of Roquetilla*
Leader of the Chichimecan Revolt

X. MEXICO: PAST, PRESENT, FUTURE

Murals on the National Palace Stairway
Mexico City

PLATE NO. 220 *Preconquest Mexico*
Left Wall, National Palace Stairway

PLATE NO. 221   *Detail: Class Struggle in Ancient Mexico*

PLATE NO. 222   *Formation of Mexico (Center Wall)*
Below: Spanish Conquest
Center: War for Independence
Top: Revolution of 1910

PLATE NO. 223   *Two Conquests*
Spanish and Yankee Invasions

PLATE NO. 224   *Spanish and French Rule*
Below: Burning Books and Branding Slaves
Above: The End of Maximilian

PLATE NO. 225 *New Spain*
Below: Rule of the Viceroys
Above: Diaz Dictatorship and Revolution of 1910

PLATE NO. 226 *Independence and Revolution of 1910 (Detail)*

PLATE NO. 227
Santa Anna, Clerical Dictatorship and Reformation of 1857

PLATE NO. 228 *Mexico Today and Tomorrow (Right Wall)*

PLATE NO. 229   *The Peasantry in Subjection*

PLATE NO. 230 *Shooting of the Agraristas*

PLATE NO. 231   *Breaking the Strike*

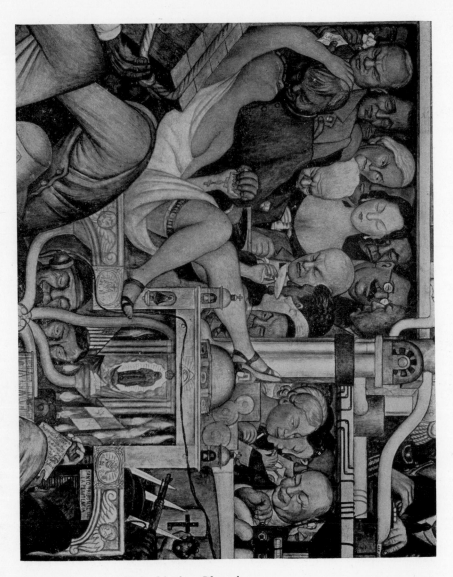

PLATE NO. 232   *Holy Mother Church*
Photo taken before acid was sprayed,
partially mutilating the fresco

PLATE NO. 233   *Love One Another*

PLATE NO. 234 *"Democratic Rights"*

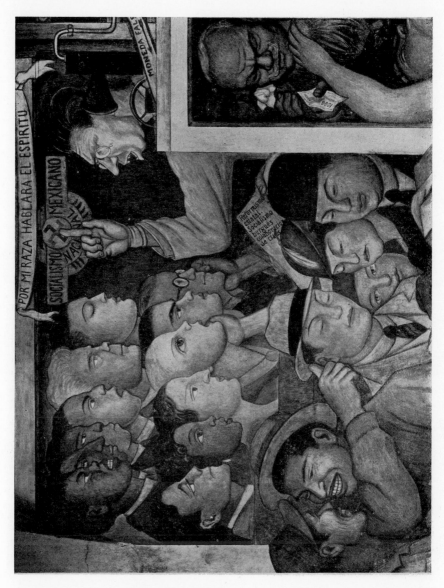

PLATE NO. 235   *"National Socialism"*
(Mexican Brand)

PLATE NO. 236   *Government by the National Revolutionary Party*
(Faces change but the pattern remains)

PLATE NO. 237 *Workers Education*

PLATE NO. 238 *Awakened Workers*

PLATE NO. 239 *Proletarian Insurrection*

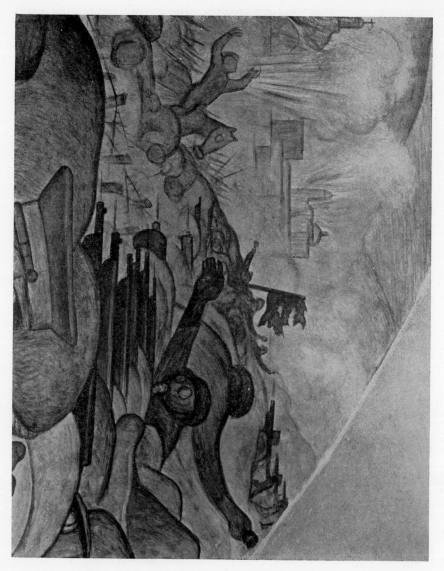

PLATE NO. 240 *Detail from Proletarian Insurrection*

PLATE NO. 241   *For a Socialist Mexico*

XI. MEXICAN CARNIVAL: YESTERDAY AND TODAY

Frescoes in the Banquet Hall of the
Hotel Reforma, Mexico City

PLATE NO. 242
Augustín Lorenzo: Carnival of Huejotzingo

PLATE NO. 243   *Augustín Lorenzo: Detail*

PLATE NO. 244   *Victory Dance of Huichilobos*
Carnival of Huejotzingo

PLATE NO. 245   *Folkloric and Tourist Mexico*

PLATE NO. 246 *The Big Boss and His Labor Lieutenant*
Detail of Folkloric Mexico

PLATE NO. 247   *Portrait of Mexico*